MAKE THE OLD TESTAMENT LIVE

MAKE THE OLD TESTAMENT LIVE

From Curriculum to Classroom

Edited by

Richard S. Hess and Gordon J. Wenham

WILLIAM B. EERDMANS PUBLISHING COMPANY
GRAND RAPIDS, MICHIGAN / CAMBRIDGE, U.K.

© 1998 Wm. B. Eerdmans Publishing Co.
255 Jefferson Ave. S.E., Grand Rapids, Michigan 49503 /
P.O. Box 163, Cambridge CB3 9PU U.K.

Printed in the United States of America

03 02 01 00 99 98   7 6 5 4 3 2 1

Library of Congress Cataloging-in-Publication Data

Make the Old Testament live: from curriculum to classroom /
    edited by Richard S. Hess and Gordon J. Wenham.
        p.   cm.
    Includes bibliographical references.
    ISBN 0-8028-4427-8 (pbk.: alk. paper)
  1. Bible. O.T. — Study and teaching (Higher)
  I. Hess, Richard S. II. Wenham, Gordon J.
  BS1193.M35 1998
  221'.071'173 — dc21   98-35494
                                          CIP

Contents

COMMUNICATION

Introduction

Compiling this collection of essays on teaching the Old Testament has been an exciting experience, for they are full of enthusiasm for their subject and an eagerness to convey it to others. They range from the problems of presenting the Old Testament to fresh undergraduates who have never read it to supervising doctoral dissertations. They span a range of institutions from seminaries to secular universities and include contributions from Europe, the USA, Latin America, Australia, and South Africa.

Those papers with a largely theoretical focus are grouped in the first, shorter part of the volume. The majority, however, have a more pragmatic pedagogical flavour as the contributors wrestle with the problem of fitting the Old Testament into the curricula of their institutions and gripping their students' attention. The core of this volume were papers delivered at a Tyndale Fellowship Old Testament study group in Cambridge, but others have been specially commissioned to ensure a more comprehensive treatment.

We trust that these essays will stimulate all engaged in teaching the Bible or theology to reflect on their own approaches to see how the subject might be made more accessible to their audience.

The book is structured in three sections beginning with a section which suggests parameters for the content of the curriculum.

The second section is devoted to the context in which such curriculum is developed, ranging from the seminary to the secular class-

room, across a wide range of abilities and cultural contexts, and with
respect to theological and confessional biases.

The final section addresses communication issues with a concluding essay by Professor Clive Lawless, who for several years was in
charge of reviewing the pedagogical excellence of the Open University.
The Open University is known in Britain for its innovative methods in
Higher Education. In his essay Professor Lawless reflects on the factors
that determine student learning and how they should influence the
design and delivery of courses in any subject. Here he focuses on
principles that should affect the teaching of the Old Testament and
scrutinises some of the suggestions made earlier in the volume, but his
reflections are applicable to many other subject areas.

We should like to dedicate this volume to Alec Motyer, who
through his teaching, preaching, and writing has done much to make
the Old Testament live today.

RICHARD S. HESS
GORDON J. WENHAM

CONTENT

Bringing Alive the Old Testament: Its Role in the Wider Curriculum

RICHARD S. HESS

Richard Hess is Professor of Old Testament at Denver Seminary. Here he examines the place of Old Testament within the curriculum of a theological college and considers the place of Old Testament study in the overall aims of the college. He also reflects on its role within the constraints and opportunities of a British B.A. degree and discusses the design of the Old Testament curriculum as a means of achieving these goals. It is a personal perspective. The author had taught the suggested curriculum for several years at Glasgow Bible College in Scotland and presents it here as a starting point for discussion.

Purpose of the Old Testament in the Curriculum

Aims and Purposes of Education

The aim of a theological college is to provide training for qualified individuals. The training prepares these people for service in the spiritual, social, and interpersonal tasks of their faith community. Within a

---

I thank Mr. Ian Ford for reading and commenting on this essay.

British context, it is assumed that this education is available to male and female school leavers who have reached the age of seventeen. This system does not require a previous college or university degree but it does assume a competency in reading, writing, and speaking English, as well as a general knowledge of Western culture.[1]

The programme's aims are concerned with the cultivation of skills in ministry and service. This is not primarily an academic concern. Most of the students attending the theological college do not intend to continue beyond their first degree to an advanced research degree in theology. This is not the purpose of the college. Therefore, the teaching of Old Testament in such an environment will not be concerned with the preparation of scholars or of students who can participate in theological research. Although these may be valuable in themselves and may be of interest to some students in the college, the focus of the curriculum, including Old Testament study, lies elsewhere. It is concerned with the enhancement of ministry skills. What are these skills? Their identification must be based upon the market as discussed below.

This essay will focus on Christian theology and especially evangelical Christian theology. This presumes that a certain value and importance is placed upon the Old Testament as a source for spiritual direction in all matters of faith and life. Along with the New Testament, this source serves as a unique authority. This is true regardless of the particular denomination(s) that the students and staff of the theological college may represent. The theological colleges that reflect such values are not thereby sources of indoctrination or propaganda, nor are they in any way different from any other educational institution. Every institution and every teacher reflect a set of values and a world view that they express through their teaching. Rather than pretending that such prior commitments do not exist, the best safeguard against in-

---

1. This distinguishes the system of education from that of the U.S., where theological college (seminary) is often reserved for those with a B.A. It is thus offered as postgraduate education, and the degree earned is the Master of Divinity. Also in contrast to the North American system, the general education knowledge necessary for a B.A. is presumed in Britain. The length of the British B.A. programme is normally three years. An important distinction in comparison with U.S. B.A. education is that the average age of students is older in British theological education. This has ramifications for educational methods, for which see the third part of this essay.

doctrination is an honest statement of one's faith and world view. In this way, no deception is involved in the actual educational process.[2]

Place of the Old Testament in a Theological College

The theological college has a primary responsibility in preparing its students to take positions of spiritual leadership and ministry in evangelical Christianity. These roles may be exercised locally or away from the home area. They may include pastors, teachers, evangelists, authors, and others. The theological college prepares people for these roles by enhancing their spiritual, academic, and practical skills. Spiritually, this involves fostering a personal relationship with God through spiritual exercises such as prayer, worship, witness, preaching, and fellowship. The cultivation of a spiritual life is the single most important task that a theological college undertakes. It permeates every other aspect of college life — and transforms it.

Since spirituality is a personal, as well as a corporate matter, its role and relationship to the place of Old Testament in the curriculum is at once crucial and yet also irrelevant. It is crucial because the spiritual life of the lecturer and the students will have an inevitable impact upon how the Old Testament is appropriated for ministry, indeed, whether it is used at all. If the Bible is a spiritual book inspired by God, then its most effective use must be found among those who possess the spirituality that can discern its true message. However, spirituality is also irrelevant. This is because the skills developed and applied in the college, as they relate to the Old Testament, must be those that submit to objective evaluation. Evangelical Christianity affirms *sola scriptura* and it argues that all interpretation of the Bible must be subject to the same canons used for the interpretation of any other piece of literature. Although the available methods of interpretation are increasingly diverse and complex (with the role of the faith community taking a more

2. More about this can be found in the important work of E. J. Thiessen, *Teaching for Commitment. Liberal Education, Indoctrination, and Christian Nurture* (Montreal: McGill–Queen's University Press, 1993). Thiessen argues for a balance in all forms of Christian nurture between instruction in Christian values and encouragement in a growth toward 'normal autonomy' in which students are able to make independent decisions.

prominent place in many approaches),[3] they remain subject to fundamental linguistic and historical elements. 'Thou shalt not kill' may evoke issues about murder, warfare, and a variety of possible nuances to the Hebrew verb. However, it will never mean, 'The sky is blue', no matter how 'spiritual' the interpreter may be.

In addition to the spiritual component, there is a practical one. This involves modelling those aspects of work and service that Christian workers might find themselves doing. In terms of biblical study, the most important application is that of the interpretation of the biblical text. As a source of faith and life, the Christian community seeks to apply the text to contemporary problems. This cannot be done without an interpretation of the Old and New Testaments. This is the chief role of Old Testament studies in the theological college, the interpretation of the Old Testament and its subsequent application to contemporary concerns.

It is in this role that the academic study of the Old Testament plays an important part. The Christian community expects that those who serve it will teach, preach, and apply the Old Testament in a manner that is not only spiritually refreshing and eminently practical, but also in a way that remains above reproach in terms of its skill. No interpretation of the Old Testament takes place in a void. All are responsible to make use of the best literary, linguistic, and historical methods appropriate to the material being studied. The academic study of the Old Testament is essential in order to guarantee that the interpreters of the text do so with the highest standards of integrity and skill that they are able to attain.

There should be no conflict between the spiritual, practical, and academic aspects of the theological college. Certainly, no student or member of staff should ever raise a false dichotomy between these. Education does not become 'more spiritual' and therefore 'less academic', or 'more academic' and therefore 'less practical'.[4] Properly un-

---

3. See, for example, S. E. Fowl and L. Gregory Jones, *Reading in Communion. Scripture and Ethics in Christian Life, Biblical Foundations in Theology* (London: SPCK, 1991); A. C. Thiselton, *New Horizons in Hermeneutics* (London: HarperCollins, 1992); and J. Goldingay, *Models for Scripture* (Carlisle: Paternoster, 1994).

4. For a vigorous defence of the highest standards of academic integrity in evangelical Christian education, see M. A. Noll, *The Scandal of the Evangelical Mind* (Leicester: InterVarsity Press, 1994).

derstood, the academic and practical aspects of training are fundamentally acts of spiritual worship. Further, the academic is necessary to support and strengthen the practical side, just as the practical is an essential outworking of the academic component. The spiritual and the academic support the goal of enabling the interpretation of the biblical text.

Relevance of the Old Testament

There are three areas in which the interpretation of the Old Testament provides relevance for the contemporary world: (1) as an example of a culture and its world view; (2) as a basis for Western civilisation; and (3) as a unique background and contribution to the Christian faith.

The Old Testament serves as an example of a culture and its world view. The book is a product of a people, of many authors writing over a period of centuries. In most cases we are not told, and do not know, when or how the material was written. Some of the earliest manuscripts that exist today were written centuries after their autographs. Among the earliest witnesses are those found among the Dead Sea Scrolls, preserved from as early as 200 BC. Already at this time other Jewish writers, and, a little later, Christian writers in the New Testament, refer to the books of the Old Testament. Sometimes they quote them. The Old Testament contains a variety of literature representing the concerns of a culture: law, administration, history, poetry, song, philosophy, and instructions on how to live, worship God, and treat other people. In it is found prophetic criticism of the society. It is not one book but many, reflecting the varied needs and concerns of a people. This has significance for us today. Present society and its problems can be better understood by looking at others such as the world of ancient Israel.

The Old Testament is also relevant to theological studies because it serves as a basis for Western civilisation. Civilisation is composed of ways of thinking and living. Morality and ethics owe much of their origin to the teachings of the Old Testament. It has made important contributions to ways of looking at the world in a variety of areas. For example, belief in one sovereign God was unusual in the ancient world. It revolutionised views of people and their value. Because they were all created in God's image (Genesis 1:26-28), everyone had worth. Thus the society included laws to protect the rights of those least able to protect themselves — orphans, widows, strangers. Possessing a common origin (Genesis 10), everyone was of equal value from the perspective of God. Thus no acts of murder could be tolerated. The decisions of people could affect the world for better or worse. Thus the story of David in 1 and 2 Samuel is one of the earliest examples of historical or biographical writing in which good and bad points of a character are noted and the reasons for actions and motivations are explored. Modern understandings of morality, justice, personhood, and self-worth are affected and informed by the Old Testament.

Most important for a theological college, however, is the unique contribution of the Old Testament to Christian faith. The New Testament looks to the Old Testament as its basis for interpreting the mission and person of Jesus of Nazareth. The Pentateuch introduces a deity who is one — loving and just. It introduces humanity as created to serve God, but also as sinful and in need of reconciliation with its Creator. The world is created by God but marred by sin and in need of restoration. The prophetic writings look forward to a future time of peace and justice in which God's law will reign from Jerusalem, the place where he lives. It describes a future ruler, in the ancient line of Israel's kings, who will establish this peace and justice between God and the people of God (*cf.* Isaiah 2:2-4; 9:6-7). Finally, the prophets speak of a servant who will bear the sins of many and, through this, bring about reconciliation between God and humanity (*cf.* Isaiah 52:13–53:12). The wisdom literature transforms the values and wisdom of the contemporary society by bringing all aspects of life under the sovereignty of God. The Psalms provide the context for praise and prayer in a variety of life's circumstances. They serve as models of worship and as a means to express before God fear and sorrow, anger and depression, joy and hope, and faith and love. For Christians, they are also important because the Old Testament, and especially the Psalms, served as the hymnal and prayer book for Jesus of Nazareth. They formed the source of his meditation. Through their study, it is possible to better understand the mind and heart of Jesus Christ.

Course Context

The nature of a theological college, especially one that seeks to award academic degrees, requires that its curriculum conforms to certain expectations common in higher education. These include several principles that have relevance for the formation of an Old Testament curriculum: modularity, progression, and integration.

Modular Structure

A modular structure allows for greater flexibility in the design of the curriculum and in its relevance to students, who are able to select and structure a personalised programme according to their requirements. Part-time students can more easily enter the programme. The essential components of a theological curriculum remain as core modules (required for all students). In addition, electives become accessible to those who wish to investigate specific areas.

The shift to a modular structure in many theological colleges has implications for the Old Testament curriculum. First, there is the greater uniformity of presentation that modules tend to impose.[5] While this has advantages for scheduling and for student expectation, it may require alterations to the curriculum so that several subjects are compressed into one module while other larger subjects are spread out over more than one module. For example, lectures on several smaller books of the Bible may form a single module rather than several series of lectures. Introductory Hebrew, on the other hand, may be divided into several modules throughout the year, rather than remain a single subject.

However, the modular system also demands a discipline. It means that lectures, assessments, and all matters related to the module are normally restricted to a single period of time. Thus students have a sense of completion of one module before proceeding to the next. This

---

5. The modular system is an essential component of U.S. higher education and it is often referred to as a 'course'. Thus one can speak of OT 101, Introduction to the Old Testament, as a course in North America. In the U.K. it would be designated as a module. The term 'course' refers to the entire programme of study leading to a degree, not just a single component of that programme.

means that there is less of a tendency to assess by examinations given at the end of a year or at the end of the course. The result is that students acquire a more complete knowledge of a module at the time that it is presented, but can more easily set it aside and not review it again. The solution is to identify the essential features of the education process and to review and develop them as the modules progress through the students' course.

Module sizes vary with the institution. The modules with which the author has worked are of uniform size. They meet three hours per week and extend over a period of eight or nine weeks, with a final week for examinations.

Progression

The element of progression assures that every module is positioned in a place in the students' course that is appropriate to their abilities and skills. It assumes that the course will provide a gradual development of difficulty in teaching and skills acquisition from the simplest to the most difficult. The progression should satisfy both the academic expectations of a degree-awarding course and the expectations of the students and of their potential career needs.

A course that seeks to prepare students to interpret the Old Testament in the light of the theological and ethical demands found in the faith communities that the students will serve involves three stages: an understanding of the basic content of the Old Testament; acquisition of the methods used in modern interpretation of the text; and the application of these methods to the interpretation of Old Testament texts. These goals reflect a natural progression in an Old Testament course. The first level emphasises knowledge of content, including its organisation and presentation. It is the essential background to appreciating the text with which the students work. The second area, that of the acquisition of methods, allows for the practice of interpreting Old Testament texts by applying these methods to various exegetical issues. It also introduces an analytic component in which the students must critically evaluate these methods and their value in interpretation. The third level develops naturally out of the second. Here the use of methods in biblical interpretation takes on a sophistication involving the creative choice and application of various methods, the integration of the broader context of the Old Testament and other theological disciplines, and the creative interpretation of Old Testament texts in the light of contemporary needs and concerns.

Integration

This element is not only important to the educational process and skill acquisition of interpreting the Old Testament, it also forms the unique component that sets the practice within the context of theology. Neither the recovery of ancient history nor the identification of literary themes and poetics alone will serve the needs of an interpretation of the Old Testament within the context of a theological college. In addition, there is the expectation that the study of the Old Testament will inform and be informed by the other theological disciplines. Questions of the following sort become relevant in such a context and serve to illustrate the distinctives of Old Testament education in the context of a theological college: Does Matthew use the Old Testament in a manner that can be said to conform with modern standards of interpretation? Was the Reformation justified in asserting the Hebrew canon over that represented by the Septuagint? Does the first chapter of Genesis argue for creation out of nothing? How does the Old Testament address the issue of abortion and the question of the beginnings of human life? Does the text approve of polygamy? How can the Psalms be used to help someone who is grieving for the loss of a loved one?

Sample Curriculum Design

The following proposal builds upon the previous assumptions regarding the goals of a theological college. It considers the concerns of course context and proposes a curriculum that agrees with the needs described there. Curriculum design here addresses the questions of the aims and objectives of modules, the teaching content, the forms of assessments and what they measure, and the place of the modules in the progression and overall design of the course. The introductory, skill, and integrative and creative segments each correspond to the three levels as described above. The Hebrew instruction includes levels II (introductory grammar) and III (readings).

(a) Introductory (Level I)

At the introductory level, an Old Testament module must provide students with a framework for all further work in Old Testament study. The module introduces the two 'worlds' of the Old Testament. There is the world of the text itself. This is the content of the Old Testament understood at its basic level, that of reading the text with a minimum of commentary. This world of the Old Testament explores the stories and teachings of the text. It presumes little or no background in the Old Testament. The focus will be on the more accessible texts found in the Pentateuch, historical books, and the prophets. An introduction to the poetry of the Psalms is also included.

The second world that students encounter at the introductory level is that in which the story of the Old Testament took place or was written. This world includes the geography and ecology of Palestine. It is an attempt to provide students with a sense of a culture and land different from their own, and thereby to place in their hands interpretive tools for the understanding of the Old Testament. A basic historical survey of political events within Palestine of the Old Testament period provides a framework for understanding the sequence of events.

These worlds are combined in the specific study of a number of Old Testament texts, such as Genesis 12, Deuteronomy 5, 2 Samuel 7, Isaiah 6–11, and the Servant Songs of chapters 40–55. Necessary to introductory presentations is an emphasis on lectures with the encouragement of questions and class discussion. Students prepare for the classes by completing prescribed readings, especially the assigned biblical text, but also the reading of other recommended literature of a biblical and theological nature.

Short objective tests given throughout the module contain questions drawn from reading assignment questions provided in advance to guide students through reading parts of the Old Testament and secondary literature. While these tests focus on the reading assignments, the written examination at the end of the module reviews the lectures discussed and presented in class. These assessments reflect the content orientation of this introductory level. This forms a necessary preparation to what follows and should not be ignored. It is not helpful to train students to do creative interpretation of texts until they understand something of the context of the Old Testament in terms of its two 'worlds'.

(b) Skill Development (Level II)

This level introduces a variety of interpretive methods and critically evaluates them. It assesses students both in their understanding of these methods and in their application of the methods in the interpretation of passages within the Old Testament. The primary concern is to interpret both the biblical texts often associated with the early period of Israel and those ascribed to prophetic and wisdom literature. Although this involves the critical scrutiny of interpretive methods, the structure of the module(s) follows that of the introductory level, *i.e.*, a survey of the Old Testament, ordering the Pentateuchal, prophetic (former and latter prophets), and other relevant texts in a traditional sequence. The Psalms and wisdom literature are considered separately. Note that the presentation of methods is integrated into the texts, not vice versa. The modules do not organise study of their texts around various methods, but work through the texts using a synthesis of relevant methods. This is important because it renders methods of interpretation secondary to the Old Testament text.

In the Pentateuchal texts and those that present Israel's life before the period of the Divided Monarchy, there is an emphasis on social science methods to recover political, economic, social, and other cultural dynamics of the early biblical world through the use of historical and archaeological methods. Students thus are able to identify and to justify their understanding of the earliest traditions of Israel's history. Literary approaches are also applied to legal and narrative texts. The Bible's prophetic and wisdom literature are then examined in order to identify major problems and issues in their interpretation. This section includes a comparative analysis of biblical and extrabiblical sources for the study of the Old Testament world of the first millennium B.C.

In addition to building on the foundation of the introductory Old Testament level, this level relates the Old Testament to other aspects of the traditional theological curriculum. Study of historical methods provides background to methods of study in church history. Study of social scientific approaches addresses questions of cultural anthropology and sociology similar to those encountered in mission studies. Study of the prophetic literature and of the wisdom literature provides backgrounds to aspects of New Testament and Christian doctrines.

Again a selection of texts from the Pentateuch, former Prophets, latter Prophets, and wisdom literature are examined in detail in order to model the critical use of methods for students. At this second level the class methods continue to include some lecture with discussion. However, there is an increased use of the biblical text where the lecturer asks individual students for their analysis of passages as the whole class works through the interpretive process. Discussions of social science approaches and especially archaeological methods lend themselves to the use of visual materials such as charts, slides, maps, etc. An important feature of this level is that the students are introduced to independent research. Practice is given in using bibliographic tools and other systems of access relevant to Old Testament studies. This is accomplished through assignments in class. Students practice locating and retrieving materials from the library and are introduced to a variety of research tools. At the same time, the process of researching and writing interpretive essays is discussed.

As always, assessments must reflect the aims of the particular level studied. A general knowledge and understanding of the Old Testament is assumed. Readings of additional Old Testament texts deepen this knowledge. The biblical text is interpreted through the application of a variety of methods. Readings dealing with methods (archaeological, sociological, linguistic, literary, etc.) follow with short objective tests designed to assess student understanding of the methods. However, the weight of the assessment concerns the student's application of these methods in the interpretation of biblical texts. This is assessed in the form of essays in which students interpret specific biblical passages. In so doing they must show bibliographic awareness of the major resources for their passage. They then analyse various methods used in interpreting the text, evaluate them, and synthesise the whole in the interpretive essay.

(c) *Integrative and Creative (Level III)*

Having gained an acquaintance with the variety of interpretive methods and skill in the interpretation of biblical passages, students can progress to specific sections of literature in the Old Testament. It is at this stage that the intensive study of Old Testament books is most appropriate, for it presupposes an understanding of their canonical context as well as an appreciation of the methods available for their interpretation. Books chosen may reflect the interest of students. From the perspective of a theological curriculum, the most important are probably Genesis, Psalms, and Isaiah. These form the major sources for New Testament references, for doctrinal sources, and for worship in the Christian community. Genesis provides the example here.

In their study of the book, students analyse a variety of interpretations of Genesis. They then interpret selected texts from the book of Genesis with a sensitivity to their literary form and structure. This surveys the whole book of Genesis and includes the critical study of its contents. It considers key texts that lie behind the Christian teachings of Creation, Fall, and Messianic hope. It provides the textual basis for theological studies touching on creation, sin, anthropology, women's studies, and the biblical view of history. It also surveys the literature and customs of the Ancient Near East relevant for comparison and contrast with the message of Genesis. Finally, it looks at the variety of literary approaches to the narrative texts of Genesis 12–50. Students interpret texts from these chapters in consultation with their peers. They discuss the implications of interpretive issues that emerge from their study in the classroom. They also prepare essays that are assessed by criteria similar to those at the previous level, though with higher expectations of performance. Thus a greater variety of methods should be applied to the interpretation and a better critical awareness of the strengths and weaknesses of these methods should be evident. In addition, the assessment adds an integrative component, in which the application of methods and issues from the other theological disciplines is integrated into the interpretation.

Teaching methods of lecture and discussion form a minor part of the module. One half of the class time is devoted to student presentations of their research in small groups. A text is introduced to the whole class at the beginning of the hour, with suggested issues for discussion.

15

The class divides into small groups that are each led by a student working on that text. This student can lead the small group in whatever way he/she wishes as long as the text is studied. At the end of the hour, the class reassembles and gathers together thoughts and ideas that have emerged on the text and issues of interpretation. The results are integrated into the study of the whole book of Genesis and its message.

(d) Hebrew

One of the most important methods for the interpretation of the Old Testament has not yet been addressed. This is the study of the original language(s) in which the Old Testament was written. It is not possible to interpret the Old Testament without a grasp of Hebrew. However, the realities of modern theological education in the English-speaking world dictate that, at best, this method remains an option for theological students. Most will not elect to study it. If it were made a requirement, it is feared that most would not attend the college course and would seek a theological course of studies elsewhere that did not require the study of Hebrew. Nevertheless, it has an important place in any curriculum concerned with the interpretation of the Old Testament.

The aims of Hebrew study in a theological college relate to the overall purpose of the Old Testament curriculum, to enhance the ability to understand and interpret the biblical text. In order to do this an understanding of the language is required. In addition, the application of the language to reading and interpreting the Hebrew Bible becomes an important goal in the teaching of the language.

No attempt to teach theological students Hebrew should compromise its standards for the sake of appeal or attractiveness. Such a decision will result in fewer students with less competency in the language, not with more students. For native English speakers with a minimum of acquaintance with foreign languages, the concept of a Semitic language is strange and a challenge to grasp. Adults will readily receive and understand a systematic presentation of the grammar.[6] Ideally, the study should introduce biblical passages for translation as soon as possible. The artificial Hebrew found in the exercises of older

6. Recent studies on androgogy confirm this understanding.

grammars should be avoided. Not only is it less attractive to students eager to 'get into the text' as quickly as possible, it is also not biblical Hebrew, but a non-native speaker's reconstruction. Thus the best grammar presentation simultaneously provides a systematic introduction to Hebrew grammar and moves students into reading biblical texts, however simple at the beginning.

Language learning is a skill in itself. Like physical skills, it is best learned with a 'coach' who is able to continually assess student progress and to correct errors before they become fixed in the minds of students. The methods used reflect these concerns and thus are different from those found in the English Bible modules. Written exercises and (both individual and group) practice in class comprise the majority of student contact time. The exercises are returned immediately, either in the same class or by the next class hour. Thus the student is able to correct any mistakes as quickly as possible. These exercises, like the drill and recitations, continually review essential grammatical structures and introduce new features of grammar. Although biblical texts are introduced from the beginning, they are selected according to the level of understanding of the student. As soon as the basic verb is understood, students move to reading an extensive selection of the biblical text, the opening chapters of Genesis for example. Student participation, in which students read, translate, and analyse the text's linguistic features, dominates the second half of the introductory level. The lecture is thus able to assess students as they participate and to provide suggestions for improving their skills.

The assessment at the level of learning the language itself includes written exercises that demonstrate the student's knowledge of basic grammar and vocabulary. Also, the reading of simple passages in the language allows the students to apply their knowledge in analysing and evaluating the meaning of the text. This may be assessed either by an examination that tests ability to translate the Hebrew text and explain important grammatical features or by an interpretive essay that discusses the meaning of the Hebrew text and demonstrates a knowledge of the grammar and word usage.

Once the essential components of the grammar are mastered (level II), the focus of the course becomes the reading and interpretation of Hebrew texts (level III). It is an axiom of language learning that regular, sustained contact with a language is preferable to a shorter more intensive exposure. Therefore, Hebrew reading modules are offered throughout the academic year and the student is encouraged to refine and develop reading and interpretive skills. A variety of Old Testament literature is chosen. Initially the student is introduced to narrative literature. Then the more challenging poetic and prophetic texts are studied. Because the texts read are never repeated, students are able to register for and to participate in Hebrew reading modules throughout their stay at the college.

As in the second half of the introductory level, the reading modules are mainly composed of student participation. However, an additional component is added to reading, translation, and grammatical analysis. At this level the students also interpret the biblical text and discuss its meaning in its original context. This incorporates the variety of methods introduced at levels II and III of the English Bible core curriculum.

The assessments focus on the student's ability to read, translate, and analyse the Hebrew texts, both orally in class and in written form in examinations and essays. The examinations include texts studied in class and require the student to analyse and evaluate various interpretations in the light of the Hebrew text. They also assess the ability to synthesise various methods and to creatively integrate methods of interpretation to make sense of the Hebrew text.

A Table in the Wilderness: Towards a Post-liberal Agenda for Old Testament Study

CRAIG G. BARTHOLOMEW

Craig G. Bartholomew is post-doctoral fellow in Old Testament hermeneutics at the Cheltenham and Gloucester College of Higher Education. He has also taught Old Testament at George Whitefield College in Cape Town, South Africa.

A Table in the Wilderness?

'Is there anyone among you who, if your child asks for bread, will give a stone?' Matthew 7:9

Jesus uses the metaphor of bread and stones in his teaching on prayer. The good father can be relied on to give that which is healthy and nourishing in response to his child's requests. If we think of Old Testament studies as something which is served up to students in our universities, colleges, and seminaries, then we could appropriate this metaphor by asking, Is Old Testament studies in its present state bread or stones? Are the Old Testament curriculums of our day healthy and nourishing?

In his preface to Thomas Oden's recent book, *Requiem*, Richard John Neuhaus declares that while Christianity does offer a feast, much theological education tends to operate a long way from that feast:

More and more 'young fogeys' like Oden are discovering the truth that is 'ever ancient, ever new' (Augustine). It is called the catholic faith, and it is a feast to which he invites us. It is a movable feast, still developing under the guidance of the Spirit. Oden is like cinema's 'Auntie Mame,' who observed that life is a banquet and most poor slobs are starving to death. Origen, Irenaeus, Cyril of Alexandria, Thomas Aquinas, Teresa of Avila, Martin Luther, John Calvin, John Wesley — the names fall trippingly from Oden's tongue like a gourmet surveying a most spectacular table. Here are arguments you can sink your teeth into, conceptual flights of intoxicating complexity, and truths to die for. Far from the table, over there, *way* over there is American theological education where prodigal academics feed starving students on the dry husks of their clever unbelief.[1]

The Christian tradition offers a table in the wilderness, but, according to this view, much contemporary theology has so succumbed to the wilderness that it has moved away from the table. For Oden, who has recently returned from the wilderness of avant-garde, modernistic theology to evangelical orthodoxy, the contemporary wilderness has been the lure of modernity. Oden's title *Requiem* relates not only to his move away from modernistic theology, but primarily to the death of modernity. Part of Oden's critique of theology is that it has bought far too strongly into the spirit of modernity, a spirit which Oden maintains is now on its last legs.

Personally I think Oden may be too quick to lament modernity; in my view the post-modern turn is not truly post-modern but rather a manifestation of the tensions and contradictions within modernity,[2] and what we are seeing is better described as late or high modernity. Either way, what the post-modern turn has done is to expose some of the prejudices of modernity and to call them to account. What was often called 'bread' in modernity is now being exposed as 'stone' by many, and of course, where theology has succumbed to the agenda of modernity, it too inevitably shares in that crisis. It is another of those situations about which Dean Inge warned — whoever is married to the spirit of this age is destined to be a widow in the next.

1. Foreword in T. Oden, *Requiem* (Nashville: Abingdon, 1995), p. xx.
2. See C. Bartholomew, 'Post/Late? Modernity as the Context for Christian Scholarship Today', *Themelios* 22, 2 (1997), pp. 25-38.

In the academy one of the results of the crisis of modernity is a situation of increasing pluralism in which a variety of approaches compete for adherence. In this pluralistic context there is increased pressure to account for one's approach. It is no longer, for example, so easy to assume the autonomy of reason as the final arbiter of truth. In my opinion this situation is to be welcomed because it encourages Christians to have a close look at the extent to which their scholarship has been shaped by and rooted in modernity, and, like Oden, to ask how compatible modernity is with Christianity.

Modernity is, of course, a complex phenomenon to which we are all indebted in too many ways to mention. A Christian approach to modernity ought not to be the attempt to recreate the pre-modern situation, as critics of modernity like Oden, Newbigin, and Lyon recognise.[3] Nevertheless, it remains true that the basic roots or world view that underlies modernity is profoundly at odds with a transformative Christian perspective upon the world.[4] Few scholars have exposed this as clearly as Lesslie Newbigin.[5] Christianity is public truth and the Cartesian legacy that Descartes bequeathed to the West is antithetical to a biblical approach to knowledge. I do not have time to argue this in detail here, but suffice to say that if Newbigin's type of analysis is correct, as I believe it is, then Oden is right. The more theology succumbs to the agenda and world view of modernity, the further it moves from the table in the wilderness.

But what, you may wonder, has this got to do with Old Testament studies? To a large extent the modern discipline of Old Testament studies is a product of modernity; and, as with theology, one of the questions we will need to ask if we are to assess the extent to which it is 'bread', is, 'to

3. See Bartholomew, 'Post/Late? Modernity', for full references to these authors. A select bibliography of Newbigin's writings can be found in L. Newbigin, *Unfinished Agenda: An Updated Autobiography* (Edinburgh: St. Andrew Press, 1993), pp. 264-67.

4. I am assuming in this argument that the transformative understanding of the Christ-culture relationship is the most biblical one. See H. Reinhold Niebuhr, *Christ and Culture* (London: Harper Colophon, 1975), for a discussion of the different Christian paradigms for understanding this relationship, and A. Wolters, *Creation Regained* (Leicester: InterVarsity Press, 1985), for a superb statement of this type of approach. It is undoubtedly true that, if one has a different understanding of the Christ-culture relationship, one may well evaluate modernity quite differently.

5. See, for example, L. Newbigin, *Proper Confidence. Faith, Doubt and Certainty in Christian Discipleship* (London: SPCK, 1995).

21

what extent has it been integrally shaped by the world view of modernity?' Among liberals and conservatives there is widespread acknowledgement of this shaping. Henry Vander Goot argues as follows:

> The integration of faith and learning in the discipline of biblical studies means that the world view investigated in the text must also be accepted as the world view from the vantage point of which the text is investigated. Only under such circumstances is the Bible's total claim properly acknowledged. Where the biblical framework is not taken to be the context for scientific study, the only other option seems to be the acceptance of a fact-value, science-faith distinction in which the two tracks of life in the ecclesia and scholarship in the university are scrupulously kept apart. Where scientific theology is not ecclesially funded, it nonetheless continues to be funded pre-theoretically and that usually by the climate of opinion which happens at any given moment to reign within the discipline. Where this latter situation obtains, one finds specifically that the conduct of theological scholarship often takes place on unconscious foundations not so easily reconcilable with the Christian story because in the modern centuries secularism has taken possession of the intellectual field. Unfortunately much modern scientific study of the Bible as an historical source illustrates this all too well.[6]

In his Oxford inaugural Ernest Nicholson is quite clear about the historical roots of the historical-critical method that has dominated Old Testament studies over the past two hundred or so years. The name of the historical-critical method indicates its source; it emerged from the historical thinking that came out of the Enlightenment, received further impulses from Romanticism, and burgeoned in the German historical school of the nineteenth century.

> To a remarkable extent, indeed to a greater extent than has often been realized or acknowledged, it was this historical thinking that provided the basis of biblical hermeneutics in the nineteenth century, and more than the theologians and biblical scholars themselves it was the leading figures of the German historical school — Barthold Gustav Niebuhr, Wilhelm von Humboldt, Leopold von Ranke, Johan

---

6. H. Vander Goot, *The Bible in Theology and the Church* (New York and Toronto: Edwin Mellen Press, 1984), p. 83.

Gustav Droysen, Theodor Mommsen, and others — who created the interpretive framework and provided the method.[7]

Of course, Nicholson and Vander Goot would evaluate this rootage of the historical-critical method very differently. But both would agree that contemporary Old Testament studies have been far more deeply shaped by modernity than most of us realise. In his inaugural Nicholson wonders whether historical criticism could be a Sisyphean toil, never really making progress, but he soon rejects that possibility. Ten years down the line that possibility cannot be so easily rejected. Historical criticism is in crisis and there is broad recognition among Christian scholars that changes need to be made in the hermeneutic we use in reading the Bible. While few would deny that immense progress has been made through historical analysis of the Old Testament, Alister McGrath is right to speak of the 'Babylonian Captivity of the Bible':

> Formerly undertaken within the community of faith, it [the study of Scripture] has been banished to a community with its own definite — although often unacknowledged and unstated — sets of beliefs and values. As a result, it is held in bondage. It is not free to challenge those beliefs, but is judged in their light.[8]

This captivity has resulted in much Old Testament study serving up stones rather than bread.[9] In a volume of this sort on teaching the Old Testament it should also be noted that this captivity is as true of the

---

7. *Interpreting the Old Testament: A Century of the Oriel Professorship* (Oxford: Clarendon, 1981), p. 16. See also W. S. Vorster, 'Towards a Post-Critical Paradigm: Progress in New Testament Scholarship?', in J. Mouton, A. G. van Aarde and W. S. Vorster (eds.), *Paradigms and Progress in Theology* (South Africa: Human Sciences Research Council, 1988), pp. 31-48.

8. A. McGrath, 'Reclaiming Our Roots and Vision: Scripture and the Stability of the Christian Church', in C. E. Braaten and R. W. Jenson, *Reclaiming the Bible for the Church* (Edinburgh: T & T Clark, 1995), pp. 63-88, 69.

9. I will not here argue in detail how contemporary Old Testament study is often 'stone' rather than 'bread'. In my *Reading Ecclesiastes: OT Exegesis and Hermeneutical Theory* (forthcoming) (Analecta Biblica, Rome: PBI, 1998) I track in detail the negative effect of historical criticism upon the interpretation of Ecclesiastes. In section four of this paper I set my proposals in opposition to the effect of modernity upon Old Testament interpretation, thus exposing some of the 'stone' of contemporary Old Testament studies.

philosophies of education that shape most of the modern institutions within which Old Testament studies are taught.[10] Price sums up the history of the philosophy of education in the following way:

> The history of philosophy of education reflects a movement evident in other phases of thought — a successive contribution on the part of antiquity to the Christian ideal for transmitting culture from one generation to another and then a gradual elimination from that ideal of supernatural and Christian elements. . . . one way of understanding the history of philosophy of education is to regard the attitude of philosophers towards the justification and explanation of educational theory as having been expressed first in Plato's classic supernaturalism, next in Augustine's Christian supernaturalism, and then in undergoing a gradual alteration into the wholly non-Christian and naturalistic view represented by John Dewey.[11]

In a recent article Ruth Jonathan acknowledges that modern liberal education's

> overarching aim has been the maximal development of the rational autonomy of each . . . to the eventual benefit of all. In ordinary language, liberal education in modern times has aimed at the freeing of each from ignorance, prejudice and superstition, so that the maximal development of their talents and tastes would give rise to a fairer, freer, more reasonable and decent — and also a richer (both culturally and materially) — world.[12]

Any Christian assessment of the current state of Old Testament studies must therefore take account of the relationship between Old Testament studies and modernity, and of the philosophy of education shaping the teaching of the Old Testament. This is a large task, and in this article we will confine ourselves to the curriculum of Old Testament

10. At least in the U.K. Philosophy of education is also undergoing the crisis in its identity typical of the post-modern turn, as recent editions of the *Journal of the Philosophy of Education* make quite clear.

11. K. Price, 'History of Philosophy of Education', in P. Edwards (ed.), *The Encyclopedia of Philosophy*, vol. 6 (New York/London: MacMillan and Free/Collier-MacMillan, 1967), pp. 230-43, 242.

12. R. Jonathan, 'Liberal Philosophy of Education: A Paradigm Under Strain', *Journal of Philosophy of Education* 29, 1 (1995), pp. 93-108, 97.

studies, returning briefly to the question of the philosophy of education at the end. The post-modern turn and the resulting pluralism in Old Testament studies necessitate this sort of examination, but even more so does the nature of Christianity as public truth. Not only does the post-modern turn call many of the roots of modernity into question, but those roots are largely antithetical to Christianity. This does not for a moment mean that nothing good has come out of modernity or the historical-critical method. Quite the contrary. But it does mean that a Christian evaluation of the contemporary state of Old Testament studies will need to be alert to the shaping influence of modernity.

Required: A Post-liberal Agenda for Old Testament Studies

The preceding discussion provides a perspective on the current state of Old Testament studies by arguing that mainline Old Testament studies has generally been too closely and unhealthily associated with modernity.[13] My suggestion is that the way for Old Testament studies to recover its health is for it to pursue a post-liberal agenda. George Lindbeck appears to have coined the phrase 'post-liberal theology' as a way of describing the family resemblance of the work of a number of Yale theologians.[14] William Placher sums up the concerns of post-liberal theology as follows:

> Postliberal theology attends to the biblical narratives as narratives rather than simply as historical sources or as symbolic expressions of truths which could be expressed non-narratively. But unlike some other theologians interested in narrative, postliberals do not let the stories of *our* lives set the primary context for theology. They insist that the *biblical* narratives provide the framework within which Christians understand the world. Christian theology describes how the world looks as seen from that standpoint; it does not claim to argue from some 'neutral' or

13. In an unpublished paper, 'Reading the Bible in Postmodern Times', I have argued that conservative biblical studies have often also been as deeply and unhealthily shaped by modernity as liberal scholarship.

14. G. Lindbeck, 'Toward a Postliberal Theology', in *The Nature of Doctrine. Religion and Theology in a Postliberal Age* (London: SPCK, 1984).

'objective' position and indeed denies the possibility of such a position. It pursues apologetics, therefore, only on an *ad hoc* basis, looking for common ground with a given conversation partner but not assuming some universally acceptable standard of rationality.[15]

The crucial insight of post-liberal theology, in my opinion, is its recognition that Christians ought to allow the Word to frame and interpret our world rather than our understanding of the world framing and interpreting the Word.[16] In other words, an integrally Christian agenda is required in Old Testament studies. Christians find it comparatively easy to see the need for Christian theology, but often find it very difficult to see how a Christian agenda could be important in other areas as well. In this respect A. Plantinga's "Advice to Christian Philosophers" is particularly illuminating. Plantinga is a leading American philosopher, and he proposes a direction for Christians in philosophy that one could call post-liberal. It recommends precisely the sort of direction that I have in mind for Old Testament studies. He suggests that

> Christian philosophers and Christian intellectuals generally must display more autonomy — more independence of the rest of the philosophical world. Second Christian philosophers must display more integrity — integrity in the sense of integral wholeness, or oneness, or unity, being all of one piece. Perhaps 'integrality' would be the better word here. And necessary to these two is a third: Christian courage, or boldness, or strength, or perhaps Christian self-confidence. We Christian philosophers must display more faith, more trust in the Lord; we must put on the whole armour of God.[17]

Plantinga is not for a moment suggesting that Christian philosophers should not be deeply involved in mainstream philosophy, but he is also insisting that

15. W. Placher, 'Postliberal Theology', in D. F. Ford (ed.), *The Modern Theologians. An Introduction to Christian Theology in the Twentieth Century* (Oxford: Blackwell, 1989), pp. 115-28, 117.

16. I would not necessarily want to endorse all aspects of post-liberal theology. In this respect see, *e.g.*, the critique of Lindbeck in A. McGrath, *The Genesis of Doctrine* (Oxford: Blackwell, 1990).

17. A. Plantinga, 'Advice to Christian Philosophers', *Faith and Philosophy* 1, 3 (1984), pp. 253-71. This article is the text of his 1983 inaugural as J. A. O'Brien Professor of Philosophy at the University of Notre Dame.

[t]he Christian philosophical community must work out the answers to *its* questions; and both the questions and the appropriate ways of working out their answers may presuppose beliefs rejected at most of the leading centers of philosophy. But the Christian is proceeding quite properly in starting from these beliefs, even if they are so rejected. He is under no obligation to confine his research projects to those pursued at those centers, or to pursue his own projects on the basis of the assumptions that prevail there.[18]

Plantinga defends the right of Christian philosophers to start from belief in God in their philosophical endeavours. He reviews theism's relationship to discussions in philosophy about verifiability, the theory of knowledge, and philosophical anthropology and concludes that theists would fare far better if they worked from their own starting point rather than trying, as has so often been done, to 'trim their sails to the prevailing philosophical winds of doctrine.'[19]

It is worth reading Plantinga's article in its entirety. Suffice it to make the point here, that we need the same kind of vision in Old Testament studies. Of course Christians need to be in touch with, and deeply involved in, the issues that mainstream Old Testament studies are throwing up. But at the same time it is vital that Christians in Old Testament studies display autonomy, integrality, and boldness in shaping an agenda which is integrally Christian. The best of evangelical Old Testament scholarship has generally manifested these characteristics and indeed evangelical Old Testament scholars have achieved a great deal over the past decades. Take Genesis scholarship, for example; we have moved from having Calvin, Young's works, Leupold, and Kidner, to all this plus Wenham and Hamilton. However, this progress has very often taken place amidst the deep connivance of liberals and conservatives with modernity, often in unhelpful ways. It is thus imperative that we reflect consciously on where we have come from and where we are going. This is particularly important in the present 'post-modern' hour, which, from a post-liberal perspective provides a unique opportunity, indeed an imperative, for Christian Old Testament scholars to reassess their discipline and to re-form it along integrally Christian lines. This

18. 'Advice to Christian Philosophers', p. 263.
19. This is Plantinga's expression. See 'Advice to Christian Philosophers', p. 258.

is not for a moment to underestimate all that has been achieved but to ask how to preserve the good in evangelical *and* liberal Old Testament scholarship, and how to develop it into the future. There needs, in my view, to be a lot of discussion among Christian Old Testament scholars about the dangers and opportunities, the areas of defence and attack in Old Testament studies today. There is a need for an agenda — not the final word, but a resounding call to serve Christ together in the delightful field of Old Testament studies today and some indication of the direction this ought to take in our situation.

A Reformational Post-liberal Agenda

Within the evangelical tradition the work of scholars like E. J. Young and the late R. K. Harrison has helped many to keep alive the possibility of a Christian agenda in Old Testament studies. Indeed, until today no work has appeared that replaces Harrison's *Introduction to the Old Testament*.[20] These scholars laboured at a time when a confessional approach to the Old Testament seemed doomed to extinction. The historical approach of liberal scholars appeared to threaten the very nature of Scripture as God's Word, and so it was here that they fought the good fight. In such circumstances their strategy was perfectly understandable. However, over the long term it is crucial that this defence is replaced by a strategy in which a Christian agenda determines the work sites. My suspicion is that many evangelicals still tend to react and to allow their work sites to be determined by others' agendas, albeit in negative mirror image, rather than to allow their work sites to emerge in relation to a 'gospel'[21] (*i.e.*, integrally Christian) agenda.

Take, for example, the current post-modernism that is being felt

---

20. In a discussion with R. K. Harrison shortly before his death, I learnt that he had revised his *Introduction* but that the publisher had thought it too long for a revised edition.

21. It cannot be stressed too strongly that I do not mean this in a naive, fundamentalist sense. I use 'gospel' to refer to the Christ event in all its depth and complexity. With its background in Isaiah etc., 'gospel' refers to the Christ event as that through which God's creation purposes are achieved and around which the whole of reality revolves. If this is an accurate description of the Christ event, then clearly it must shape OT studies in some way.

all over the academy, including in theology and biblical studies.[22] There is no doubt that Christian scholars ought to take this new trend seriously.[23] However, it would be a mistake for Christian scholars to expend all their energy there and to neglect work sites that their own perspective makes important. Alvin Plantinga is most perceptive in this respect. He calls much of this post-modernism creative anti-realism and says,

> creative antirealism is presently popular among philosophers; this is the view that it is human behaviour — in particular, human thought and language — that is somehow responsible for the fundamental structure of the world and for the fundamental kinds of entities there are. From a theistic point of view, however, universal creative anti-realism is at best a piece of laughable bravado. For *God*, of course, owes neither his existence nor his properties to us and our ways of thinking; the truth is just the reverse. And so far as the created universe is concerned, while it indeed owes its existence and character to activity on the part of a person, that person is certainly not a *human* person.[24]

In this light it is not surprising to hear Plantinga say that

> [t]he Christian or theistic philosopher, therefore, has his own way of working at his craft. In some cases there are items on his agenda — pressing items — not to be found on the agenda of the non-theistic philosophical community. In others, items that are currently fashionable appear of relatively minor interest from a Christian perspective. In still others, the theist will reject common assumptions and views about how to start, how to proceed, and what constitutes a good or satisfying answer. In still others the Christian will take for granted and will start from assumptions and premises rejected by the philosophical community at large.[25]

---

22. See, *e.g.*, D. R. Griffin, W. A. Beardslee, and J. Holland, *Varieties of Post-modern Theology* (New York: SUNY, 1989). In the U.K. 'post-modernity' was the theme of the January 1996 SOTS conference.

23. A. Thiselton, *Interpreting God and the Postmodern Self* (Edinburgh: T & T Clark, 1995), p. 16, rightly notes of the more extreme versions of post-modernism that, 'These perspectives constitute the most serious and urgent challenges to theology, in comparison with which the old-style attacks from "common-sense positivism" appear relatively naive'.

24. Plantinga, 'Advice to Christian Philosophers', p. 269.

25. Plantinga, 'Advice to Christian Philosophers', p. 270.

Of course it is vital that Christians respond to current scholarly trends. Responding to modernistic Old Testament scholarship is, however, different from allowing modernistic Old Testament scholarship to set the overarching agenda. In this respect the distinction in Reformational philosophy between transformational as opposed to reformational scholarship is helpful. 'Transformational' and 'reformational' are two terms from reformational philosophy,[26] each of which tries to get at the heart of what Christian scholarship should be about. Johannes Klapwijk has argued over the past few years that Christian scholarship should be transformational.[27] This approach to scholarship should, in his view, be based on assessment, arrest, and appropriation with the central category as transformation. He resurrects the notion of 'spolatio' (spoiling the Egyptians) and focuses the direction of transformational philosophy in terms of sanctification compared with the secularisation of secular philosophy. The transformational approach recommends that Christians work where the key sites of action are and try and transform these sites towards a Christian direction. 'The idea of transformational philosophy excludes by definition, however, the possibility of a separate alternative circuit of Christian scholarly praxis because it proceeds on the basis of the dynamic notion of possessio.'[28] If I understand Klapwijk correctly, he wishes to focus Christian scholarship away from the development of integrally Christian scholarship and towards transforming secular ideas.

The reformational approach, associated with the Dutch philosophers Dooyeweerd[29] and Vollenhoven, sees by comparison the need for the development of scholarship that is driven by integrally Christian roots. If one imagines scholarship as a building then the structure should emerge out of and take its direction from Christian foundations.

26. Reformational philosophy is that tradition of Reformed philosophy that has developed in the neo-Calvinist line of Herman Dooyeweerd and Dirk Vollenhoven. The word 'reformational' was coined by the Canadian aesthetician Calvin Seerveld, to describe philosophy in the Reformed tradition which consciously seeks to be shaped by a Christian world view.

27. J. Klapwijk, 'Reformational Philosophy on the Boundary Between the Past and Future', *Philosophia Reformata* 53 (1988), pp. 101-34.

28. J. Klapwijk, 'Reformational Philosophy', p. 105.

29. The best contemporary explanation of Dooyeweerd's philosophy is that of R. Clouser, *The Myth of Religious Neutrality* (Notre Dame: University of Notre Dame Press, 1991).

The reformational approach recognises the importance of dialogue with and transformation of existing work sites but insists that the edifice of (for example) Old Testament studies must be developed as a whole along integral Christian lines. For a reformational scholar it is not enough to see where the work sites are and then to try and work Christianly there. More fundamental questions surface, such as: If I take a Christian perspective on reality seriously and see my work in Old Testament studies as service of the Lord Christ, then where ought the work sites to be in Old Testament studies today?

Obviously both transformational and reformational Old Testament scholarship are needed. And both approaches presuppose that Christian scholarship ought to be Christian. However, it does seem to me that the dominant requirement is reformational Old Testament scholarship; and my suggestion is that evangelical Old Testament scholarship tends to be transformational rather than reformational.[30] This seems to me a dangerous path to pursue. Much evangelical scholarship has been of this sort; let so-called 'liberals' set the agenda and then evangelicals will fight according to their agenda and try and defend the cause where they create the battle. Within Old Testament scholarship this has often been the pattern, with evangelicals taking a reactive rather than a proactive stance, so that in the process both evangelicals and liberals tend to have been deeply in the grip of modernity.

The problem with this is that one never gets round to doing positive scholarship that is integrally Christian. Christian scholarship needs, of course, to be deeply in touch and in dialogue with secular trends, and to be busy with transformation, but this cannot be the heart of our direction. Re-formation of the sciences should remain our primary concern; this will always involve transformation but it will be more than that in its construction of integrally Christian scholarship. As Calvin Seerveld has said, synthesis may be our practice but it should never be our policy.[31] Scripturally led believers do have a head start in their orientation to the truth, and as Kuyper indicated, 'What we really

30. This is of course a generalisation. In the present crisis in Old Testament studies there are encouraging signs of evangelicals and others striking out in bold, new directions, some of which I refer to in section 4 of this paper.
31. In a personal conversation.

need is a seedling of scientific theory [read "OT theory"] thriving on Christian roots. For us to be content with the act of shuffling around in the garden of somebody else, scissors in hand [to cut the other's flowers], is to throw away the honour and worth of our Christian faith.'[32]

In our Old Testament scholarship we are called to love God and serve our neighbours. Another way of expressing this is that we are to serve up good, nutritious bread to our neighbours, baked as best we are able. Historical criticism has been so shaped by modernity that it has generally not produced bread but stones; the danger with transformational Old Testament scholarship is that it produces at best only less dangerous stones! It never has the time for the inner reformation of Old Testament studies so that we can start producing some loaves, however inadequate and immature — this will only happen if we allow a Christian perspective to determine our agenda in Old Testament studies.

The 'great' thing with 'post-modernity' is that no one knows where the Old Testament work sites should be anymore anyway! There is widespread agreement that Old Testament studies are in a state of flux and uncertainty with no signs of an emerging paradigm-consensus.[33] There is no longer one historical-critical agenda, if there ever was one. David Clines will give you one agenda and certain work sites, John Collins will tell you that the historical-critical work sites are still the place to operate from, Brevard Childs will encourage you to focus on the final canonical form, and so on. We are now in a situation where you have to account for your work sites![34] I welcome this because it encourages Christians to account for their agenda in Old Testament studies rather than accepting a non-Christian agenda and trying to work Christianly within it.

32. A. Kuyper, *De Gemeene Gratie,* 3 vols. (Kampen: Kok, 1902-5), vol. 3, p. 527.
33. See *Biblical Interpretation* I (1993) for a number of papers dealing with the present state of Old Testament scholarship.
34. See J. Levenson, *The Hebrew Bible, the Old Testament and Historical Criticism* (Louisville: Westminster/John Knox, 1993).

Some Contours of a Post-liberal Agenda

If we were to pursue a post-liberal agenda in Old Testament studies, what shape would such an agenda take? That is of course a huge question. In this final section I want to merely make some suggestions about the sort of contours such an agenda might take.[35] I should mention at the outset that I am assuming that Old Testament study is a theoretical discipline within the academy/university.[36] It is a different activity from Bible study or devotional use of the Old Testament, however closely related it is and should be to these other activities. An Old Testament lecture is not, and should not be, a Bible study or quiet time. Theoretical, precise analysis characterises Old Testament studies, whereas attentive, whole-person listening characterises devotional reading of the Bible. In relation to this it is important to

35. The tentative nature of this section needs to be stressed. My main concern in this paper is to make the point that we are in urgent need of a post-liberal agenda in Old Testament studies. It should also be stressed that I do not regard a post-liberal agenda as one which would simply erase all that has gone on in Old Testament studies over the past one hundred years. In my opinion huge advances have been and are being made, and a post-liberal agenda would want to secure and build on these.

36. I do not have space in this article to reflect in detail upon the differences between a university and a theological college. In my view Old Testament studies should be integrally Christian in both, insofar as they are being practiced by Christians. This is not to deny non-Christians the right to do Old Testament studies of course! A democratic society should allow societal pluralism to manifest itself in all sectors of society including the university. The point is that such a pluralism would also allow Christians the right to let their most basic beliefs shape their scholarship. I am arguing that Christian Old Testament scholars in the university and the theological college should positively and critically let their basic beliefs shape their scholarship. Some basic beliefs have to fulfill this function, and it is difficult to see why these should be non-Christian rather than Christian, since neutral, objective basic beliefs are an impossibility. The difference, in my view, between Old Testament studies in the university as compared with the seminary relates to the more theoretical nature of the university compared with the more practical nature of the seminary. (*Cf.* J. J. Venter, 'Yesterday and Today; the Task of the University', in *Social Theory and Practice, Koers* XL 4, 5, 6 (1975), pp. 402-18, on the theoretical task of the university.) The important point is that taking Christian presuppositions seriously in Old Testament studies in the university does not mean turning the university into a seminary or Bible college. A university might, for example, have a practical theology department which reflects theoretically on Christian praxis, but its task is not to teach the practical skills of preaching.

remember that God has not given us his Word primarily for theoretical analysis. It is given to all God's people — not just to scholars — and is to be received by God's people in a trusting, listening manner that will equip us for service of the King in his world. Old Testament study is thus a secondary activity in relation to the purpose of Scripture, and ought to be directed towards deepening the primary activity of listening to Scripture.[37]

1. Post-liberal Old Testament study would have far more of a kerygmatic focus.

In his creative application of speech-act theory to biblical hermeneutics Nicholas Wolterstorff declares,

> So I recognize that that interpretative practice which reads and interprets the Christian Bible so as to discern what God is saying thereby is only one among many alternative, contested practices. Though it was the dominant interpretative practice in the Christian community for about 1500 years, it is my impression that it has pretty much disappeared from the academic community and now puts in its appearance mainly in homiletical and devotional settings.[38]

If Scripture is God's Word, then clearly from a Christian perspective the neglect of approaching it as such is a serious indictment of the academy. Brevard Childs makes a related point to Wolterstorff's when he insists that

> The final task of exegesis is to seek to hear the Word of God, which means that the witness of Moses and Jeremiah, of Paul and John, must become a vehicle for another Word. The exegete must come to wrestle with the kerygmatic substance which brought into being the witness.[39]

37. Vander Goot, *The Bible in Theology*, explores this relationship between pre-theoretical and theoretical approaches to Scripture in detail.

38. N. Wolterstorff, *Divine Discourse. Philosophical Reflections on the Claim That God Speaks* (Cambridge: Cambridge University Press, 1995), p. 131.

39. B. Childs, 'Interpretation in Faith', *Interpretation* 18 (1964), pp. 432-49, 443.

Childs's canonical project is a massive attempt to recover this kerygmatic aspect of Scripture in Old Testament studies. As he has noted again and again, it is an aspect of Scripture that historical criticism does not do justice to. Interestingly, the neglect of the kerygmatic focus[40] of the Old Testament is a characteristic of much liberal and conservative Old Testament scholarship. Especially within liberal Old Testament circles, the historical-critical agenda has continually tended to focus on the stages underlying the final form of the text and away from the text as a unified whole. So much so has this been the case that Francis Watson says of biblical studies,

> To work with the final form of the texts, removed from this diachronic framework and envisaged now as relatively autonomous linguistic artefacts, is therefore to propose a major reorientation or paradigm-shift within the discipline.[41]

Historical criticism tends to have biblical scholars devoting all their energies to the stages underlying the final form of the text, and rarely getting to expound the kerygma or message of the text as a whole.[42]

This is clear, for example, in the history of the interpretation of Ecclesiastes where there is no single, major critical commentary on the present (final) form of Ecclesiastes.[43] It is true that there has been a

---

40. 'Kerygma' has received sustained attention in theology this century, particularly by Barth, Bultmann, and Dodd. I am using 'kerygmatic' in the general sense of a focus for interpretation upon the message/communicative function of biblical texts. This general usage needs to be nuanced in relation to these other theological uses, but I cannot pursue this here. Suffice it to note that the kerygmatic focus I am proposing is inseparable from important and complex hermeneutical issues. Speech act theory is particularly useful in terms of developing a nuanced approach to biblical texts which takes account of their communicative function. On the relevance of this for evangelical biblical interpretation see A. Thiselton's very useful 'Authority and Hermeneutics: Some Proposals for a More Creative Agenda,' in P. E. Satterthwaite and D. F. Wright (eds.), *A Pathway into the Holy Scripture* (Grand Rapids: Eerdmans, 1994), pp. 107-41.

41. F. Watson, *Text, Church and World, Biblical Interpretation in Theological Perspective* (Edinburgh: T & T Clark, 1994), p. 15.

42. There are obvious exceptions to this. The journal *Interpretation*, for example, was founded to focus on the kerygma of the Bible. A responsibility of a post-liberal approach would be to search out these positive strands in the history of Old Testament interpretation and critically appropriate them in the present.

43. For a detailed assessment of this history see my *Reading Ecclesiastes*.

growing sense of the literary unity of Ecclesiastes this century, but the legacy of the extreme source criticism of Ecclesiastes at the turn of the century lingers, in that the epilogue continues to be excluded from this unity without serious reexamination. Michael Fox's work[44] is an important exception to the failure to wrestle with the literary shape of Ecclesiastes, although he has not written a major commentary on the book. Fox is one of a few contemporary commentators who insist on taking the frame of Ecclesiastes seriously as an integral part of Ecclesiastes.[45] Fox's reading of the epilogue in relation to the main body of the book is debatable, in my opinion, but his focus on Ecclesiastes as a literary text is crucial if the kerygma of Ecclesiastes, *i.e.* the canonical text as we have it, is to be discerned.[46]

Although conservative Old Testament scholars have tended to stress the unity of Old Testament texts much more strongly, often in reaction to historical criticism, this has not, however, meant that they have focused their interpretative endeavours on the kerygma of the individual texts. Consider the Tyndale commentaries for example — this is in general their weak area. They are often full of useful particular comments and exploration of major themes in the Old Testament books, but they generally have little detail on the communicative function of the text as a literary whole in its original context or today. A Christian hermeneutic would insist on bringing all its weight and exegetical spade work to bear here. This is not to suggest that the historical and literary and thematic dimensions of texts should be neglected but that, in terms of biblical interpretation, they should be subordinate to the explication of the kerygma of the text.

Consider, for example, the book of Kings. What was its message to its original hearers? For all the value of contemporary commentaries this question rarely receives sustained attention. The focus has been on

44. 'Frame Narrative and Composition in the Book of Qoheleth,' *HUCA* 48 (1977), pp. 83-106; *Qoheleth and His Contraditions* (Sheffield: Almond, 1989). For an assessment of Fox's reading of the epilogue see C. Bartholomew, *Reading Ecclesiastes*.

45. G. Ogden, *Qoheleth* (Sheffield: JSOT), is also very helpful in taking the shape of Ecclesiastes as a whole seriously.

46. In *Reading Ecclesiastes* I have tried to show just how significant it is for the interpretation of 'Ecclesiastes' if 'the book' is read without the epilogue as an integral part.

the underlying events rather than on the kerygma of the text in its final form. The historical aspect of the text is important, but Kings is not primarily a history book; it is kerygmatically focused.[47] This is why Leah Bronner's work on the Elijah, Elisha narratives is so useful.[48] It sets them against what we know of Baal and they spring to life as we see that all that is predicated of Baal is actually true of Yahweh! Reflection on this perspective as addressed to the exilic and post-exilic community, the audience for whom the book was written, leads one into the communicative dynamic of the text.[49]

The Old Testament books surprisingly come to life when approached as kerygmatically-focused in their historical contexts. I think of Gordon Wenham's work on Genesis which, in my view, receives its dynamic from inquiring after Genesis' message/kerygma in its ANE context, especially with respect to Genesis 1–10.[50] This may seem obvious but historical criticism and reactionary evangelical scholarship generally did not move one in this direction and thus distorted rather than deepened Christian use of the Old Testament. Especially for the Old Testament student it was easy to feel caught between a source-critical approach which fragmented the text or an inerrantist approach which ignored the complex literary genres of Genesis. If their defence of the historicity of the Old Testament sometimes prevented conservative scholars from doing the hard work on its kerygma, so too did their concern for the unity of the testaments sometimes get in the way. For E. J. Young, for example, the main message of Jonah is prediction of

47. The relationship of synchronic to diachronic analyses of Old Testament texts remains controversial. It seems to me that we must be cautious about setting them against each other. The best analysis of their relationship has, in my opinion, been done by Meir Sternberg in his discussion of the relationship between discourse analysis and genetic analysis. See M. Sternberg, *The Poetics of Biblical Narrative. Ideological Literature and the Drama of Reading* (Bloomington: Indiana University Press), pp. 7-23.

48. See L. Bronner, *The Stories of Elijah and Elisha as Polemics Against Baal Worship* (Leiden: Brill, 1968).

49. Iain Provan's *1 & 2 Kings* (Old Testament Guides, Sheffield: SAP, 1997) rightly and most helpfully analyses the historical, literary, religious, and didactic elements in the interpretation of Kings. See also his *1 and 2 Kings*, New International Biblical Commentary (Massachusetts/Carlisle: Hendrickson, Paternoster).

50. On the creation narratives see also the excellent work by J. Stek, 'What Says the Scriptures?', in H. J. van Til (ed.), *Portraits of Creation: Biblical and Scientific Perspectives on the World's Formation* (Grand Rapids: Eerdmans, 1990), pp. 203-65.

Christ![51] This may defend a conservative view of Scripture but it prevents one from positioning oneself among the Hebrew group to whom this masterful kerygmatic story of the disobedient prophet is being told, with the insight gradually dawning that Jonah is a paradigm of Israel and the real question is where you are in relation to Yahweh's will and word!

Literary and narrative approaches have of course been very helpful in moving the focus from the underlying events to the final shape of the text. Indeed it is through narrative and carefully crafted literature that many of the authors of the Old Testament books present their message. The kerygmatic nature of the Old Testament should, however, alert us to the fact that a literary approach which stops short of clarifying the kerygma of the text is insufficient. Consider Jonah, for example. That there is skilful narrative technique is clear. But it seems to me that Jonah is finally kerygma rather than story, or perhaps I should say that story is employed in the service of kerygma. We never know what happened to Jonah — did he come round to God's way of thinking or not? He seems to have gone full circle and not to have learnt at all. This, I suggest, is not a good ending for a story — but it is for a kerygmatically focused story/sermon, in which the key issue is not what happened to Jonah but . . . where are the hearers in relation to God's Word and will?!

Christian Old Testament studies should privilege the present form of Old Testament texts but they should privilege them kerygmatically or communicatively, and refuse to make the literary or historical aspect of these texts the dominant one.[52] A hermeneutic is required which takes full account of the literary and historical aspects and explores their relation to the dominant kerygmatic aspect. Sternberg's *Poetics*[53]

---

51. E. J. Young, *An Introduction to the Old Testament* (Grand Rapids: Eerdmans, 1960), p. 280. Young writes that '[t]he fundamental purpose of the book of Jonah is not found in its missionary or universalistic teaching. It is rather to show that Jonah being cast into the depths of Sheol and yet brought up alive is an illustration of the death of the Messiah for sins not His own and of the Messiah's resurrection. . . . Thus the experience of Jonah has as its basic purpose to point forward to the experience of that One that is "greater than Jonas." '

52. *Cf.* the discussion of the relationship between the literary, historical, and theological aspects of the New Testament texts in N. T. Wright, *The New Testament and the People of God* (Minneapolis: Fortress, 1992).

53. Sternberg, *The Poetics of Biblical Narrative*.

and N. T. Wright's *The New Testament and the People of God* are the most helpful indications of this sort of direction available at present.[54] J. C. McCann's *A Theological Introduction to the Book of Psalms: The Psalms as Torah*[55] is a marvellous example of what can happen when the historical, literary/canonical, and kerygmatic dimensions of a biblical text are integrated. The discovery that the Psalter has something of an overall literary shape has opened up all sorts of new directions in study of the psalms,[56] and McCann develops these insights such that one begins to hear the Psalter as Scripture in a fresh and powerful way, and in a way that fits naturally with the New Testament.

And indeed, the recovery of a kerygmatic focus to Old Testament study needs to be extended beyond individual books and texts to the whole Old Testament and to the Scriptures as a whole. Historical criticism has always led to fragmentation of texts and has a built-in antipathy to the unity of the Old Testament and the Bible. It does not take much discernment to realise the implications of this for any doctrine of Scripture as God's (univocal) Word. Old Testament and biblical theology have taken a systematic hammering from historical criticism and there are few work sites in these areas remaining from the historical-critical paradigm.[57]

Unfortunately transformational conservative scholarship has neglected to create many either. Following current fashions conservatives tend to work thoroughly on small texts from the Old Testament, quietly and uneasily holding to the unity of Scripture but having no powerful emerging Old Testament and biblical theologies to support that belief.

There are some encouraging exceptions to this trend. One exception is Moore College in Australia, where Graham Goldsworthy, Bill

---

54. Sternberg operates with a communicative model of textuality. From personal discussion with him I gather, however, he would not agree with me in describing the Old Testament texts as kerygmatic.

55. J. C. McCann, *A Theological Introduction to the Book of Psalms: The Psalms as Torah* (Nashville: Abingdon, 1993).

56. See, *e.g.*, J. C. McCann, ed., *The Shape and Shaping of the Psalter* (Sheffield: JSOT, 1993).

57. Tom Wright notes, for example, in his update of Stephen Neill's *The Interpretation of the New Testament*, that "[t]he connection between the Old and New Tetaments remains a matter of interest, but strictly on the sidelines as far as the mainstream of New Testament scholarship is concerned." In *The Interpretation of the New Testament 1861-1986* (Oxford/New York: Oxford University Press, 1988), p. 365.

Dunbrell, and others have made biblical theology an integral part of their curriculum for many years now, and in the process a steady stream of publications has emerged from this school.[58] Of course these have their weaknesses but they seem particularly valuable in attempting to get at the inner unity of Scripture. Certainly for any community wanting to uphold Scripture as God's Word, works of this nature are indispensable. James Barr and Langdon Gilkey apparently sounded the death knell of the biblical theology movement, but there seems to have been a neglect of cautious assessment of the strengths and weaknesses of that movement and the insistence on not giving up on Old Testament and biblical theology. Karl Barth has said that the best apologetics is a good systematics, and undoubtedly the best defence of the unity of Scripture would be a series of Old Testament and biblical theologies. Scobie has recently published a number of stimulating articles on the possibility of and shape a biblical theology might take, but this discussion is rare in biblical studies nowadays.[59] It is also heartening to see Francis Watson attempting to revive biblical theology in his recent *Text and Truth*.[60]

2. Post-liberal Old Testament scholarship would have more of a communal nature.

It is increasingly difficult for an individual to write a single Old Testament theology or a major Old Testament introduction in his/her life-

---

58. I am told that this tradition of biblical theology goes back to D. W. B. Robinson, former Archbishop of Sydney and at one time Vice-Principal of the College. It was certainly nurtured by former Principal D. B. Knox. See as examples G. Goldsworthy, *Gospel and Wisdom* (Carlisle: Paternoster, 1987 [1995]), W. J. Dumbrell, *Covenant and Creation: An Old Testament Covenant Theology* (Exeter: Paternoster), *The End of the Beginning: Revelation 21–22 and the Old Testament* (Australia: Lancer, 1985).

59. See, for example, S. Scobie, 'The Structure of Biblical Theology', *Tyndale Bulletin* 42, 2 (1991), pp. 163-94.

60. *Cf.* also C. R. Seitz, *Word Without End. The Old Testament as Abiding Theological Witness* (Grand Rapids: Eerdmans, 1998). Walter Brueggemann has regularly gone against the stream in producing a number of books on Old Testament theology. See his *Old Testament Theology. Essays on Structure, Theme, and Text* (Minneapolis: Fortress, 1992) and most recently see his monumental *Theology of the Old Testament: Testimony, Dispute, Advocacy* (Minneapolis: Fortress, 1997).

time today. An advantage of this is that it serves to remind us that Christian scholarship should be communal. The battle for Christian Old Testament scholarship will never be fought successfully by a series of individuals; it must be a deeply communal venture. Francis Watson correctly says in his plea for a theological biblical hermeneutic that 'what is needed above all is not individual performances but communal agreement as to how a theologically-oriented exegesis could be established, developed and practised. Clearly, such a consensus will not in the foreseeable future comprehend more than a minority of biblical scholars.'[61]

Modernity has been/is deeply individualistic and so is modern scholarship. Originality and individual performance are the goals. A Christian perspective will not ignore these but will also want to find a place for tradition, faithfulness, communal work and service. The great thing is to serve up nutritious bread and this requires communal projects. If Old Testament theologies are a great need of the day that will probably involve a group of like-minded international Christian Old Testament scholars who share a commitment to post-liberal Old Testament scholarship working together. Communal Old Testament scholarship will also involve nurturing and passing on the vision to new generations of Old Testament scholars.

3. Post-liberal Old Testament studies would be more interdisciplinary.

By this I mean a number of things. First, like all disciplines, Old Testament study works with philosophical tools, *i.e.*, with an ontology and an epistemology. It needs to ensure that these are Christian and will thus need to be in dialogue with Christian philosophers and theologians. One thinks, for example, of Watson's serious plea for a theological hermeneutic in his *Text, Church and World*. In this creative text he includes detailed exegesis of parts of Genesis in order to show how a theological hermeneutic would work with the biblical text. In my view hermeneutic questions are theological and philosophical, so it would be most helpful if Christian biblical scholars could dialogue with Chris-

61. F. Watson, *Text, Church and World*, p. vii.

tian theologians and philosophers in order to raise their consciousness about their philosophical and theological presuppositions. Conscious self-reflection on methodology is fast becoming an imperative and it is important to ask what a Christian methodology/ies should look like. Recent decades have seen major advances made in Christian perspectives in philosophy,[62] and Old Testament scholars could easily dialogue with scholars like Plantinga and Wolterstorff in these areas. Within New Testament studies, Tom Wright's *The New Testament and the People of God* is an excellent example of the fruit that taking philosophy seriously in biblical studies can bear. Sadly not much of this sort of work has yet been done in Old Testament studies.

Second, Scripture is God's Word for all of life and thus biblical studies has unique potential for dialogue across disciplines, much of which potential has not been exploited. How, for example, does Old Testament ethics relate to theological ethics and philosophical ethics? And does Old Testament law have any insights to offer contemporary legal studies — if so how does one go about relating these disciplines?

Third, other disciplines also bear on Old Testament studies, and not least on the teaching of the Old Testament, which is the main theme of this collection of essays. Within the university and the theological college Old Testament studies is taught within an educational milieu that has developed over centuries. As we noted, this educational ethos is not neutral, and particularly in the university context has been deeply shaped by modernity, as a who's who of influential educational philosophers over the last few hundred years soon demonstrates. Within Old Testament studies the dominance of historical criticism fits hand-in-glove with the rationalistic modern university.[63]

Christians teaching the Old Testament will therefore need to be aware not only of non-Christian influences on Old Testament studies, but also of the ideologies shaping the philosophy/ies of education in their teaching context. Increased specialisation and separation of disci-

---

62. See, *e.g.*, A. Plantinga, 'Christian Philosophy at the End of the Twentieth Century', in S. Griffioen and B. M. Balk (eds.), *Christian Philosophy at the Close of the Twentieth Century. Assessment and Perspective* (Kampen: Kok, 1995), pp. 29-53.

63. See J. Levenson, *The Hebrew Bible,* for a stimulating analysis of religious interpretation of the Old Testament compared with that of historical criticism. He shows how the modern university and historical criticism have been shaped by the same ideology.

plines in the modern 'multiversity' means, for example, that Old Testament specialists will not readily think of the influence of philosophy of education upon their discipline. However, a Christian agenda will mean being sensitive to these influences and the importance of thinking through the university from a Christian perspective.

Certainly there is much in modern educational philosophy to hold onto, but the crisis of post-modernity is being felt in the philosophy of education as well. Roger Lundin begins his excellent text on post-modernity with two chapters on the crisis of education in the U.S.A.[64] And a similar crisis and flux is evident in U.K. education, as a perusal of recent editions of the *Journal of Philosophy of Education* demonstrates. Paul Hirst, whose modern analytical approach to education has deeply influenced British education, has recently moved away considerably from his previous educational philosophy.[65]

Perhaps the most significant implication of modernity for religion has been the latter's privatisation. Freedom of religion is allowed but religion is privatised and confined to people's private and church lives. Reason and human autonomy are understood to reign in the public spheres of life such as politics, economics, and education. Here religion is thought to be inappropriate and divisive. As regards Christian education it must be noted that many Christians have argued that this model of liberal pluralism *is* Christian. Education, interpreted through this grid, is to be for all and ought to be open and unprejudiced in its search for truth. I have nowhere seen the view that Christian education ought to be neutral and objective more clearly articulated than by Hirst.[66] The following quotes give some sense of his influential position in the 1970's.

> The belief that religion does in fact significantly influence any part of the curriculum in Catholic schools, other than that of specifically religious education, can be seriously doubted. (p. 3)

64. R. Lundin, *The Culture of Interpretation. Christian Faith and the Postmodern World* (Grand Rapids: Eerdmans, 1993).

65. See the articles and especially Hirst's contribution in R. Barrow and P. White (eds.), *Beyond Liberal Education. Essays in Honour of Paul H. Hirst* (London and New York: Routledge, 1993).

66. P. Hirst, 'Education, Catechesis and the Church School', in L. Francis and D. W. Lankshear (eds.), *Christian Perspectives on Church Schools* (Leominster: Grace-wing Fowler Wright, 1993 [1979]), pp. 2-16.

This second, sophisticated view of education is thus concerned with passing on beliefs and practices according to their objective status and with their appropriate justification. It is dominated by a concern for knowledge, for truth, for reason, distinguishing these clearly from belief, conjecture and subjective preference. (p. 5)

On this second view, the character of education is in the end determined simply by the canons of objectivity and reason appropriate to the different forms of knowledge and understanding that we have. What is involved in teaching say the sciences, history, the arts, is determined by the nature of these pursuits themselves and not by characteristics that are in any way dependent on any religious presuppositions. Though certain Christians at times try to argue otherwise, I suggest we have now reached a point in our understanding of the nature of the sciences, the arts, mathematics, philosophy and so on, that their autonomy and independence of any specifically Christian presuppositions must be granted. (p. 5)

The . . . concept of education I have been articulating is . . . marked above all by:
    a. a commitment to the autonomy or independence from religious beliefs of the pursuits of objectivity and reason; and
    b. a commitment to developing a rationally autonomous person whose life is self-directed in the light of what reason determines. (pp. 7-8)

Hirst's is a quintessentially modern view of Christian education. It should be noted that he is arguing this perspective as a Christian. Christian catechesis is, in his view, a private matter that can complement objective education.[67]

The 1970's Hirst, in my opinion, is completely wrong about the neutrality of education and its independence from religion.[68] In the context of the post-modernism debate there has emerged a recognition of the extent to which modernity is a particular tradition with its own prejudices. Encouragingly, Hirst himself has recognised the extent to

67. Hirst's model is a good expression of the nature-grace understanding of the Christ-culture relationship. For a discussion of this see R. H. Niebuhr, *Christ and Culture* (London: Harper Colophon, 1975).
68. See R. Clouser, *The Myth of Religious Neutrality*.

which his 1970's position was shaped by a particular perspective. In the 1993 collection of essays celebrating his career, Hirst remarkably acknowledges that in the 60's and 70's British philosophy of education and he himself were under the spell of 'a hard rationalism', a spell which, says Hirst, has now been broken. According to the 1993 Hirst 'we must shift from seeing education as primarily concerned with knowledge to seeing it as primarily concerned with social practices.'

Although Hirst is not arguing for religion as foundational in the sense that I would, the contrast with his 1978 position is remarkable. He says, for example, that

> A great mistake of the 'rationalist' approach was that it saw theoretical knowledge as the only type of knowledge that is properly significant in determining both the ends and means of rational practice and thus of the good life. . . . If practical reason is given its proper place in determining the ends and the means of the good life, with the achievements of theoretical reason seen as in general ancillary, the notion of rational choice that the conduct of the good life requires can no longer be that of detached, neutral judgement of either ends or means. . . . There can be no detached clean slate position from which all possibilities can be assessed. . . .[69]

Hirst has recognised the problems with the myth of neutral, objective education. Sadly though, the notion of neutral objectivity still tends to reign supreme in the general practice of education, often even among Christians. Even as a growing awareness has developed in the U.K. that we all have presuppositions and that inevitably our communal baggage shapes our scholarship, few have discerned the responsibility for Christians to allow their presuppositions to shape their academic pursuits as the rest of their lives.[70]

69. P. Hirst, 'Education', p. 193.

70. It should be noted that some very good work is being done on the theory of education from a Christian perspective. See, for example, J. Shortt and T. Cooling (eds.), *Agenda for Educational Change* (Leicester: Apollos, 1997), E. J. Thiessen, *Teaching for Commmitment: Liberal Education, Indoctrination, and Christian Nurture* (Leominster: Gracewing, 1993), and the journal *Spectrum* — since 1997 known as *Journal of Education and Christian Belief*. The work is being done, but there are few places in higher education in the U.K. where an attempt is being made to integrate such theory of education with a post-liberal agenda for Old Testament studies.

A Time for Setting the Table

As Christians in Old Testament studies we are working all the time with some kind of agenda for Old Testament studies, but is it a conscious and integrally Christian one? Time and again students come to their teachers seeking guidance in discerning where to focus their energies. Now it is wrong for a supervisor to impose his interests upon the student, but it is equally wrong to give no guidance. In discerning our God-given vocation John Stott once helpfully commented that we need to discern our God-given gifts and then ask how those gifts can best be stretched to meet the needs of the day. Imagine you are working with a student who has the gifts and the call to service of the Lord Christ in Old Testament studies. What would you say to her in her quest to stretch her gifts in relation to the needs of the day? Any attempt to answer this question will force one to confront another question: what are the needs of the day in Old Testament studies? Where are the urgent holes that need to be plugged until more thorough work can be done?

I have argued here that a post-liberal agenda is the sort of direction that Old Testament studies should aspire to. There is much at stake in the discipline of Old Testament studies and it is valuable to pause every now and again to check our bearings. This paper is a call to check the direction of current Christian Old Testament scholarship in our 'postmodern' context. What are our gifts and what are the needs of our day? How are we to work together in order to serve up bread and not stones in our scholarly work on the Old Testament? The post-modern condition makes it important to undertake such reflection now. If not, the danger is that Christian Old Testament scholarship will drift into a reflection of post-modern pluralism with little communal agenda until perhaps a new consensus emerges where it will make its uneasy home once again. However, the opportunity is there for Christian Old Testament scholars to seize the present and to use the present flux to chart a fruitful way ahead in our field. What Lundin says of modernity and post-modernity in general is true of Old Testament studies:

> Christian belief presents distinct alternatives to Enlightenment rationalism and the pragmatic irrationality of postmodernity. . . . As Christians engage contemporary theories, they ought to do so criti-

cally, recognizing the need to renew their own vocabulary as well as to learn from the critiques offered by postmodern culture. If they do anything less than that, if they neglect their own heritage or view it solely as a source of corruption and oppression, Christians are in danger of selling their own birthright — their saving vocabulary of sin and grace, judgement and forgiveness, death and resurrection — for a cold pottage of jargon and obscurity.[71]

Such an agenda in Old Testament studies could only be achieved by a group with a common vision — a common world view and commitment to post-liberal Old Testament scholarship — who work communally to serve our neighbours by giving them bread and not stones. 'In sum, we who are Christians and propose to be Old Testament scholars and teachers must not rest content with being Old Testament scholars who happen, incidentally, to be Christians; we must strive to be Christian Old Testament scholars. We must therefore pursue our projects with integrity, independence, and Christian boldness.'[72]

71. Lundin, *The Culture of Interpretation,* p. 30.
72. This is an adaptation of Plantinga's conclusion in 'Advice to Christian Philosophers'.

A Theological Approach

JAMES McKEOWN

James McKeown is lecturer in Old Testament at Belfast Bible College. Here he examines the teaching of Old Testament theology in the context of a theological college. Some of the benefits that may be expected from studying this subject, in spite of the methodological difficulties involved, are outlined and followed by a discussion about the contents of a course that would maximise these benefits.

There is now a great deal of scepticism about the feasibility of producing a coherent Old Testament theology. R. N. Whybray regards it as a non-existent mythical beast analogous to Lewis Carroll's 'snark'. He suggests that the failure of the hunters to kill the snark was due, not only to the fact that the hunters had not agreed about the nature of the beast they were hunting, but also to the fact that the beast did not exist.[1] He suggests that the mythical beast of Old Testament theology may be sought with 'bund' or threatened with a 'Heilsgeschichte' to no avail!

Whybray is not suggesting that there is no theological teaching in the Old Testament; in fact he is quite happy to speak about theologies

---

1. R. N. Whybray, 'OT Theology — A Non-Existent Beast', in B. P. Thompson (ed.), *Scripture, Meaning and Method* (Hull: University Press, 1987), p. 168.

rather than theology; the theology of Deutero-Isaiah, the kerygma of the Yahwist, etc.[2] What he objects to is the idea that it is possible to present Old Testament theology in a way that embraces the entire Old Testament in a coherent and comprehensive manner.[3]

This scepticism is not shared by everyone. W. E. Lemke draws attention to the number of full-length theologies written since 1970 and suggests that when one adds to these the hundreds of thousands of articles and monographs dealing with some specific topic or aspect of Old Testament theology, one can only conclude that the discipline is 'alive and well'.[4] However, the health of a discipline is not necessarily linked to the number of articles written about it, and, in spite of this proliferation of literature, we do not seem to be any closer to a consensus about how the methodological problems of producing an Old Testament theology may be solved.

Unfortunately these difficulties and uncertainties affect the teaching of the discipline which is now often side-lined to a list of options that a student may choose from. This is to be regretted since Old Testament theology is the ideal discipline to give students an overview of the Old Testament message and an understanding of the development of theological concepts. Courses in Old Testament introduction and verse-by-verse exegesis are very valuable but they offer no opportunity to give the students an understanding of the Old Testament as a whole. As T. D. Alexander points out,

> Studying the biblical texts by means of commentaries can be compared to looking at the separate pieces of a jigsaw puzzle. While we may find something of interest in each piece, it is only when all the pieces are put together that we get the complete picture.[5]

An Old Testament theology course is an excellent canvas for the presentation of this 'complete picture'. It can enable students to gain a useful perspective on the entire range of Old Testament literature and can show them how the message of the Old Testament develops. This

2. Whybray, 'OT Theology', p. 169.
3. Whybray, 'OT Theology', p. 177.
4. W. E. Lemke, 'Old Testament Theology', *Anchor Bible Dictionary*, 6, p. 454.
5. T. D. Alexander, *From Paradise to the Promised Land: An Introduction to the Main Themes of the Pentateuch* (Carlisle: Paternoster Press, 1995), p. xv.

is particularly beneficial in the context of an evangelical theological college where students may have a rather distorted view of the Old Testament because of the haphazard and uncritical way that the Old Testament is approached in Christian pulpits. We shall now discuss three main ways in which a course in Old Testament theology can be helpful in this context.

Old Testament Theology and Uncritical Approaches to the Hebrew Bible

The teaching of Old Testament theology should help students to shake off the shackles of uncritical approaches to the Hebrew Bible. Students who come from an evangelical background have tremendous advantages when they enter theological studies. Their knowledge of the content of the Bible is usually very good and they will probably have already memorised a number of important texts. On the other hand, they will have disadvantages that may be easily overlooked. In particular they may have been introduced to the Old Testament as if it was merely a collection of proof texts that point forward to Christianity. Christological interpretations of the Old Testament are not new. The Epistle of Barnabas interpreted the red heifer as a type of Christ and the scape goat with the scarlet wool typified Christ with his scarlet robe at his trial.[6] A similar imaginative approach still prevails in some circles and as a result major Old Testament themes are distorted. A favourite pulpit device that students may have been subjected to is the idea that Christ was personally present in many of the Old Testament stories: he is the Angel of Yahweh, one of the three visitors to Abraham's tent, and, of course, Melchisedek. Verses such as Genesis 3:15 may have been given christological interpretations with no thought to the meaning of the pericope in its context.[7] The historical context of passages such as Isaiah 7 may have been completely ignored in an attempt to make the material rele-

---

6. R. L. Smith, *OT Theology: Its History and Method* (Nashville: Broadman and Holman, 1993), p. 25.

7. Work such as that done by T. D. Alexander shows how the Old Testament can be interpreted in its context and still reflect a christological interpretation. See, *e.g.,* 'From Adam to Judah: The Significance of the Family Tree in Genesis', *EQ* 61 (1989), pp. 5-19.

vant to the Christmas message. This Christianising of the Old Testament is also evident in the way that matters relating to the cult are treated. For example, sacrifice is often approached christologically and afforded a centrality and importance unwarranted by the Old Testament.

I am not suggesting that we can be totally impartial in our approach to the Old Testament and avoid reading it from a Christian standpoint. The fact that we use the term 'Old Testament' makes it clear that our approach is Christian. However, students can be taught to avoid the extremes outlined above. Rather than try to divorce the minds of our students from their Christian orientation we can equip them with the necessary hermeneutical know-how to interpret the texts in their historical, cultural, and cultic contexts.

The process of re-educating students will be facilitated by an introduction to the meaning of key theological words. This is particularly important for those who are not required to learn Hebrew. An introduction to Hebrew thought forms and to the main Hebrew idioms will reduce the danger of a superficial approach to the text. It is important to make the students aware of the difficulties and complexities that exist so that they will not read Christian or modern Western content into Hebrew words or phrases. The differences between Hebrew thinking and that of the modern Western Christian mind should be introduced in areas such as, 'righteousness', 'salvation', 'peace', 'justice', 'truth', 'faithfulness', etc. This may be reminiscent of a systematic theology but I am not suggesting this. Rather, these key concepts should be dealt with in a way that does justice to their literary and historical contexts.

Old Testament Theology, the Hebrew Bible, and the Christian Church

A course in Old Testament theology should show how the message of the Hebrew Bible may be relevant to the Christian church. Concomitant with the task of showing how to avoid superficial approaches to the Old Testament is the important challenge of showing how it can be relevant for the church. Old Testament theology not only provides us with a means to sweep away uncritical ideas about the theological message of the Old Testament, but it is also an excellent pedagogical tool to introduce sound hermeneutical principles. The Old Testament will not receive the atten-

tion it deserves unless we can show that it has a role to play in the twenty-first century. There is, of course, disagreement about what this role should be. Some understand Old Testament theology as a purely descriptive task. This view has been strongly supported by K. Stendahl.[8] He advocates a framework for Old Testament theology which 'does not borrow its categories from the New Testament or later Jewish or Christian interpretations'.[9] J. L. McKenzie's theology reflects his concern to interpret the Old Testament in its own right, allowing no significance to later Christian developments, and he claims to have written his book on Old Testament theology 'as if the New Testament did not exist'.[10] Stendahl and McKenzie's approach undoubtedly avoids extreme messianic interpretations; McKenzie is convinced that 'messianism is a Christian response to the Old Testament and should be treated as such'.[11]

However, it is extremely unlikely that, as Christians, we can produce a theology of the Old Testament that is purely objective and free from Christian presuppositions. In spite of McKenzie's efforts to produce a theology of the Old Testament with no reference to the New Testament his approach is still a Christian approach and this is undoubtedly how a Jewish reader would understand it. Clearly it is impossible for Christians to suspend their faith and study the Old Testament in a vacuum.[12] The suggestion that the text can be approached without the presuppositions or the faith of the interpreter having any influence is naive.[13]

Moreover, avoiding uncritical approaches does not necessarily lead to a purely descriptive approach. If the Bible is not simply a collection of ancient documents but carries authority as God's word with relevance for Christians today, then Old Testament theology should clearly reflect this and be constructive as well as descriptive.

8. K. Stendahl, 'Biblical Theology', *IDB*, 1, pp. 418-32.
9. Stendahl, 'Biblical Theology', p. 423.
10. J. L. McKenzie, *A Theology of the Old Testament* (New York: Macmillan, 1974), p. 319.
11. McKenzie, *A Theology of the Old Testament*, p. 23.
12. J. Goldingay argues that Old Testament theology 'cannot be a purely descriptive discipline — it inherently involves the contemporary explication of the Biblical material!', *Approaches to Old Testament Interpretation* (Leicester: InterVarsity Press, 1990), p. 23.
13. Lemke, 'Old Testament Theology', p. 455.

E. A. Martens argues that since the Bible is God's word, 'a theology of the Old Testament should point beyond the description of the message to an indication of its importance for today's believer'.[14] Lemke makes a similar observation and points out that,

> If theology is in any sense concerned with 'truth for us' or truth for the religious community in which the Old Testament is a foundational faith document, then Old Testament theology cannot be content merely to describe the religious ideas which the ancient Hebrews held at some point in their history. Inevitably it must press on to discern what the abiding truth is today for those who consider themselves to be the spiritual descendants and heirs of ancient Israel.[15]

So, in spite of the difficulties involved Old Testment theology is an excellent discipline to develop an understanding of the relevance of the Old Testament for the Christian church without imposing New Testament paradigms on the Hebrew text. If our students leave college with a grasp of the message of the Old Testament and of how to make it relevant without distorting its contents, they will be more likely to use it in their ministries and to communicate its value to others.

Old Testament Theology and the Main Themes of the Old Testament

An Old Testament theology course should be used to highlight the main themes that run through the Old Testament. There is value in studying themes and concepts in a way which highlights their development and diversity. We should always remember that we are not trying to construct a systematic theology with everything tied neatly in the conceptual theological bundle to which it belongs. The systematic approach gives the impression that the Bible is a kind of ancient Yellow Pages that you can look up for information under various headings. All the colour and interest of the biblical material is reduced to various shades of grey and its dynamic cut and thrust is submerged in the stagnant

14. E. A. Martens, *God's Design* (Grand Rapids/Leicester: Baker/Apollos, 1994), p. 11.
15. Lemke, 'Old Testament Theology', p. 455.

waters of an unyielding system. Rather, Old Testament theology should reflect the nature of the material that it is dealing with and interpret material in the light of its historical, cultural, and cultic backgrounds. Since we are not trying to create a logically coherent conceptual system of doctrinal belief, we can come to terms with the complexity of the text without having to ignore apparent developments or ambiguities.

In doing so we shall avoid the main criticism levelled at the dogmatic-didactic approach which borrowed the old dogmatic theology categories and sought to systematise the Old Testament message in the God–man–salvation scheme. While there are obvious pedagogical advantages in bringing together scattered information about a particular subject under one heading, the damning indictment of such an approach is that the message can be distorted if it is removed from its original context. As R. E. Clements observes, 'It is essential . . . that an Old Testament theology should retain a proper consciousness of the literary setting of the material it utilises, rather than to seek a body of quite abstract doctrines'.[16] Thus, a satisfactory scheme for organising the biblical material is unlikely to be found in a framework that is alien to the data that it is being used to present. As G. F. Hasel argues,

> The approach to the Bible that searches for an *internal* key, one that grows out of the Biblical materials themselves, can alone be expected to be adequate and proper for a theology or theologies which is or are present in the Bible itself.[17]

Eichrodt very successfully broke away from the categories of dogmatic theology and developed a scheme around the concept of covenant. This paved the way for a great deal of discussion about the concept of an 'organising centre' for Old Testament theology and some very useful work has been done in this area. However, while many are convinced that the Old Testament message may be studied from the standpoint of its central theme, no consensus about what this should be has emerged.[18] If there is such a thing as a central theme, why is its identity

16. R. E. Clements, *Old Testament Theology* (Basingstoke: Marshall, Morgan and Scott, 1985), p. 15.

17. G. F. Hasel, *Old Testament Theology* (Grand Rapids: Eerdmans, 1982), p. 138.

18. Some who did not agree with Eichrodt that covenant was the centre of the Old Testament, nevertheless, postulated other centres such as: Holiness of God

so elusive? Should a single all-embracing theme not be immediately obvious and are we not justified in concluding that the failure to find this theme means that it does not exist? It is unrealistic to expect that one theme or centre will be adequate for material that reflects not simply a system of belief but a nation's history and lifestyle. Why must we squeeze the vast amount of Old Testament data into one central concept? Scobie's complaint that it is 'difficult to understand the obsession with finding one single theme or "centre" for Old Testament or New Testament Theology' is understandable.[19] To take one particular doctrine or concept as representative or central is unlikely to succeed any more than one thread of a tapestry could possibly be used to describe adequately the entire work. This is not to pour 'cold water' on the excellent work that has been done. Some of the attempts to find a key to Old Testament theology shed very valuable light on the Old Testament and suggest useful approaches since they reflect some aspect or theme which is found in the text. Since these themes or centres have arisen from the text some of them will be very useful in teaching Old Testament theology providing they are not permitted to be mutually exclusive. They point us in the right direction for teaching Old Testament theology; that is, towards a thematic approach.

Although the main themes of a particular book may be studied in courses on Old Testament introduction, most syllabuses do not include themes that are found in several books and in different historical settings. Old Testament theology is the ideal discipline through which to identify and study the origins (if known), development, and significance of themes in a way that other disciplines are unlikely to achieve. The fact that Old Testament theology is not limited to one book or time gives it

---

— J. Hanel, E. Sellin; Sovereignty of God — J. Heller; Kingdom of God — B. Hessler, G. Klein; Rulership of God — H. Seebass; Communion — Th. C. Vriezen; Promise-rest — W. C. Kaiser; Election — R. C. Denton, H. Wildberger. Other suggestions have focused on a larger centre than these single-centre suggestions. R. de Vaux argues for a dual-centre approach and he finds this in the dual idea of election-covenant. R. Martin-Achard goes for a threefold 'axis', that is, three lines of thought, the doxological, the polemical, and the soteriological, around which the Old Testament may be grouped. S. Terrien argues that it is the Hebraic theology of presence which provides a key to understanding the Bible. E. A. Martens uses a fourfold approach. He sees the key to Old Testament theology in God's fourfold purpose — deliverance, community, knowledge of God, and land.

19. *TynB*, 42, 2 (1991), p. 178.

the flexibility to embrace varied aspects of biblical themes and to show how these themes are affected by the genre of literature, their historical context, and the overall objective of the passage in which they appear.

Seeking to organise the teaching of Old Testament theology around a number of main themes may be open to the objection that we are moving towards systematic theology. However, this is not the intention, and the main difference will lie in how the themes are identified. For the systematic theologian the main categories will arise from the need to deal adequately with issues that are current and pressing for his readers. On the other hand the choice of themes for Old Testament theology will arise from the text itself and from the historical context.

Designing an Old Testament Theology Course

How should a course in Old Testament theology be designed? We have argued that an Old Testament theology course should enable students to break away from a Christianising approach to the Old Testament while at the same time showing them how the Old Testament can be relevant and normative for the Christian church. We also suggested that Old Testament theology is an excellent tool for introducing the main longitudinal themes in the Old Testament. If we accept these objectives, we must now turn our attention to how they can be achieved through an Old Testament theology course. We have already seen that there is no generally agreed methodology and even a definitive definition is elusive. Our first priority should be to find a way of organising the material that does justice to the biblical texts in their cultural and historical settings and which highlights the main longitudinal themes of the literature. This points us in the direction of an approach that is both historical and thematic.

Before making my own proposals I shall present two outlines which represent historical and thematic approaches to Old Testament theology.

The historical approach to Old Testament theology is exemplified by Hogenhaven's work.[20] Though we might expect that the historical approach he adopts would lead him to organise the material in accor-

20. J. L. Hogenhaven, *Problems and Prospects of OT Theology* (Sheffield: JSOT Press, 1987).

dance with his understanding of the chronological development of Israelite religion, he argues that since the primary concern of Old Testament theology is with the literature rather than with the religion of Israel, it is the literary genres of the Old Testament that provide the 'most appropriate guideline' for the structure of Old Testament theology.[21] The outworking of this can be seen in his suggested model for a course-book on Old Testament theology:

Introduction
Theology and the Bible — and the discipline of biblical theology
  A. **Wisdom in the Old Testament**
  1. Proverbs — the main themes of 'wisdom', 'world order', retribution, divine justice, the theological redaction of Proverbs
  2. Job — the suffering of a righteous man and the problem of divine justice
  3. Ecclesiastes — questions as to the reality of a just 'world order'
  B. **Psalmic Literature in the Old Testament**
  1. The Psalter — hymns, individual prayers, collective psalms, didactic poems, other psalms
  2. Lamentations — the crisis of 587 and the attempt at a theological response
  3. The Song of Songs — sexual love and its interpretation
  C. **Narrative Literature in the Old Testament**
  1. The traditions — the Primeval history, the Patriarchal narratives, the Sojourn in Egypt, the Exodus, the Revelation at Mount Sinai, the Wandering in the Wilderness, the Settlement in Canaan
  2. The 'history works' — the Deuteronomistic history, the Chronicler, the final redaction of the Pentateuch
  D. **Law in the Old Testament**
  1. The major collections — the Book of the Covenant, the Holiness Code, the Deuteronomic laws, the Priestly laws
  2. The ethical summaries
  3. The theological redaction of the laws in the Pentateuch
  E. **Prophecy in the Old Testament**
  1. The narratives on the earliest prophets

21. Hogenhaven, *Problems and Prospects*, p. 96.

2. The prophetic books in the Old Testament — the eighth-century prophets, the prophets in the era of the Babylonian exile, the post-exilic prophets, the book of Daniel

In contrast let us look at an outline of the themes in Old Testament theology as presented by Dyrness. He divides his work into the following themes:

1. The Self-Revelation of God
2. The Nature of God
3. Creation and Providence
4. Man and Woman
5. Sin
6. The Covenant
7. The Law
8. Worship
9. Piety
10. Ethics
11. Wisdom
12. The Spirit of God
13. Prophecy
14. The Hope of Israel

Both approaches have much to commend them. However, the problem with Hogenhaven's approach is that dividing the literature into categories fails to do justice to themes that are not limited to one particular genre of literature. On the other hand the approach of Dyrness is open to the criticism that it is reminiscent of systematic approaches that force the Bible into a pre-determined set of categories that may distort the overall message. Dyrness does acknowledge that at times in his work he has 'fallen into the trap of systematisation',[22] but nevertheless as a basic introduction to the message of the Old Testament his book is useful. I would like to find an approach which combines the best of Dyrness with Hogenhaven while hoping to avoid the problems that their respective theologies face.

22. W. Dyrness, *Themes in OT Theology* (Downers Grove: InterVarsity Press, 1979), p. 11.

In order to avoid Dyrness' putative 'trap' and also to avoid a purely historical approach, I suggest an approach which concentrates as much as possible on unifying themes. Choosing these will not be particularly easy. It is important that the themes are not chosen because they are important to New Testament theology or to any other aspect of post Old Testament study. The repetition of key words and the recurrence of motifs and ideas will provide a clue. The following does not pretend to be a comprehensive course on Old Testament theology but rather a course that samples main theological themes and acquaints the student with the idea that the Old Testament can be viewed as a unit rather than as a collection of books.

A. **Introduction to Old Testament Theology**
   1. A study of the history of the discipline and of the methodological problems involved
   2. Questions related to organising Old Testament theology
B. **Hebrew Thought Forms**
   1. An introduction to Hebrew language and thought
   2. A study of important concepts, including 'righteousness', 'justice', 'love'
C. **The Character of God and His Dealings with Humankind**
D. **The Concepts of Blessing and Cursing**
   1. In creation
   2. In relation to Israel
E. **The Theme of Land**
   1. Yahweh and the land
   2. Humankind and land
   3. The nation of Israel and land a. Patriarchs b. Exodus and conquest
F. **The Theme of Chosen Seed**
   1. The concept of a special line of descent
   2. The covenant with Israel
   3. The covenant with David
G. **Alienation and Reconciliation**
   1. Historical Survey of these themes in relation to Israel's history
   2. The role of the cult
H. **The Future of Israel**
   1. National expectations

2. Prophetic hope
3. Apocalyptic
I. **Major themes from Wisdom and the Psalms**
1. The well managed life[23]
2. Major questions related to everyday life

This scheme is not intended to be definitive but is simply a suggested agenda for teaching Old Testament theology in a way that allows the dynamic of the faith of Israel to shine through. This approach should enable the student to see the Old Testament, not as a compendium of doctrine, but as a record of the living encounters of individuals and of a nation with God in the rough and tumble of everyday life in the Middle East before the coming of Christ. If the Old Testament is understood in this way, its original message can be appropriated and reapplied to the modern situation without distortion.

23. Kidner uses the phrase 'a life well managed' to describe the contents of Proverbs in *Wisdom to Live By* (Leicester: InterVarsity Press, 1985).

CONTEXT: SEMINARIES, UNIVERSITIES, SOCIETIES

Correctly Handling the Word of Truth — Teaching the Old Testament as a Christian Book

PAUL BARKER

Paul Barker teaches part-time at Ridley College, Melbourne, Australia, where he was originally a student. It is an independent Anglican theological college founded in 1910 with an evangelical constitution. Its most famous Principal was Leon Morris who retired in 1979. Ridley has about three hundred students, a quarter of whom are full-time. Not all are Anglican and only about one tenth are candidates for ordination. Most are pursuing theological studies for personal interest and lay ministry, some are missionary candidates, and some are training for youth ministry. Paul Barker returned to teach there after completing his Ph.D. at Cheltenham and Gloucester College in the United Kingdom where he also taught part-time for a period of three years. Here he reflects on his experience and suggests how Old Testament study should be integrated into the curriculum.

In order rightly to handle the word of truth, the Old Testament needs to be taught in a distinctive way, something which is not always done. This chapter aims to highlight principles for teaching the Old Testament as the word of truth. There seems to be a substantial legacy in the teaching of Old Testament derived from liberal-critical presuppositions, the effects of which are not always recognized. Thus this essay makes an appeal to teach the Old Testament in a way integrated with the New Testament, emphasising a biblical theology of the Bible. Further, it argues for more emphasis to be placed on correct interpretation because the task of teaching is incomplete if exegesis, and not interpretation, is its goal. Suggestions for a syllabus are made as well as some comments about helping Christian students cope with academic study. Some of these principles are then applied to the secular teaching environment.

Teaching Old Testament in a Theological College

Integration

As a student I experienced some isolation of the Old Testament. The aim of the courses was to understand the Old Testament as the Old Testament. It was thematic, critical, and exegetical in approach for the sake of understanding the texts at hand. It deliberately restricted itself to attempting to understand the Old Testament in the setting of ancient Israel and against the ANE background. This is common in the teaching of Old Testament and is a serious weakness.

Old Testament and New Testament

First, because for Christians the Old Testament is part of our canon of Scripture, the teaching of the Old Testament must be integrated with the New Testament. Yet often little attempt is made to teach the unity of the Bible. This seems a fundamental weakness in the teaching of Old Testament. Despite the modern, scholarly uncertainty about whether we are dealing with the Hebrew Bible or the Christian Old Testament, the Old Testament and New Testament are in fact united in truth, not least through Jesus. This is not just a personal or confessional stance. The unity of Old Testament and New Testament is a statement of truth. Perhaps we should call the Old Testament the 'older testament' or, as Goldingay does, the 'First Testament'.[1] Perhaps having biblical studies lecturers who teach both testaments would help. But if Old Testament is taught as a separate discipline from New Testament, we do not do

---

1. J. Goldingay, *Models for Scripture* (Grand Rapids: Eerdmans, 1995), p. 2.

justice to its testimony and message. We limit its God-given horizon. The New Testament's view that all of the Scriptures give testimony to Christ needs to be taken seriously. Somewhere in theological college, the gap between the testaments must be bridged in a way it has not always been done in the past.

Yet this gap is not bridged by merely addressing the issue of how the New Testament uses the Old Testament. Though this needs to be done, it can, in fact, create a discrepancy with what is taught about the Old Testament itself, *i.e.*, that the Old Testament is complete in itself. Thus it can create a sense that the New Testament writers used the Old Testament irresponsibly or that Christianity is not the natural sequel to Old Testament Judaism. What is needed, within the teaching of Old Testament itself, is an understanding of the Old Testament as directed towards the New Testament — the Old Testament recognising its own need for something more.

The most satisfactory way this is done, in my experience, is through a biblical theology approach.[2]

Why is such an approach useful? Students need help to see the big picture of the eternal purposes of God being worked out in history, purposes which, from the beginning, have their direction towards and culmination in Jesus. They need to be taught the consistency of God, as a gracious covenant-keeping God in both testaments. They need to see the consistency of God's concern for the whole world in both testa-

---

2. Along the lines outlined in G. Goldsworthy, *Gospel and Kingdom* (Carlisle: Paternoster, 1981); *According to Plan* (Leicester: InterVarsity Press, 1991); W. J. Dumbrell, *The End of the Beginning: Revelation 21–22 and the Old Testament* (Sydney/Carlisle: Lancer/Paternoster, 1985); *Covenant and Creation: An Old Testament Theology* (Sydney/Carlisle: Lancer/Paternoster, 1984). See also M. Strom, *Days Are Coming* (London: Hodder & Stoughton, 1989). Contrast the older biblical theology approaches of W. F. Albright and G. E. Wright *et al.* Moore Theological College in Sydney has pioneered the teaching of this sort of biblical theology, though similarities exist with Westminster Seminary, Philadelphia, also. This approach stems from D. W. B. Robinson, former Archbishop of Sydney and one time Vice-Principal of Moore. Though Goldsworthy has published in this area and has been influential, I am told that his models derive from Robinson. The late D. B. Knox, former Principal of Moore, took this approach to George Whitefield College in Cape Town when he became Principal there. For the first time in 1995, Ridley, under the influence of the present Principal formerly on the staff at Moore, has introduced a biblical theology unit into its teaching. However, in both places this unit is not part of the degree. It is taught as a no-credit extra.

ments. They need to see that the Old Testament cult is from its inception a shadow of what is to come. They need to see that the old covenant acknowledges its own impotency and that it awaits the new. A biblical theology approach will also keep God's actions central in the narrative of the Old Testament and demonstrate that the Old Testament is not a moralistic resource for Sunday school but God's word about himself and his eternal purposes. The Old Testament is too often taught along descriptive Old Testament religion lines. At least, that's where the bulk of the literature rests. There needs to be more theological appraisal of what is going on in the Old Testament cult and religion as an anticipation of New Testament.

Here is but one example of this. In Deuteronomy 27 instructions are given about the ceremony to be held at Mt. Ebal and Mt. Gerizim after the conquest of the land. One of the intriguing things about this ceremony is that the plastered stones and altar are to be set up on Mt. Ebal, the mount of curse. Why there? Barely any commentaries make a theological comment about this.[3] Yet it seems to me that the choice of this mountain is making a theological statement about the inevitability of sin and the provision of sacrifice for atonement, making the same points as Paul in Galatians 3 for example.

Genre

Second, when I was a student I found the study of genre was surprisingly weak. I do not mean genre identification and description but how to read various literary genres and what literary shape they have. This lack was especially apparent with regard to narrative and prophecy. Alter, Sternberg, and Polzin were almost unheard of. Literary devices for understanding meaning and purpose in a text were never discussed. Certainly the optionality of Hebrew contributed to this. At the least, what I have in mind is the sort of work done by Fee and Stuart in *How to Read the Bible for All Its Worth*.[4] This a good book at a student level for giving guidelines for understanding and interpreting various genres

---

3. An exception is J. Ridderbos, *Deuteronomy* (BSC; Grand Rapids: Zondervan, 1984), pp. 248-49.
4. G. D. Fee and D. Stuart, *How to Read the Bible for All Its Worth* (London: Scripture Union, 1982, 1995).

in the Old Testament. Associated with this, exegetical method was never taught systematically. We were expected to exegete passages in an exam and occasionally in class. Yet exegesis was presumed to be caught, not taught. Nothing like Douglas Stuart's *Old Testament Exegesis* was ever recommended or used.[5]

One of the weaknesses of modern Old Testament exegesis is its atomistic approach, in part a legacy of the liberal fascination with form-critical, pre-final forms of the text. Evangelicals should be preoccupied with the final form of the Old Testament. This makes a big difference in exegesis.

Description and Prescription

This leads into a third point, that of the message or prescription of the text. This is another place where academic study often stops short. Sometimes it seems as though the academic discipline of Old Testament study is restricted to the description of the times and culture of ancient Israel and a description of how the text fitted therein and of the text itself. It seems often that any attempt at the text's prescription for today, its application beyond ancient times, is not in fact regarded as academic-scientific but a question of faith, and hence out of place in the lecture room. There is a weakness, then, in bridging the gap from exegesis to application — two different but related skills.

There are, perhaps, two main reasons for this divorce of exegesis and application. The first is the influence of historical-critical methodology with its liberal presuppositions. Now historical and linguistic issues are important and cannot be ignored. Historical-critical approaches have had many positive effects. Yet we must be careful not to let historical-critical approaches totally set the agenda, for their great weakness is in theological and literary areas. Historical-critical approaches restrict the Old Testament. The Bible is for our training in righteousness, reproof, etc. Thus when it is taught, it must be taught as such. It cannot be taught as only an ancient document. Historical, or linguistic or cultural, knowledge is not the aim of teaching the Old Testament. Rather, righteousness is.

Another way of putting this is to say that truth must be integrated

5. D. Stuart, *Old Testament Exegesis* (2nd ed.) (Louisville: Westminster, 1984).

with ethics, for truth and ethics, orthodoxy and orthopraxy, are two sides of the same coin.[6] Academic study fails when it attempts to divorce the two. Thus academic study must be prepared to view the text as proclamation; and teaching it in its fullness requires receiving its message or gospel or kerygma. Thus academic study must sit under the text. It must teach its message. Exegetical, critical, and thematic study does not always address this issue. For example, when I was a student there was very little in the way of guidelines for determining the prescriptive message of a narrative. What is its kerygma? The Bible cannot be understood apart from receiving its gospel demands. We must teach it kerygmatically.

The other main reason for the gap between exegesis and application is the growing 'evangelical-charismatic pneumatology', that truth for today is conveyed subjectively and directly by the Spirit, often, in practice, independently from biblical exegesis. Hunter, quoted by Hafemann, argues that many evangelicals believe that 'the meaning of a text or story (from the Bible) would necessarily vary for each believer since everyone would be approaching the Bible from a different life situation'.[7] Hafemann and Hunter argue that exegesis is often seen as an irrelevant exercise in biblical interpretation because it is not linked to application. Exegesis, dealing with what God said, is not seen as linked to what God says today. Thus, the Bible speaks to us today in many and various ways, and interpreting a text for today is not regarded as an academic, scientific, or objective exercise, as far as any can be. Interpretation of Scripture has become a matter of personal choice and subjectivity. It means for me what I want it to mean. Without wishing to ignore the fact that exegesis is itself in part interpretative, many regard exegesis as an academic enterprise but not so interpretation.[8]

For both these reasons, perhaps, the commentaries often do not

6. See R. P. Stevens, 'Living Theologically: Toward a Theology of Christian Practice', *Themelios* 20 (1995), pp. 4-8.

7. See S. J. Hafemann, 'Seminary, Subjectivity, and the Centrality of Scripture: Reflections on the Current Crisis in Evangelical Seminary Education', *JETS* 31(1988), pp. 135-36.

8. J. L. Crenshaw, *Trembling at the Threshold of a Biblical Text* (Grand Rapids: Eerdmans, 1994), p. 6, scoffs at the commonly held assumption that historians are objective, theologians biased. He argues, 'Describing religion without taking its spirit into account is as futile as trying to get a rose to bloom after cutting the roots off the plant'.

help. They rarely go beyond the first step, and so neither do we nor our students. Even evangelical commentaries like the 'Tyndale' series stop short of proclaiming the message of the text. The 'Word' series pays lip service to explanation of the text. The 'Interpretation' series goes further, but often not in evangelical ways. 'The Bible Speaks Today' series is one exception. Some syllabi are more along the 'Tyndale' lines and extremely reluctant to go any further than descriptive exegesis. What we must do, as evangelical teachers, is show that exegesis is both the necessary but also first step. We must show that the Bible itself is kerygmatic and speaks today. We must also show that to understand it today, we must first understand what it originally said.

Old Testament and Preaching

Fourthly, and leading on from the previous point, there must be an integration between the teaching of Old Testament and preaching. Preaching was taught as a practical subject, by practitioners rather than biblical studies lecturers. That is a mistake, though I suspect a common one. James Crenshaw acknowledges that his students frequently complain that the classroom prepares them well for the exegetical task but poorly for the move from text to sermon.[9] When I was taught preaching, it was notably weak on theological or hermeneutical assessment. Sermon critiques always majored more on issues of style and delivery than on theological accuracy. Likewise modern preaching is more concerned with charisma and eloquence than truth. I suspect that behind this lies the perception I mentioned above, that interpretation for today is subjective, a matter of personal choice or direct Spirit leading.

Thus there seems to be almost a contradiction. We strive very carefully to discover the determinate meaning for the original audience but are far less cautious in looking for the meaning for today. With regards to the application we are practical indeterminists. One of the exercises to give a class from time to time is to get them to respond to sections of devotional commentaries or Scripture Union (daily Bible reading) notes to see whether they agree with their interpretations and applications. Alternatively, get students to write their own devotional notes. It is all too easy to 'force' a simple message of comfort and faith

9. Crenshaw, *Trembling at the Threshold*, p. 136.

from any part of the Bible. Evangelicals must resist this trend towards free interpretation. There are right and wrong interpretations of Scripture and we need to teach how to distinguish between them. We must be prepared to point out what is wrong use of Scripture.

We, in theological colleges, must be preachers as well as teachers. We must not only model good preaching but show students how to become good preachers. We must persuade our students that it is the word which is powerful, accurately interpreted, applied by God's Spirit, and not the style, winsomeness, humour, or anecdotal ability of the preacher which is the most important. There is so little Old Testament preaching done in our pulpits, and what is done is often so bad, that there is a big job to be done for theological students.

A Revised Syllabus

In the light of these comments, if I were constructing an Old Testament syllabus for a theological college today, I would incorporate the following:

(i) First-year overview of all the Bible, covering historical and geographical background, basic issues of all major books, key themes and major emphases of each book. This would concentrate on reading the Old Testament in its original context with some attempt at application for today and reading the Old Testament through the New Testament.

(ii) Separately, I would have a first-year biblical theology course which discussed issues of the relationship between the testaments and traced the major biblical theology themes: covenant, presence of God, salvation, kingship, gospel and kingdom, etc.

(iii) Apart from further courses on specific Old Testament texts, critical methodology, language, exegesis, I would have a second-year course working on the interpretation of texts. This would be taught by biblical studies teachers but with the aim of applying the Old Testament to modern times. This could work through books such as *The Modern Preacher and the Ancient Text*, *Postcard from Palestine*, and those of Fee and Stuart.[10]

10. A. Reid, *Postcard from Palestine* (Sydney: St. Matthias Press, 1989); S. Greidanus, *The Modern Preacher and the Ancient Text* (Grand Rapids: Eerdmans, 1988).

(iv) There would be an entirely separate practical course in public speaking, voice control, etc.

(v) A third-year course would then draw together the practical and hermeneutical second-year strands in preaching. Works such as *Expository Preaching*[11] and Greidanus' book would be important here. I acknowledge that not every student is called to be a preacher but the hermeneutical principles apply just as well for those who will be Bible study group leaders, Sunday school teachers, religious education teachers, etc. This final year preaching course must be taken by biblical studies teachers.[12]

(vi) Ideally, of course, Hebrew would be compulsory, and enough of it to get to the point of being useful.

(vii) Another issue is where to teach biblical inspiration. Usually this is taught as a separate topic in systematics or dogmatics. However, a case can be made for teaching this within biblical studies, especially dealing with separate genres and inspiration, as Goldingay does, for example.[13] Thus the doctrine of inspiration could be a theme which recurs at different points in the Old Testament (and New Testament) syllabus, even over a couple of years.

(viii) Finally, a worthwhile element of a course would be reflection groups. Here, throughout the course, a group of students would meet with a lecturer, perhaps every fortnight or three weeks, to reflect on the implications of what has been taught. Such sessions would integrate topics, ministry, ethics, and pastoral issues.

(ix) This last point also leads into another, namely that some issues and topics could well be team taught. For example, the problem of evil could be addressed by lecturers from Old Testament, New Testament, philosophy of religion, ethics, and pastoral fields. One benefit of such an approach is to demonstrate the integrity of truth, that the study of Old Testament, for example, impinges on systematics, ethics, and preaching. Team teaching helps students to make connections between areas of study and thus develop their own more integrated Christian perspectives.

---

11. H. W. Robinson, *Expository Preaching* (Grand Rapids: Baker, 1980).

12. Of course, somewhere in the whole degree, work would need to be done on understanding contemporary culture. This was also lacking in my training.

13. Goldingay, *Models for Scripture*.

One of the recommendations for Old Testament study is the addition of a section on Old Testament theology. This could be in three parts: themes (covenant, worship, people of God, land, kingdom of God, nations, suffering, eschatology), nature of Old Testament theology (unity and diversity, the search for a centre of Old Testament), Old Testament and the Christian (Old Testament and biblical theology, Christian approaches to the Old Testament). Such an addition, if approved, will greatly enhance the teaching of Old Testament and go some way to meeting some of these points. This will certainly increase the biblical theology approach and help students see the place of the Old Testament within the Bible. A second alteration, in recognition of the rarity of studying Hebrew, is the scrapping of textual criticism from the later unit and the addition of a fuller section on the canon and process of canonisation of the Old Testament. Other minor changes proposed include the selection of texts for exegesis.

Study and Faith

Every year, theological study both challenges and confuses students' faith. In part this reflects a background of simple faith, a fear of liberalism, reason or academic questioning. In part it reflects deficiencies in the academic approach. This often begins in Genesis 1–11 where many recoil from ANE parallel texts as though they threaten the Bible's authority. Discussion of authorship, source, and redaction theories also sometimes seems to threaten students. Many come to college wrongly expecting elevated Bible studies and devotional talks. We need therefore to be pastoral teachers.

Presuppositions and Observations

Many students feel that an academic approach to the Bible is an attack on it, even in an evangelical environment. I used to run seminars for first years a month after the new year began to help them find their way through academia. All of us know that much that is written is dry and arid, sceptical and critical of truth. Yet we also know that there are occasional oases in the liberal desert. We can learn from our liberal and non-believing colleagues. Believers do not have a monopoly on truth. In these seminars, I found it helpful to simply distinguish between presuppositions, observations, and conclusions. Many scholars have theological presuppositions we do not share or even fundamentally opposed to ours, yet their observations about the Old Testament can be insightful and illuminating. When we reject their presuppositions, their conclusions will also likely be ones we do not share. They work with an equation $A + B = C$. We may reject A (the presuppositions) for A'. But if the observations are worthwhile, our equation will become $A' + B = C'$, not C. If we just reject liberal scholarship, we will throw out B, the good observations, along with the rest. Helping students see these distinctions will aid their appreciation of good observations while not being threatened by liberal presuppositions and conclusions.

In particular, students need help dealing with the historico-critical method. Helping them understand the presuppositions of such methodology is more important than often assumed. So much of Old Testament studies of the last century has begun from positions alien to an evangelical one. Though we have all gained from the insights and observations of many Old Testament scholars, fundamentally much of their method is flawed. This raises the difficult issue of how far we work with the prevailing method and how far we abandon it. More needs to be done in setting evangelical models of Old Testament methodology free from the constraints of liberalism. Because the vast majority of Old Testament literature that students will read is from a liberal perspective, it is crucial that they know how to read it carefully. But we also need alternative, evangelical works. Where is an evangelical equivalent to the JSOT Old Testament Guides which are freed from the liberal agenda? Where is an evangelical introduction to Old Testament study, equivalent to Rogerson, for example?[14] In our teaching of Old Testament, we need to set the agenda and not be driven by a liberal agenda.

Autocracy of Truth

Students should be encouraged to see that truth is not democratic. What determines truth is God, not a majority scholarly view. Otherwise stu-

---

14. J. Rogerson, *Beginning Old Testament Study* (London: SPCK, 1983).

dents can easily get the impression from their reading that liberal views are right. Further, they can be helped in seeing that the truth of God's word stands and cannot be shaken by academic study. What is being studied is God's truth and no matter how deeply it is examined, critiqued, or prodded, it will always be found to be truth. I therefore want students to question, probe, and pursue problem areas, and not to shy away from deep questions as Tomlinson accuses evangelicals of doing.[15]

Thinking on Truth

Following on from this point, I also urge students to realise that academic study of the Bible is part of 'thinking on truth' or developing and transforming our minds. I want students to integrate their academic study with their devotional reading of the Bible. I encourage students to have the 'same Bible' for both, not meaning the edition, but recognising that what they learn about the Bible must not be put aside in their quiet times. This relates to points made above about the integration of truth and ethics, or, in other terms, mind and heart, thinking and practice. Academic study of the Bible should stimulate faith. I encourage students with my own situation that, despite all the liberal literature I have studied and read, all the formal theological study I have done, my faith in God and the reliability and power of his word grows, not diminishes.

Teaching Old Testament in a University

Quite obviously there are major differences between a seminary and a university. There are different aims and objectives, different communities, different student aims, different priorities for lecturers (research, publications over teaching and pastoring, perhaps). Clearly not all the above comments about preaching, for example, apply in a university. Yet there is a sense in which our fundamental approach should be the same in either institution. I shall make just a few, uncomprehensive comments in the light of some part-time teaching at a university over three years.

15. D. Tomlinson, *The Post-Evangelical* (London: Triangle, 1995).

The Teacher and Advocacy

In one respect it was a rude shock teaching my first class in a university. It was a first-year class on 'Interpreting Biblical Literature'. Though I anticipated that my students would now, unlike at a seminary, include non-believers, I hadn't anticipated the ignorance and antagonism of many. I was very cautious of pressing a Christian view too dogmatically at first, anxious to appear objective and dispassionate. However, I strengthened my stance each subsequent time I taught this class, for the Bible cannot be rightly interpreted other than by Christians. Certainly non-Christians can use good literary, linguistic, and textual methods to aid interpretation, but ultimately, interpretation of the Bible cannot be divorced from receiving its gospel and obeying its commands. Interpretation is not merely an intellectual exercise; it is also an ethical one. 'Academic' should not be equated to 'intellectual' here. Teaching the Bible must mean engagement with both intellect and ethics. If we omit the latter, we do not teach it properly, thus not objectively, and that is failing academically. I acknowledge where I am coming from and make no apology for it and I do not want to deceive anyone. I also make it clear I do not expect all students to have the same stance.

Crenshaw suggests there are three stages of knowledge — description, experience, and internalisation. The first two are easy. The third is the difficult one because it involves ideology. Christianity, he rightly says, demands an internalisation and hence the advocacy of ideology. He questions whether this is appropriate in a university context but notes that one cannot remain neutral where ideology is concerned. A teacher without ultimate commitments is only half a teacher. Yet Crenshaw states that he leaves the process of internalisation to the students. Of course we cannot do the internalising for them, but if we stop short of the demands of Scripture to internalise, if we stop short of advocacy, then we only half teach.[16]

No teacher can teach purely objectively. The Christian must not give up the right to teach the truth from a Christian standpoint. We must realise that the push to teach description only is as subjective, indeed more so, as teaching from an explicitly Christian point of view.

16. Crenshaw, *Trembling at the Threshold*, pp. 137-38.

The push to teach all religions as equal is also just as subjective. We need to take a stance on these issues and resist the marginalisation of Christianity. In a class on Amos, I make no apology for showing how the New Testament resolves some of the issues of Amos, how the cross reconciles the tensions between judgement and hope, and how we today are to read and sit under and preach Amos. That is because Amos was never written to be only a book for the eighth century but was written for us, and our students, whether they are believers or not. It was never intended as a totally discrete text but as part of a canon of Scripture under God's providence and serving his eternal purposes. Amos is not taught properly if the teacher ignores the fact that the book addresses us.

Ignorance and a Biblical Theology Model

The widespread ignorance of the Old Testament among under-graduates means a necessary difference from theological college where more background can be assumed. One of the frustrations is the lack of time to correct this, for many students may only do one Old Testament module of a semester in length. Where, for example, university B.Ed. students do a compulsory workshop on 'Interpreting Biblical Literature' I change, where possible, the syllabus to cater more for the ignorance about the Bible. Rather than starting with a session on the reliability and inspiration of Scripture, I start with a theological over-view of the contents of the Bible, in just two hours. In some respects this is, in fact, a presentation of the gospel. It is really a biblical theology approach.

I have also used the model of an Agatha Christie mystery novel. The Bible has the same structure. All begins well. Soon a problem is unearthed, a murder in one, sin in the other. The consequences of sin are discussed, mainly in terms of separation from God, banishment from the garden. Then the Old Testament is considered in terms of clues looking for a solution to the problem of sin. Not all the clues are fully explained at first. Some threads don't seem to hang together. Various avenues seem to come to dead ends. I try and pick out the thread of God's presence with his people as that motif relates to the separation caused by sin. Then I compare the New Testament with the drawing room scene with Hercule Poirot explaining all. In both Old Testament and Agatha Christie, sense is made, at the end, of all the strange clues. This helps explain reading the Bible forwards (Old Testament then New Testament) and backwards (New Testament then Old Testament). Obviously a weakness of this model is that Agatha Christie is fiction and the Bible is not. However, the benefit of this model, and I am sure there are many adequate variations and alternatives, is that it proclaims the Bible's message. That must be first and foremost, before description, background, analysis, and anything else. Only when that big picture is presented is there an adequate interpretative framework for the interpretation of the bits. I have also found that even long-standing Christians have rarely seen the Bible in such a light.

It is possible to lecture in a course in Genesis giving a brief biblical theology of major themes from Genesis 1–3 in the rest of the Bible. Themes like Eden, life, rest, presence of God, nature of humanity, can be traced through both Old Testament and New Testament, making no apology for the latter, and finish by showing their resolution in the new Jerusalem in Revelation 21–22. This can be very brief but student response can be very encouraging to having expressed things in such a way.

Difficulties

Community

There are many more difficulties teaching in a university context than at a theological college. Personally I much prefer the latter. Teaching is generally not done in community in a university. There is often hardly a community of the faculty, let alone one of lecturers and students. At theological college there is a greater integration of learning, pastoral care, and worship. There is a commonality of purpose which is not possible in a university. Staff don't pray together, preach, worship together, or pastor students. The university exercise is intellectual but not personal or ethical. Perhaps monthly research seminars for biblical studies students and lecturers could be introduced where reading and discussing papers can contribute to communal learning.

It is important to prevent research and teaching being too isolated a task.

Religious Pluralism

Biblical studies is always under threat of marginalisation. The Bible is officially regarded as just one of many sacred texts and evangelicals have a difficult job to proclaim its uniqueness. All these are battles that have to be fought in an age of growing pluralism, political correctness, and relativism. These battles can distract from the actual teaching.

One of the difficulties in the modern university is that theology or religious studies is one area among many. One of the things which we need to encourage students to see is that God is central to all of life and that the world, and therefore other academic disciplines, cannot be understood correctly without reference to him. Teaching students to develop a Christian perspective on all of life is much more difficult in a university than a theological college. Yet that should be part of our aim, for it is part of the aim of Scripture.

Old Testament and Proclamation

Many of the things above that apply to seminary teaching also apply to the university. We need to integrate the Old Testament and New Testament in our teaching. We need to teach the Old Testament as proclamation, not as history, religion, or moralism. We also must be even more careful in teaching critical methodology for these students will have less background, less know-how, and less contact time to develop an adequate framework for critiquing such things. I have had a number of students in recent years who have resisted totally any critical methodology, as part of their defence of the truth of the Old Testament. In a theological college there is much more opportunity for personal formation to deal with that. In a university, and especially as a part-time lecturer, there is much less. However, it is worth remembering that because the Bible is evangelistic, teaching it cannot help but be, at least implicitly, evangelistic also. If not, we are distorting its message and thus not teaching it objectively. Also, because the Bible is God's powerful word, a two-edged sword, teaching the Bible can penetrate people's hearts and not only inform their minds but make them wise for salvation and train them for righteousness.

May we, wherever we teach, be workers who do not need to be ashamed and who correctly handle the word of truth.

A Star-Spangled Old Testament: Teaching in the American Seminary

ROBERT L. HUBBARD, JR.

Robert L. Hubbard has taught Old Testament in an evangelical seminary in the United States for over two decades. After nineteen years at Denver Conservative Baptist Seminary, Colorado, he moved to North Park Theological Seminary of Chicago, Illinois, the seminary of the Evangelical Covenant Church of America. Thus most of this essay derives from experience at the former seminary. He offers these reflections in the hope that they will aid his pedagogical colleagues in other contexts to become more effective teachers of the Bible's most misunderstood half.

During the so-called Cold War, a story circulated about the Soviet motorcycle policeman assigned to catch speeders along a certain Russian highway. He skilfully hid himself out of sight behind a large billboard advertisement. Sadly, only plodding peasants and slow-moving oxcarts passed his hiding place. After a month on the job he had yet to cite a single speeder. Finally, a mystified friend asked him what purpose his job served. 'I don't know', the policeman shrugged, 'but this is the way they do it in America'.

In exploring the teaching of Old Testament, this essay eschews any similar sweeping claim that 'this is the way they do it in America'. Its focus is more modest — on the teaching of the Old Testament in the context of an evangelical seminary in the United States but it makes no assumption that this is the way it should be done elsewhere. It is my conviction that if Christians understood the Old Testament better, their view of God would be richer — and so would their walk with God. By the same token, the ministries of churches would be more holistic if they paid greater attention to the other half of the whole counsel of God.

Not surprisingly, the topic of teaching the Old Testament has received very little published reflection.[1] Books and essays on preaching from the Old Testament abound[2] which may be due to the simple fact that more people preach than teach from it each week — or at least they aspire to! Certainly, there are more pulpits from which the Old Testament may weekly sound its voice than there are lecterns. But a congregation is not a class, nor is a sanctuary a lecture hall. Whatever their similarities, teaching and preaching are not the same endeavour, so it is right to seek specialised discussion on teaching the Old Testament. Along this line, several studies discuss how to teach the Bible as literature in secular universities[3] and another treats Bible instruction in a local congregation.[4] But essays on teaching the Old Testament in other contexts (theological schools or seminaries, for example) are very rare indeed.[5]

1. For discussion of rationales for the study of the Bible in general, see W. Brueggemann and D. A. Knight, 'Why Study the Bible?' *Council on the Study of Religion Bulletin* 11 (1980), pp. 76-81.

2. *E.g.*, D. Gowan, *Reclaiming the Old Testament for the Christian Pulpit* (Edinburgh: T & T Clark, 1980); E. R. Achtemeier, *Preaching from the Old Testament* (Louisville: Westminster, 1989); *Preaching the Old Testament* (Nashville: Abingdon, 1991); G. L. Klein, *Reclaiming the Prophetic Mantle* (Nashville: Broadman, 1992); *et al.* See also R. K. Harrison's four part series 'The Pastor's Use of the Old Testament', in *Bibliotheca Sacra* 146 (1989).

3. *E.g.*, the course outline for undergraduates pursuing majors other than literature by N. M. Tischler, 'Bible Literature for Secular Non-Humanists', *Christianity and Literature* 30 (1980), pp. 96-102; J. G. Catlin, 'Bugs in the Garden: Teaching "the Bible as Literature" in Oklahoma,' *Christianity and Literature* 31 (1982), pp. 58-66. For the teaching of the Bible as literature in secondary schools, see the articles by J. S. Ackerman and T. S Warshaw in the supplement of *Religious Education* 67 (1972).

4. R. Bender, 'Teaching the Bible in the Congregation', in W. M. Swartley (ed.), *Essays on Biblical Interpretation: Anabaptist-Mennonite Perspectives* (Elkhart, IN: Institute of Mennonite Studies, 1984), pp. 291-302.

5. *Cf.* L. E. Porter, 'Teaching the Old Testament Prophets: Their Place in the Agreed Syllabus', *EvQ* 26 (1954), pp. 130-45; J. S. Chesnut, 'Problems in Teaching

That scarcity notwithstanding, the topic remains a significant one, not only because of the importance of the Old Testament for the life of the church, but also because of the importance of the pedagogical context in shaping how one teaches. Thus, the present volume fills a lacuna in professional secondary literature on education, facilitating further reflection on the topic of the teaching of Old Testament and its related subjects.[6] This present essay is admittedly impressionistic in character, aiming to give readers unfamiliar with the seminary scene in North America an introduction to it through the eyes of one pedagogical practitioner, and hopefully providing more than just the 'confessions of an Old Testament professor'!

The American Educational System

To begin, a brief sketch of the larger educational scene in the United States may be helpful.[7] The United States has both private and public institutions of higher learning. Public institutions include universities and colleges owned and operated by individual states (*e.g.*, the University of Michigan, the University of California, Rutgers State University of New Jersey, etc.). They are funded primarily by state legislatures from state tax revenues and are accountable to boards of regents either appointed by state officials (*e.g.*, governors, commissioners of education, etc.) or elected by the public. Whether counted as a whole category or by individual schools, their student population is by far the largest in the world.

Unlike many European countries, the United States has no official state religion supported financially from the public treasury. Indeed, the First Amendment of the United States Constitution says that 'Con-

---

the Old Testament', *JBR* 30 (1962), pp. 284-90. For a more recent discussion from a specifically feminist perspective, see C. Hess and E. Hess, 'Reflections on Teaching the Bible in a Sexist World', *Koinonia* 1 (1995), pp. 55-67.

6. It is interesting to observe that the annual meeting program of two major, primarily North American, scholarly societies (the American Academy of Religion: Society of Biblical Literature) now offers a study group focussed on the academic teaching of biblical studies.

7. I regret that limitations of space and of my own knowledge require that I omit treatment of the educational systems of Canada and Mexico, the closest neighbours of the United States.

gress shall make no law respecting an establishment of religion, or prohibiting the free exercise thereof . . .'. The federal government can neither set up a state religion nor interfere in the religious practices of the people. Religions are free to proselytise and practise in the public religious marketplace as each sees fit. That general social policy of religious pluralism directly determines how Old Testament is taught in public universities. To my knowledge no public university has a Department of Theology in which the subject might be taught, because one associates 'theology' specifically with Christianity. Hence, to have such a department might imply the establishment of religion in violation of the First Amendment. If it is taught at all, the Old Testament would be incorporated in courses on the Bible as literature, the ancient Near East, world religions, ancient history or philosophy, etc.

Private institutions of higher learning continue to flourish in the United States. These are schools founded and funded primarily from private sources of revenues.[8] Some are purely secular in character (*e.g.,* the Claremont Colleges, Carleton College, etc.), but many have an explicitly religious character (*e.g.,* the University of Judaism, Catholic University of America, Texas Christian University, etc.).[9] In the latter category also fit schools and seminaries whose primary mission is to train clergy for their supporting religious bodies (*i.e.,* Hebrew Union College-Jewish Institute of Religion, St. Mary's Seminary, the Lutheran School of Theology, etc.). These schools offer degrees at the post-baccalaureate level to students already having completed undergraduate studies or the equivalent. Indeed the policy of the separation of church and state in the United States means that each religious body, not state universities, is responsible for the training of its clergy. Free of constitutional constraints those explicitly religious schools may teach the Old

8. Some private schools receive government funds for specific purposes, *e.g.,* for scientific research, etc. In general, colleges and universities that identify themselves as specifically Christian are reluctant to accept government funding, however, because to do so may obligate them to abide by government policies, for example, nondiscrimination in the hiring of employees. They fear that financial entanglement with the government might prohibit them from refusing to hire individuals on the basis of religious beliefs which significantly differ from those of the employing school.

9. Some schools originally founded as religious institutions have either severed or loosened their ties to specific religious groups and would now identify themselves as 'secular' institutions, *e.g.,* Harvard University, Northwestern University, the University of Southern California, etc.

Testament as they see fit, normally from the perspective of their own religious tradition. In some cases, that tradition may mean that their course content differs very little from that of the public university down the street; in others the differences may be monumental.

The American Evangelical Seminary Student

As noted above, this essay focuses on the teaching of Old Testament within the setting of an evangelical seminary. Since education involves the interaction between teachers and students, a profile of the American evangelical seminary student seems in order at the outset.[10] Again, what follows intends to be impressionistic and reflective rather than precisely statistical and objective. Its strength lies in the general portrait it paints, its weakness the subjectivity and limitations of the author-observer's experience.

The very make-up of the population of American theological schools has undergone subtle but significant changes in the last two decades. In the 1970's most students started seminary studies the very fall after earning their undergraduate degree. In other words, only a summer separated undergraduate studies from seminary matriculation, and most students were in their early twenties. To be sure, the intervening summer was often an eventful one, with many students getting married, labouring to learn a biblical language for the first time, or both. Two decades later, however, the entering seminary student is in his or her early to mid-thirties. Driving this startling rise in average age is another phenomenon, the second career student.

For an increasing number of seminary students the ministry represents a second career. Some have entered seminary after years, if not whole careers, as doctors, dentists, certified public accountants, lawyers, educators, military officers, advertising executives, and business owners. Some even supported themselves financially during their theological studies by continuing their professions, and earning high salaries even though they were only working part-time.

10. For the broader picture of American theological students, see the issue 'Profile of Contemporary Seminarians Revisited' of *Theological Education* (Supplement) 31 (1995).

This quality of student population poses both pedagogical challenges for the professor and curricular challenges for the theological school. The students' richer life experiences mean that they ask different (often, tougher!) questions in class. They are also less intimidated by professors than younger students, especially if they are older than the teacher, and may feel more freedom to push him or her hard on some issues — all within the bounds of genuine respect for the professor, of course. Further, 'pat answers' which fail to reckon with their experience of complex issues are less likely to persuade or satisfy more mature students than peers junior to them. It all makes for some lively classroom discussions, often with students sharing insights drawn from their own rich past histories. Pedagogically, the teacher will have to allow time, whether in class or outside it, for such discussions — and to be prepared to interact intelligently.

As for curriculum, older students tend to select a shorter, more practical curriculum of study, *i.e.*, a two-year Master of Arts degree rather than the traditional three-year Master of Divinity degree. Most have families to support while earning their degrees, financial demands which mean that they take fewer hours per term and take more years to finish. They also tend to be less in a hurry to get somewhere than their younger fellow students. That is, having spent some years in the work-a-day world they seem to savor the chance to study, think, and reflect, as if they regard this educational phase as a refreshing interlude between their past and future phases of employment. Of course, their preference for shorter degree programs confronts them with a difficult decision concerning whether or not to learn a biblical language (or whether to learn only one). Previously they tended to avoid the study of Hebrew (but not Greek), but recently more such students brave introductory Hebrew classes, thereby attempting to learn both languages.

Another factor behind the phenomenon of second-career students is the expanding diversity of religious ministries in this country (or, put differently, the increasing specialization of ministry). This expansion has occurred in both church and para-church contexts. Two decades ago, virtually all students intended to become pastors, youth workers, or foreign missionaries. Today, besides those more typical students, basic Old Testament classes may serve students in counselling headed toward private practice as therapists, others aimed at church, youth, or camping ministries, still others hoping to teach Bible in a Christian secondary school, and quite a few uncertain about their future vocation. The diversity of student vocational goals requires that, in illustrating the usefulness in ministry of course subject matter, the professor must employ a wider variety of examples than would have been necessary two decades ago.

Students Come from Everywhere

The Old Testament teacher also confronts increasing biblical illiteracy among students. In former years most students came to seminary having grown up in a local church. Years in Sunday school and small-group Bible studies had educated them thoroughly in Bible content.

Granted, their undergraduate studies may have been a long way from theology — e.g., in agronomy, economics, engineering, or art history — yet they still not only knew the Bible's major figures and events, but they could also quote (or at least paraphrase) many important biblical passages, even lengthy ones. Involvement in university Christian groups had matured their faith and shaped in them a Christian world view. For them, in-depth discussion of the theology of familiar texts was a relatively easy, if not an exhilarating exercise, one that deepened their understanding of old, long-treasured friends.

Recently, however, increasing numbers of students come to seminary without growing up in a church at all. These are students who became Christians and were nurtured spiritually through university evangelism ministries like Campus Crusade or InterVarsity Christian Fellowship. They show the fiery fervour of new converts and often know much about the Bible. But their biblical literacy and theological depth run a mile wide — and only an inch deep. In teaching Old Testament, it can no longer be assumed that students know their Bibles. The pedagogical challenge thus is to enrich the understanding of both the more biblically literate and less biblically literate.

On the other hand, seminary students who have grown up in churches may show what may be regarded as one of evangelicalism's less appealing traits. I call them 'modern Marcionites', that is, they tend to ignore the Old Testament — or at least anything but the Psalms.[11]

---

11. Marcionites were followers of Marcion, a Christian heretical leader (2nd century A.D.) who promoted the radical discontinuity between Christianity and

Some come from religious traditions whose aim is to replicate exactly the teachings and practices of the New Testament church today, a view which reduces the Old Testament to irrelevancy. Others follow dispensationalism, a hermeneutical schema which teaches that the relationship between God and humanity was dominated by law in the Old Testament and grace in the New Testament.[12] They love to learn Greek and exegete Paul's letters, but they see little or no reason to learn Hebrew and exegete Moses and the prophets. They may even hold a faculty post at a prestigious evangelical seminary!

Fortunately, unlike the demons whom Jesus expelled, their 'name is [not] Legion' — they are not many in number (Mark 5:9; Luke 8:30). But, obviously, they pose a pedagogical challenge to any teacher with a passion for the truth of the Old Testament. Such students can be approached, first, by arguing from New Testament evidence that the Old Testament was the Bible of Jesus, the apostles, and the church which they founded (*e.g.*, Matt. 4; 2 Tim. 3:15-16; Rom. 15:4; *et al.*).[13] The hope is to drive a mental wedge between their prior learning and the new learning they are about to experience in the course. Second, in teaching try to show them how much the Old Testament has to teach Christians today. If this is successful, they will quietly reformulate their view concerning the relationship between the testaments and, more importantly, get excited about what they are discovering in the Old Testament.

Finally, American theological students share a major trait of American culture in general: they are very pragmatic. They want course content that is practical, ready-to-apply, stuff that works, that has relevance to ordinary life, and that shows them 'how-to' live and minister in the future. Greatly prolonged discussions of abstract theories of composition — the Judahite redaction of Amos, for example — are likely to create a classroom full of glazed, drowsy eyes and diplomatically-stifled yawns. Topics deemed 'academic' — to retrace the history

---

Judaism, arguing that Jesus was not the same as the God of the Old Testament. His canon contained only parts of the Gospel of Luke and Paul's ten letters. For an overview of his career and influence see J. J. Claheatix, 'Marcion', *ABD* 4, pp. 514-16.

12. For a recent survey of dispensationalist thought, see W. R. Willis *et al.* (eds.), *Issues in Dispensationalism* (Chicago: Moody, 1994); R. L. Saucy, *The Case for Progressive Dispensationalism* (Grand Rapids: Zondervan, 1993).

13. In my view, the classic defense of Old Testament authority remains J. Bright, *The Authority of the Old Testament* (Grand Rapids: Baker, 1975).

of an Old Testament tradition through convoluted layers of growth, or even to rehearse how a text-critical reading came to be — probably will leave a class bored, if not actually restless. Few questions will be asked — except for one by a brave but frustrated student: 'Is this going to be on the exam?' The ultimate pragmatism! For them pragmatism means that the ultimate test of truth is the applicability of a topic to the practice of personal piety or to the life of the church. They tend to learn and believe things that work or apply to life.

Such pragmatism confronts teachers of the Old Testament with some key questions. To what extent should Old Testament be taught as an academic field of study? How much higher criticism do future clergy need to know? Or, put more pointedly, should modern higher criticism be taught in a seminary at all? On the other hand, to what extent do I teach Old Testament as part of the Christian Bible? How practical, if not devotional, should Old Testament classes be? How many perspectives (*e.g.*, feminist, post-modernist, liberationist, etc.) should one course represent at a time? Here the institutional independence of American private schools grants a freedom not shared by European teachers whose students ultimately must sit for exams graded by university faculty. In writing syllabi, the teacher is only accountable to the students and the school.

On the other hand, it is worth considering whether the external accountability endured by European colleagues might benefit American evangelical seminaries. It might prevent their professors from focusing their course content too narrowly on 'safe' and 'relevant' topics, or from skirting some controversial issues which they should cover. Such external accountability might stretch their students intellectually in ways that would not otherwise be possible. In the end, it might serve to tone up the too often flabby intellectual muscle of American evangelical clergy.

One approach is to always seek to give the student a balanced diet — enough criticism to stretch the mind, enough devotion to stir the spirit. Select textbooks with that balance in mind by pairing books of different views — one book with which most evangelical students will feel 'comfortable' alongside one whose views will stretch them.[14]

14. For example, for an introductory course on Old Testament prophets I often pair the moderately conservative W. S. LaSor *et al.*, *Old Testament Survey* (Grand Rapids: Eerdmans, 1982), with the more mainline works like J. Bright, *A History of*

Furthermore, teachers are regarded as representatives of an academic discipline whose methods, positions, and discussion they are obligated to present. Integrity demands that they present those views as fairly as they can but with proper dispassionate critique rather than as the proverbial 'straw men' to be toppled triumphantly.

At the same time, the ultimate goal should always be to teach students to listen as carefully as possible to the biblical text. Discussions of higher critical themes serve that goal by forcing students to wrestle with the biblical text, that is, the biblical evidence which underlies those theories. Such discussions teach the most important lesson which students should learn, namely, to be able to hear what the biblical text is saying.

The Globalization of American Theological Education

Increasingly, American church bodies are reckoning with the expanding ethnic populations in their midst. It is not uncommon for a local Protestant church to have two or three congregations — most often, Anglo, Korean, and Hispanic — worship in the same building at different times. Signs written in each congregation's language announce the schedule of services and list the pastor's name and phone number. Vibrant congregations have long been at the heart of African-American culture, and the latter has fostered its own network of educational institutions for the training of clergy and laity alike.

Recently, however, seminaries which traditionally served Anglo students have sought to build bridges to serve the needs of other ethnic groups. In the last two decades, special programs targeted to their needs have begun to appear, normally coordinated by a faculty member from that cultural group. As a result, an increasing number of students from African-American, Hispanic, and Korean congregations have begun to attend formerly all-Anglo schools. A similar increase in the number of women pursuing theological degrees has occurred. In schools open to the ordination of women, women may comprise nearly half the student

---

Israel (3rd ed.) (Philadelphia: Westminster, 1981), G. von Rad, *Theology of the Old Testament*, vol. 2 (New York: Harper & Row, 1965), or J. M. Ward, *Thus Says the Lord: The Message of the Prophets* (Nashville: Abingdon, 1991).

body; in others the percentage will be less but still significantly greater than in years past.[15] Even seminaries less open, if not opposed, to women in ministry, have recently seen an increase in the number of women preparing for non-ordained ministries such as Christian education, missionary, service, counselling, youth ministry, and university evangelism.

Over the last decade, the Association of Theological Schools (ATS), the agency which academically accredits seminaries in the United States and Canada, has promoted the globalization of theological education.[16] Globalization remains one of the accreditation standards which ATS institutions must meet.[17] Broadly understood, 'globalization' refers to concerns for ethnic, economic, and gender diversity and for the contextualization of education which acknowledges and is reshaped by that diversity. In other words, globalization means not only that a school will promote ethnic and gender diversity among its faculty, staff, and students, but that cross-cultural and gender-inclusive perspectives will also influence curricula and course content.[18]

The change in student population has had an immediate impact on the vocabulary of the teacher. No longer can professional advice in

15. In addition, I can also recall having had as students at least three married couples who entered seminary so that both husband and wife might pursue a degree. All three men pursued the Master of Divinity and ordination, while the three women completed Master of Arts degrees without seeking ordination. It is not uncommon among some American Protestant denominations for a married couple to serve as fully-ordained co-pastors of a local congregation after graduating together from seminary.

16. For early discussion see D. W. Shriver, 'The Globalization of Theological Education: Setting the Task', *Theological Education* 23 (1986), pp. 7-18; D. S. Schuller, 'Globalization in Theological Education: Summary and Analysis of Survey Data', *Theological Education* 23 (1986), pp. 19-56. D. S. Browning, 'Globalization and the Task of Theological Education in North America', *Theological Education* (Supplement) 30 (1993), pp. 15-29, offers a more recent assessment.

17. See Standard IX in the ATS *Bulletin* 41 (1994), p. 30; *cf.* also its *Handbook of Accreditation* (rev. 1993), p. 33.

18. From 1989 to 1994, about a dozen schools from Roman Catholic and various Protestant traditions (including two evangelical schools) participated in a five-year program to foster globalization in their schools. The Pilot Immersion Project — The Globalization of Theological Education (PIP-GTE) featured two-week summer immersions overseas and in each school's local area. Each school then planned how to implement globalization in its operation, a process which continues to this writing.

class be prefaced with the common phrase, 'Now. when you men get out in ministry . . .'. Instead, language inclusive of women and course content aimed at their professional needs are necessary. Further, a larger female presence has positively affected the way the Old Testament is taught. In discussing the author or editor of a biblical book or corpus, it is necessary to speak inclusively about 'he or she' rather than only the former.[19] Also, their presence has subtly stimulated an interest in the Bible's female characters, people who otherwise may have been bypassed. I have yet to offer a course on 'Women of the Bible', but I find myself using the lives of more biblical women as examples of biblical truths.[20] More subtly, I think the presence of women in my classes has moderated the way I treat the Bible's less admirable women (*e.g.*, Eve, Gomer, Jezebel). For example, I try to balance my criticism of Jezebel's conduct with similar criticism of Ahab and other Israelite kings. I have also become very sensitized to the Bible's male domination — a reflection of its cultural origins, to be sure, but nonetheless an issue with which theological students must wrestle.

The same sensitivity applies to the ethnic diversity of my classes. I must candidly confess, however, that I feel myself back in kindergarten here. My sisters and my wife have sensitized me to women's concerns, but I still feel blinded by my privileged Anglo upbringing to the worlds of some of my students. Fortunately, in my present teaching post I have more ethnic students than in the past, and I am trying to solicit their feedback concerning ways to tie my teaching in to their cultural experiences better. Also, I have periodically had the privilege of visiting and ministering among several ethnic groups other than my own always with great profit for my growth in globalization. In addition, several recent volumes in biblical studies written from various ethnic perspectives open windows on how the latter read biblical texts.[21] My own

---

19. Candidly, I suppose another factor in this inclusivity was my conclusion that the author of the book of Ruth may have been a woman; *cf.* my *The Book of Ruth*, NICOT (Grand Rapids: Eerdmans, 1988), p. 24.

20. In 1994, however, I did publish a series of six devotional articles on 'Women in the Old Testament' in the June to December issues of *Moody Magazine*. My subjects were Rebekah, Abigail, Naaman's maid (2 Kings 5), Naomi, Ruth, and Esther.

21. C. H. Felder, *Stony the Road We Trod: African American Biblical Interpretation* (Minneapolis: Fortress, 1991); J. L. Gonzalez, *Santa Biblia: The Bible Through Hispanic Eyes* (Nashville: Abingdon, 1996).

personal small steps notwithstanding, the challenge of relating the Old Testament to all of my students marks the cutting edge of my pedagogy. Under God's good hand, I may one day advance to the next stage.

Conclusion

'I don't know', the Russian policeman shrugged to his friend, 'but this is the way they do it in America'. This essay has explored how one Old Testament seminary teacher 'does it in America'. As in semantics, so in pedagogy — context is crucial to effective teaching. To a great extent, the kinds of seminary students — their cultural background, biblical literacy, past experiences, church denomination, and vocational goals — determine how the Old Testament is taught. Perhaps this assumption constitutes a pedagogical counterpart to the reader-response aspect of biblical exegesis. In other words, teaching is most effective when it triggers productive, enriching responses in the heads and hearts of the students.

Granted, my philosophy affirms that I represent an academic field whose major consensuses I must present, even if with critique. But, at the end of the day, a passion to see students fall in love with the Old Testament and, through it, with the God who gave it, is the reason I teach. Hopefully, these reflections have provided colleagues in other places and already aflame with the same passion, with fuel to spark that love in their own students.

A Religious Book in a Secular University

T. DESMOND ALEXANDER

Desmond Alexander lectures in Old Testament at The Queen's University of Belfast. In this essay he gives a personal refection on the issues surrounding the teaching of the Old Testament. He does not attempt to provide a model course. Rather, it is hoped that the issues raised will provide a stimulus for further reflection and discussion.

Introduction

This essay, concerning an evangelical Christian approach to the teaching of the Old Testament at a university, falls into two parts.[1] The first half briefly considers the challenge of teaching biblical studies in a secular context, recognising that within most university departments of biblical studies, or their equivalent, there are teachers, probably in the majority, who reject unreservedly the traditional Christian view of the Bible as divine revelation. The second part highlights various factors which have, or ought to have, a bearing upon the shape of any Old Testament syllabus.

1. I would like to express my gratitude to Dr. Philip Johnston for reading and commenting helpfully on an earlier draft of this paper which was read at the Old Testament Study Group of the Tyndale Fellowship in July 1995.

T. DESMOND ALEXANDER

Teaching the Old Testament in a Secular Environment

The academic and critical study of the Bible in Britain is largely undertaken in departments in secular universities. (The situation in the United States is, of course, rather more complex.) In many cases, universities have statutes which prohibit denominational religious teaching. In such university departments, the teaching is based upon research, which is itself based upon the fundamental tenet of the critical method, namely, that scholars are free to follow in their work what they sincerely believe to be the truth, even if that begins to question the religious and academic assumptions that they hold.[2]

While these words highlight, on the one hand, the freedom with which all university lecturers may approach their studies (a freedom which I for one much appreciate), on the other hand, they also reflect a significant presupposition which underlies much research and teaching within our universities — all truth is to be ascertained by human reason. While at one level such a presupposition may seem quite innocent, it is important to appreciate that it reflects a particular philosophical outlook that may be traced back to the period of the Enlightenment in the eighteenth century. Furthermore, the main tenets of the Enlightenment, regarding (a) the central rôle of human reason in the quest for truth,[3] and (b) the

---

2. J. Rogerson, 'An Outline of the History of Old Testament Study', in *Beginning Old Testament Study* (London: SPCK, 1983), pp. 23-24. Professor Rogerson is well-known as the head of probably the largest biblical studies department in the British Isles.

3. According to Christian Wolff (1679-1754), one of the leading theological and philosophical proponents of the Enlightenment, the path to absolute truth was through 'pure reason'. Those adopting this outlook 'distrusted all authority and tradition in matters of intellectual inquiry, and believed that truth could be attained only through reason, observation and experiment'. See 'The Enlightenment', in *The Oxford Dictionary of the Christian Church* (2nd ed.) (London: Oxford University Press, 1974), p. 458. Linked to this was the belief that 'man can understand the universe by beginning from himself without any recourse to outside knowledge, specifically outside knowledge or revelation from God'. F. A. Schaeffer, *The Church Before the Watching World* (London: InterVarsity Press, 1972), p. 17. Whereas prior to the Enlightenment human reason had been generally viewed as subject to divine revelation, divine revelation now became subservient to human reason. The Enlightenment was 'a system founded upon the presupposition of faith in the omnipotence of human ability' (Karl Barth) quoted by W. Detzler, 'The Enlightenment (Aufklärung)', *The New International Dictionary of the Christian Church*, p. 343.

rejection of divine revelation,[4] continue to determine to a large degree how the Bible is studied in secular universities, and also, although hopefully to a lesser extent, in theological colleges.

Given the general ethos of the British university system, scholars working in the area of Old Testament may hold very different, and often contrary, views regarding the interpretation of the biblical text; frequently such differences are but a natural consequence of the presuppositions with which these scholars approach their studies. Within the university environment evangelical scholars form a small minority, many choosing or finding openings in theological colleges which have a decidedly less secular and more inviting ethos. As a consequence, in university departments of theology and biblical studies evangelical scholars often find themselves as lone voices in a wilderness of scepticism, teaching alongside colleagues who may have a tendency to mock what they perceive to be 'antiquarian' beliefs. (I am amazed at the way in which the views of evangelical scholars are often caricatured, seeing little in common between what others think I believe and what in reality I do believe.)

While the general ethos of the university system gives considerable freedom to staff in the way they approach their own research, various factors limit this freedom when it comes to the content of their teaching. Courses are normally designed in conjunction with other colleagues and often require the approval of external examiners. Much rests, therefore, on the attitudes and outlooks of all those involved. Not surprisingly, as regards the content of the courses they teach, younger evangelical scholars may find their supposed 'academic free-

---

4. The period of the Enlightenment also marked, according to Schaeffer, an important ideological and philosophical shift in German universities towards 'modern naturalism'. Whereas earlier scientists (such as Copernicus, Galileo, and Newton) had 'believed in the uniformity of natural causes in a *limited system open to reordering by both God and man*,' it now became fashionable to think of the uniformity of natural causes in *'a closed system, a concept which makes everything that exists a cosmic machine'* (Schaeffer, *The Church*, p. 13). This latter view of science is incompatible with the biblical view of God (and man). As Schaeffer comments, 'God is not a slave to the cause-and-effect world He has created, but is able to act into the cause-and-effect flow of history' *(idem)*. Unfortunately, faculties of theology in German universities were soon deeply influenced by 'modern naturalism', a trend which was widely followed elsewhere. All this was to have an important bearing on the study of the Bible.

dom' considerably restricted, much depending upon the hierarchy under which they operate. In the light of this, well-established evangelical scholars have an important rôle to play in supporting younger colleagues.

A further challenge exists for evangelicals who teach the Bible within universities. The Bible, by its very nature, is a text which anticipates a response from those who read it. By emphasising this aspect evangelical scholars are likely to be accused of promoting their own beliefs. On the other hand, any study of the Bible which fails to appreciate its dynamic nature cannot do full justice to the text itself. Until we hear the text speaking to us, we can hardly say that we have understood it.

Designing an Old Testament Syllabus for the Modern University

In approaching the teaching of the Old Testament within a university context there are two basic aims which should be fulfilled: students should be enabled to know, understand, and evaluate (1) the biblical material and (2) the different methods of approaching the Bible. Since it is unlikely, given the time allowed for undergraduate study, that a student will actually come to terms with the entire Bible and all that has been said about it, no course of study will fulfil completely these two aims. At best all that can be done is introduce students to parts of the Old Testament and in doing so equip them for further independent study. Selectivity is clearly an important factor in designing any syllabus — what to include and what to exclude.

Alongside restrictions which arise due to the length of time available for teaching a course on the Old Testament, there are various other considerations which need to be taken into account. Six issues are highlighted here, although others could be added.

a. To recognise that the multifaceted nature of biblical studies creates a major problem in trying to arrive at a balanced syllabus.

Apart from the possibility of devoting considerable time and energy to the learning of the biblical languages, a student of the Bible must contend with a multitude of different disciplines: *e.g.,* archaeology, comparative religion, ethics, history, literature, philosophy, social anthropology, sociology, theology. It is difficult to think of any other academic subject which covers such a wide range of fields. How does one do justice to all the various areas that contribute in their own distinctive way to our understanding and appreciation of the Bible?

b. The problem of finding the correct balance between studying the biblical material as a primary source, and examining what others have to say about the Bible, that is, the secondary sources.

It appears that often the latter is done almost to the exclusion of the former. As a result students know and are able to evaluate what scholars X, Y, and Z have to say about the biblical text, yet they remain ignorant of the biblical text itself. While it is important that students should be familiar with recent and current scholarship, it must always be remembered that the primary object of our study is the Bible itself. Moreover, the results of biblical scholarship need to be constantly tested against the primary source.

c. The importance of helping students understand and evaluate the different methodologies used by scholars in dealing with the text.

These are primarily such methods as textual, source, form, redaction, traditio-historical, and literary criticism. Not only do students need to be introduced to these different methods, but most of all (a) they need to be made aware of the different questions which they seek to address, and (b) they need to be enabled to evaluate the usefulness and relia-

97

bility of these methods. For example, it is important that students should be familiar with the application of source criticism to the study of the Pentateuch. They need to understand how the different sources have been isolated and dated. Furthermore, they must see how the study of these sources has led to a re-writing of the history of ancient Israel and all that this entails for our understanding of the Old Testament material. All this is necessary if students are to understand and engage with contemporary scholarly writings. Yet, it is essential that students appreciate the hypothetical nature of the source analysis of the Pentateuch and all that depends upon it. As teachers it is imperative that we help our students to distinguish between fact and hypothesis. Unfortunately, in my experience this is no easy task; it is often time consuming and from the student's point of view confusing. Why, they ask, should we devote so much time to studying something which at the end of the day is highly speculative and of dubious worth? For me, as a teacher, this raises the question: to what extent do I allow the agenda in Old Testament teaching to be determined by the fashion(s) of the age, and to what extent do I allow it to be determined by focusing on approaches which, although possibly less adventurous, are methodologically sound and sensible? Thus, for example, in looking at the book of Genesis it may be wiser to concentrate on the book as a literary unity rather than focus on the sources which are supposed to underlie the present text.

d. The importance of teaching students how to read the text.

This might appear unnecessary; after all, students are expected to be able to read before coming to university. Yet, I am convinced that many of the problems which arise in the study of the Bible result from an inability to read the text intelligently. Students need to be taught about ancient Near Eastern literary conventions and styles. They need to appreciate that documents written over two thousand years ago in a culture far removed from our own cannot be simply read as modern short stories. We have to understand the culture(s) and world view(s) of the ancient writers, insofar as that is possible. All this places a further demand on the lecturer in biblical studies.

e. The need to encourage within our students a recognition that our knowledge of the biblical world is often partial and uneven.

Since it is in the nature of the academic enterprise to try and push the boundaries of our knowledge ever backwards, there is the inherent danger that we constantly move further and further into the area of speculation and hypothesis. In the light of this it is essential, and very biblical, that as scholars we constantly remind our students of the limitations of human knowledge and understanding. While doing so, it is vital to affirm those things which can with some certainty be known. In this regard, we must teach students the importance of evaluating the questions they ask of the biblical text. I am reminded of a saying collected by Charles Caleb Colton (1780?-1832), 'Examinations are formidable even to the best prepared, for the greatest fool may ask more than the wisest man can answer'. Unless we and our students address appropriate questions to the Bible, we may not get the right answers back. For example, it is not particularly helpful to ask, What does Genesis 1 tell us about the mechanics of creation? This is not primarily what the opening chapter of Genesis is about. A more appropriate question might be: what does the opening chapter of Genesis reveal about God's relationship to the world and humanity? Knowing the right question to ask is important if we are to handle the Bible correctly.

f. The common practice of separating the study of the Old Testament from the study of the New Testament.

Yet, if we, as evangelical Christians, believe that the Old Testament finds its fulfilment in Christ, then it should be a natural consequence of our teaching that any meaningful study of the Old Testament would naturally involve some discussion of the New Testament.

Conclusion

In the light of these issues it is clear that the task of deciding how to construct an Old Testament syllabus is challenging in itself. Many other issues of a more practical nature could be considered. I hope that the foregoing remarks may provide food for thought, especially for evangelicals teaching the Bible in our universities and colleges of further education. By God's grace may we all become better teachers of the holy Scriptures which make us 'wise for salvation through faith in Christ Jesus' (2 Tim. 3:15).

Teddy-Bear Sacrifices:
Selling the Old Testament
in a Religious Studies Department

GORDON J. WENHAM

Gordon Wenham moved from the department of Semitic Studies in Belfast to the religious studies department in Cheltenham — an experience presenting something of a culture shock. The curriculum was totally different, teaching and assessment methods differed, and last but not least, student interest in, and knowledge of, the Old Testament was markedly lower. All these factors have led him to devise a new and distinctive approach to teaching the Old Testament which he outlines here.

What is different about teaching the Bible in a department of religious studies from teaching in a theology department or theological college? How do these differences impinge on the content of the course, the teaching methods employed, and the assessment? What stance should the lecturer in religious studies adopt towards his subject and his students? Are there any ideas that though they have been born in a religious studies environment could be applied in other contexts or institutions? These are some of the questions this essay seeks to answer.

Religious studies is a fairly modern phenomenon reflecting the theological pluralism of our century. When Ninian Smart established his department of religious studies at Lancaster in the 1960's, on which many other departments were modelled, a phenomenological approach to religious studies was fashionable. This aimed to study all religions in the same way, by looking at their beliefs, rituals, history, and so on. To try to see the religion as adherents to that religion do, but not to decide whether a particular faith was true or valid. Description not evaluation was the game — or so it was said — though putting all religions on the same level in this way implied they were all equally right, or since they disagreed with each other, all equally wrong. The only scholarly stance was a detached one.

Biblical study sits uneasily within this framework, with the Bible's strong claim to inspiration and its exclusivist approach to truth. In most religious studies departments biblical study is marginalized and focuses on historical criticism, for that provides a framework for understanding the emergence of the three monotheisms of Judaism, Christianity, and Islam. At Cheltenham, however, religious studies has been tilted in a more Christian direction, with courses on church history, modern theology, and Christian ethics, with relatively little on world religions apart from the three monotheisms. Within this framework, biblical studies — and particularly study of the Old Testament — has a more prominent role. It also demands that the Old Testament be studied in an unconventional way. Let me explain.

Religious studies attracts a broader range of students than theology and especially than theological colleges. Many choose religious studies because they want to study non-Christian religions. In my first-year classes about a third are active committed Christians, one third are sympathetic or occasional churchgoers, and about one third are curious agnostics. In subsequent years the proportion of Christians is greater, as agnostics are more likely to do non-biblical options. But students' backgrounds are only surveyed on entry, so I cannot be so precise. About half the students have done religious studies at A-level, but this may well be without any biblical element, though a few may have studied part of the Old Testament in depth — usually Israelite history and the prophets. While they are very ignorant of the Old Testament and its contents, they are also dubious of its value or interest.

Traditional theological courses presupposed an acquaintance at least with the Old Testament story and tended to plunge into a study of its history and the main critical problems. My first year of study at University involved the history of Israel and a study of the prophets Haggai and Zechariah, hardly central figures in the Old Testament story.

I am sure if I had not been brought up on the Bible, such a menu would have put me off the Old Testament for good!

One of the first tasks of the teacher should be to make the students actually read and enjoy the Old Testament. I entitle this course 'Making Sense of the Old Testament' and it usually attracts more than half of the first-year entry. In our modular degree structure, religious studies students have to take only one biblical course and that could be a New Testament course or a second-year Old Testament module. In the very first lecture then I seek to reassure them that, despite its name, study of the Old Testament should be central to everyone's education. I read them the remarkable letter of Lady Stansgate, who tells how when she visited Peking University in about 1980 she noticed a Bible on the desk of every student. 'On being asked if the students there were Christians, the lecturer who guided us replied with some embarrassment. "Oh no! They are all studying in the English faculty," and then added by way of explanation, "You cannot possibily understand the history and literature of the British people if you do not study the Bible".[1] I then ask, if Chinese communists see the Bible as so central to English culture, why is it so neglected in British schools? I list some of the figures from British history, *e.g.*, Alfred the Great, Cromwell, Lord Shaftesbury, Margaret Thatcher, Tony Blair, and English literature, *e.g.*, Shakespeare, Milton, Hardy, T. S. Eliot, whose work was clearly influenced by the Bible. I draw attention to the importance of the Old Testament for understanding the New Testament, Judaism, and Islam and suggest that 'Making Sense of the Old Testament' should really be compulsory for all students of religion, if not all humanities students!

'Making Sense of the Old Testament' comprises a mere twenty-four hours of teaching, so one must be selective. In order to allow students to appreciate parts of the Old Testament there are many parts of the subject one must leave out. But what should be selected? The usual approach has been to focus on the first millennium B.C. and its literature, hence the emphasis on Israelite history and prophecy. This partly reflects the post-Wellhausen consensus that the prophets were the real founders of Israelite religion, that the law came after and is a degenerate development on the way to the hidebound legalism of later Judaism.

1. *The Times*, 4 October 1984, p. 15.

Whatever may be thought about this critical approach, I believe the prophets are the least suitable point for an initial study of the Old Testament. To appreciate their message contextually one has to be aware of their historical setting, which is often difficult to reconstruct, and if it can be reconstructed exceedingly complex; just think of Hosea or Jeremiah. Not only is the background difficult, the oracles themselves often jump from one topic to another, and are often surmised to have a complex tradition history. You need patience and a good commentary to make sense of them, and a wonderful memory to retain it. A student coming to the Bible for the first time cannot be expected to read the prophets on his own and make sense of it. One needs to begin with the prose books. They are not only easy to follow, but the new narrative criticism[2] has reminded us just how brilliant examples of the story-teller's art they are.

First-Year Course

There are thus two obvious places to begin, either with the books of Samuel and Kings or with the Pentateuch. I have chosen the latter: indeed apart from some introductory remarks the first-year course is built around the Pentateuch and wisdom literature. These books (1) offer the clearest entree into the religious and social world of the Old Testament; (2) they are foundational for all biblical theology; and (3) address many modern concerns very immediately. It is also essential to have some knowledge of the Pentateuch to understand Judaism, which is included in the second-year course. This came to me very vividly, when in my first year at Cheltenham I asked some of my students to explain the blessing which mentions Sarah and Rebekah, Rachel and Leah. None of the class, save an Anglican priest, knew who these women were! The old course on the Old Testament which they had taken had not involved them reading the Pentateuch.

Therefore Genesis is a good place to begin. Chapters 1–11, when contrasted with the parallels in other Near Eastern literature, suddenly

---

2. J. Licht, *Storytelling in the Bible* (Jerusalem: Magnes Press, 1978), and R. Alter, *The Art of Biblical Narrative* (New York: Basic, 1981), are the most accessible for beginning students.

come alive as revolutionary theological statements about God and the world.[3] The difference between the capricious polytheism of the Gilgamesh epic and the moral monotheism of Genesis emerges starkly when their flood stories are contrasted. Genesis 1 and 2 portray the creation of mankind as the climax of the creation, not an afterthought as in the Atrahasis epic; furthermore it is God who feeds man in Genesis, not *vice versa* as in much oriental thought. The idea of sin and the fall provides another contrast with the optimistic belief in progress shared by ancient Babylon and the modern world. These beliefs in one God who cares for man, despite his sinfulness, are foundational to the rest of the Bible, and are even more splendidly demonstrated in the incarnation.

Moving through the Pentateuch book by book, I focus on the final form of the text: source criticism is not mentioned until the very last lecture. The aim is to let the text speak for itself, so that the students may see what it is saying about God and his relationship to Israel. These lectures are heavily indebted to D. Clines' *The Theme of the Pentateuch*[4] and to theologies which see covenant as central. Genesis 12–50 takes one week, and then another week is spent on Exodus 1–20 with special attention to the Ten Commandments. Here it is good to have a little digression about antinomianism and point out its incompatibility with New Testament teaching. Ask the students to rearrange the Ten Commandments in order of importance as reflected in our modern criminal law. Usually they put them in roughly reverse order to the Bible's order, with the prohibitions on stealing or murder preceding those on lying or adultery and with sins against God hardly figuring at all. The Ten Commandments reverse today's sense of priorities. They put God first, family next, and property last. Jesus maintains an order of priorities similar to the commandments when he says, 'If anyone does not hate his own father or mother . . . , he cannot be my disciple' (Luke 14:26).

The ritual law, the point at which most people give up if they try to read the Bible all through, takes a whole lecture. It is important

---

3. G. J. Wenham, *Genesis 1–15* (Waco: Word, 1987), pp. xlv-liii. E. C. Lucas, *Genesis Today* (London: Scripture Union, 1991), offers a helpful broad introductory treatment of Genesis 1–11.

4. D. J. A. Clines, *The Theme of the Pentateuch* (Sheffield: JSOT Press, 1978). T. D. Alexander, *From Paradise to the Promised Land* (Carlisle: Paternoster, 1995), is the book that comes nearest to my approach in the first half of my course.

discuss the significance of ritual in every culture[5] including our own, and point out that ritual needs to be acted out not just read. So I ask some of the class to act the rite of the spurned widow in Deuteronomy 25:5-10, and then the suspected adulteress in Numbers 5:11-31. In today's culture both provoke much mirth! Then we slaughter a cuddly toy as a burnt offering and discuss the theology of sacrifice, explaining how sacrifice embodies and teaches the central ideas of the covenant.[6] This approach to ritual transforms what is usually regarded as the dullest part of the Old Testament into the most interesting. Often students mention this lecture as the one they remember best. The final lecture deals with Deuteronomy, but that is more conventional. Again the focus is on the structure and teaching of the book, not the critical issues often raised.

The next section of the course deals with the differences between Old Testament society and our own, or more precisely between Israelite family life and ours. We look at marriage customs, how marriages were arranged and celebrated, inheritance customs, and the importance of genealogy in determining your status in society. We also have a look at male and female roles.[7] These topics engage student interest deeply, and to provoke them to think more deeply about it and not just dismiss the biblical patterns as quaint and out of date, I go out of my way to stress the merits of their life style. Obviously modern students bridle at the idea of arranged marriages, but I ask if they have not heard of computer dating agencies. Surely sensible parents could do a better job than a computer using inadequate data? Contrast the competitive rat-race of our individualistic society with the static but cooperative culture of ancient Israel. There at least in theory everyone saw themselves as part of a team, as part of a larger family, of a tribe, of a people. Our society professes a belief in individual autonomy, yet is very inter-dependent (we go to supermarkets, depend on the national grid, water companies, and multinationals); whereas they believed in cooperation and interdependence, though in some ways they were more indepen-

5. G. J. Wenham, *Numbers* (Leicester: InterVarsity Press, 1981), pp. 25-39.
6. G. J. Wenham, 'The Theology of Old Testament Sacrifice', in R. T. Beckwith and M. J. Selman (eds.), *Sacrifice in the Bible* (Carlisle: Paternoster, 1995), pp. 75-87.
7. Basic material on this topic in R. de Vaux, *Ancient Israel* (London: DLT, 1961), pp. 19-55 and W. Neuer, *Man and Woman in Christian Perspective* (London: Hodder, 1990), pp. 59-87.

dent than we are. (They grew their own food on their own land.) Within this society there was a hierarchy of authority, in which nearly everyone was subject to someone else, so that the subordination of wives to husbands was no more surprising than the submission of adult men to their father, the head of the extended family.

This digression illustrates something that is very important in teaching Old Testament today: the lecturer must sell it to his listener. Detached description may be scholarly but it is boring. As a student I detested Nineham's form-critical approach to the gospels, but he was interesting because he was determined to try and convince us that it was right. Whereas Moule's much more balanced approach to New Testament theology was not so interesting. If we are not enthusiasts for our Old Testament, we can hardly expect our students to be. I do not want to be misunderstood. I am not advocating a confessional approach to teaching the Old Testament in a religious studies department, though that would be quite appropriate in a theological college. What I want to do is to make my students understand how a believing Israelite would see the world and what he might think of our society and its attitudes. I hope this may lead my students to reconsider their own attitudes, which many have unthinkingly adopted. But I am not trying to impose my values or the Bible's on them. I think this approach works. The subsequent year's courses on Judaism and the Old Testament are some of the largest in our department.

Two lectures are devoted to the books of Proverbs, Job, and Ecclesiastes. These books are well suited to first-year study.[8] Though one has to know something about Old Testament society not to misread them, you do not have to understand the in's and out's of biblical history, as you have to in studying the prophets. Furthermore their eternal relevance is obvious. We still have to cope with awkward neighbours, death and suffering, and we wonder about the meaning of existence. These are the issues that the wisdom books discuss, and whether students accept the answers these books offer, I hope the challenge to fear God and keep his commandments will not be missed.

The final lecture deals with Pentateuchal criticism. It seems quite wrong to start with these historical-critical issues, when most of my

---

8. D. Kidner, *Wisdom to Live By* (Leicester: InterVarsity Press, 1985), offers an engaging approach to these books.

students have the haziest of ideas as to what the Pentateuch contains, let alone what it is trying to say. Yet they will come across the sigla J, E, P from time to time, so at the end of the course, I initiate them into these mysteries and preserve a semblance of academic respectability. But basically I leave discussion of diachronic issues to the second and third years. The emphasis in the first year is on the content, arrangement, and theology of these books of the Old Testament. These are the most important areas of study and are at the same time easiest for newcomers to the study of the Bible to cope with.

Second-Year Course

In the second year of religious studies students may take three courses with some Old Testament content — Hebrew Poetry and the Psalms, Introduction to Hebrew, and Introducing Judaism. All these are taught in two-hour blocks over twelve weeks. Two hours once a week is not ideal for Hebrew, and they do not go very far. They cover only the first ten lessons of Lambdin,[9] read some short passages from the Old Testament, and learn how to use concordances, lexicons, and Old Testament dictionaries. However, those who take to Hebrew may study it throughout the third year instead of writing the long essay required of other finalists. To make for variety and interest, introduce a little modern Hebrew in the second-year class. To ask your fellow student his name or whether he has a camel ensures that the language does not become just an arcane crossword puzzle.

Rather than put the Psalms in the third year and a course on the prophets in the second year, I reverse the sequence as students cope more easily with the Psalms than with the prophets. This works very well. This course looks at the nature of Hebrew poetry, then surveys the various Psalm genres, and discusses some of their theological themes.[10] But the most interesting feature of this course is its use of student-assessed seminars. Courses are assessed on the basis of forty

9. T. O. Lambdin, *Introduction to Biblical Hebrew* (New York: Scribner's, 1971).
10. Core texts for this course are T. Longman, *How to Read the Psalms* (Leicester: InterVarsity Press, 1988), J. Day, *The Psalms* (Sheffield: Academic Press, 1987), and J. C. McCann, *A Theological Introduction to the Book of Psalms* (Nashville: Abingdon Press, 1993).

per cent course work, usually an essay, and sixty per cent exam, but in the Psalms course each student has to lead seminars on two Psalms. Since the class has to be divided into four or five groups for the seminars, the lecturer cannot be present at them all. Each listener in the seminar group is given a sheet to mark the leader's performance and the lecturer just has to collate the marks. To ensure parity of marking, the groups need to be monitored and the leader's seminar notes taken in. This procedure has ensured remarkably high attendance at the seminars, lively presentations by the students, and good exam performance. It comes highly recommended.

The other second-year course is entitled 'Understanding Judaism'. It is the largest course (up to seventy students), attracting students interested in biblical studies as well those interested in world religions. In this course[11] it is easy to glance at the celebration of the sabbath and the passover, skim over the history of the Jews from the exile to the present day, and look at food laws, rites of passage, and prayer. Much of this comes straight out of the Old Testament; some of it illuminates the New Testament; and with the Holocaust and the British Mandate comes very close to home. The mass of audio-visual material available, visits to synagogues, kosher dishes cooked by students, and the fact that the Middle East is often in the news makes this the most immediate course to teach. In discussing the Jewish approach to prayer and other religious practices, it is possible to make comparisons with analogous Christian activities, thereby touching on areas not handled elsewhere in the course, which are vital to Christian piety. For these reasons a unit on Judaism could well figure in Christian theology courses, for it seems to intersect with and integrate so many areas of study.

Third-Year Course

These are more conventional. They are based on specific books of the Bible. At last in a course on Amos the students have a chance to study biblical prophecy! My earlier attempts to survey the whole prophetic

---

11. Of the many books available D. J. Goldberg and J. D. Rayner, *The Jewish People: Their History and Their Religion* (London: Penguin, 1989), fits my purposes best.

canon failed, as the complexity of the historical setting and the confusing arrangement of the prophetic books were too difficult to master. The course on Amos has two aims: (1) to discuss prophecy in general and illustrate these general observations from Amos; and (2) then in seminars (marked like the Psalms course) to carry out an exegesis of a complete prophetic book. It seems to work. In the other half of the year we study Genesis, chosen because for many years this has been my prime area of research. Until my commentaries appeared, the students certainly were subjected to a number of ideas not easily accessible elsewhere. But whether it is really wise to spend time on Genesis when we have never dealt with one of the major prophets, I am not sure.

To conclude. Within the constraints of the very limited time allocated to Old Testament in a religious studies department, this programme makes the most of it. But I am aware of some major weaknesses, which have yet to be solved satisfactorily. First, how can one ensure that students read round the subject and not just enough to write an essay and question spot for the exam. They tend to think that if work is not assessed it is not important. But even if our degree structure allowed more assignments to be set, there would not be the time to mark them.

A second regret is that due to government pressure to increase class sizes, there is very little time to get to know the students we teach. Apart from giving back an essay, there are some students I have no contact with except as listeners to my lectures. I think this is sad, but I cannot see any other way of operating. In the last few years I have led an Israel study tour for a fortnight. Up to twenty per cent of the students I teach have gone, and I think for many this constitutes the best educational experience in their degree programme. Not only do they learn a great deal about the Bible and its world, but I get to know the students better and *vice versa*. Unfortunately not many can afford to come, even though we stay in the cheapest accommodation.

My final regret about our institution is that it provides so little opportunity for worship and community life. The Bible exists to lead us to God, to provoke us to prayer and action, yet we stop short of that. Traditional theological colleges make worship compulsory. Religious studies departments approach faith in a more detached fashion, which means that participation in worship could not be required. But that does not mean we might not do more to facilitate it on a voluntary basis.

From Student to Scholar: Surviving as an Old Testament Ph.D. Student

REBECCA DOYLE

Rebecca Doyle came to the United Kingdom from a seminary in the United States to undertake her post-graduate degree. As a foreign student in England, her perspective naturally differs from the experiences of a home student.

As I reflect on what has happened these last few years, one experience sits crystal clear in my memory. . . . There I was sitting across the room from a distinguished British gentleman. The office was full of books with a large desk and a couple of armchairs. This gentleman had been recommended by a scholar who had come to my seminary as a guest speaker. He was the best person to lead me through research in my area of interest. I had been told that I should write a letter explaining my interest in studying with him. Now here I was, six thousand miles away from home, meeting him for the first time — and he was talking seriously about things that had been dismissed as unimportant by my lecturers at seminary. Waves of amazement swept over me as I began to realise that this was going to be an adventure.

Reflection for writing this paper was aided by a publication for PGs (postgraduates) when it printed an article entitled 'PhD — The Game/Reality (?!)'. It is a fun idea and almost too real for comfort. Each person is to move according to the throw of the dice and the instructions given by the square in which he or she lands. It starts off, 'Beginning, Throw away sanity to start'. Then square 1 reads, 'Your supervisor gives you project title, go on three spaces'; square 3, 'You are full of enthusiasm, have another turn'; square 5, 'Go to library, you can't understand catalogue, miss turn'. It goes on this way, losing or gaining spaces. How many spaces have I lost each time I have not found a book mentioned in a crucial footnote? At one point it says, 'Beat supervisor at squash, back 7 spaces'. Fortunately, I do not play squash, though I am at the mercy of other parts of the process. I have had several bouts of losing all motivation to read or write because I have been bored or frustrated with my work. There are eighty spaces to the game in total. Number 79 reads, 'You are asked to resubmit thesis, back to 60' and 60 reads, 'You are offered a job, you may continue or retire from game'. The last square is, 'Your PhD is awarded, congratulations, now join dole queue'. The caption that follows the rules at the bottom of the page reads — 'Remember this is just a game, although some play it for real'.

I would like to capture my own personal experience (with a few notes from conversations with friends) in three rather broad and overlapping categories: (1) The Department (meaning the particular place where I am studying); (2) The Process (what I have been doing in the Department); and (3) The Life (how I have been doing it).

The Department

In my first term of the first year, the first-year postgraduates (PGs) took an induction course designed to introduce us to the department and to the nature of doing research. It was very helpful. The latest course that the first-year postgraduates have been required to attend is far more rigorous than the one that I took. This has been instituted by the university as a general policy in the Arts faculty (I don't know about other faculties), and is a progressive move towards putting together a programme that moves students through the paces a little faster and smoother. Our department was large enough to warrant teaching it as an in-house module. By contrast to the present first-year postgrads, I stumbled my way to putting together a bibliography of relevant theses and articles using *Dissertation Abstracts* and *Religion Index One*. They were required to present a bibliography for part of the induction course.

I have heard them talk at great length about what their methodology is and how or if it will work. Was this part of the induction course that I took? I did not dare discuss my methodology with anyone apart from my supervisor. I assumed all along that since he says it is viable, it must be so. Articulation of what I have been doing and why freezes on my tongue and in my heart. (Excuse a bit of hyperbole.)

From talking to colleagues in other institutions I have begun to realise that this department may well be unusual. At least, in that all of the PGs who lived locally were expected to be in the department at least once a week for a postgraduate seminar (PG seminar). The room got a bit tight and the air a bit heavy if we all showed up. This does happen, however, when someone like Walter Brueggemann comes to share with us about his 'wild and woolly holiness'. Because a wide range of people have made presentations in these seminars it has helped to keep the whole range of biblical studies before us. The format has changed slightly over the four years that I was there but the priority of giving students opportunity to take part in discussion of issues has not altered. We were able to explore a wide range of methodologies and perspectives with eminent scholars. This offered an invaluable wealth of experience to our study in this department. One year we split up into smaller groups arranged by subject, meeting once fortnightly. The thought had been to provide a format for deeper discussion in a less intimidating atmosphere. The experiment seemed to succeed.

This department is not primarily a PG department, though from a PG's perspective it seems to be. Unless, of course, as a PG you take the opportunity to get some teaching experience. Sometimes, in order to prepare for a first or second year undergraduate class, pulling your head out of your books is like pulling your wellies out of deep mud, but it is a taste of the 'real world'. Putting together material that is not specifically related to a research topic and dealing with students at their level helped to keep it all in perspective. As my supervisor pointed out to me — learning to juggle responsibilities and scholarship at the same time is a lesson better learned earlier than later. Besides, it put a few extra pence in the pocket.

Access to Material

Then there were the times that I tried to get my hands on a book or an article mentioned in a footnote. My area of research is more specialised than the provisions of the university library. So, I have been dependent on ILL (Interlibrary Loan), which often means waiting a matter of weeks or maybe months. Occasionally, a memo returns that the article is unavailable in the U.K. or not at all. Much to my delight and amazement I found a wonderful library. This has been one of the few places where I can find material, books as well as journals in my area of research, on the shelves. A week or two on occasion in Cambridge has easily surpassed what I could have done solely using the ILL system. Occasionally a coveted book came off my supervisor's own bookshelves. Books are not the only necessity in this age of technology, however. Research is enhanced by CD ROMs, Bible search packages, laser printers, the Net, etc. It was learn-as-you-go and the hope that the department and the university would get that latest version or model of whatever it is. Consider what we can do with the simple flick of a couple of fingers or a click of a mouse!

The Process

I wish I had read Estelle Phillips' book[1] before I began this. It all started with what I thought was my topic. In my first term my supervisor asked me to do a paper just to get acquainted with the subject. During that first term my supervisor met with me a couple of times to talk about the area that I wanted to research and 'we' (meaning myself with the assistance of my supervisor's wisdom) came to the conclusion that my first title was too broad and needed to be refined. The remainder of my first year was spent in trying to work out what I was doing and how to do it. At one point during this first year, while applying for a scholar-

---

1. E. Phillips, *How to Get a PhD, Managing the Peaks and Troughs of Research* (Milton Keynes: Open University Press, 1988). I am fairly certain that there is a more recent and updated version. A second volume is by D. Stemberg, *How to Complete and Survive a Doctoral Dissertation* (New York: St. Martin's Press, 1981). However, these seem to be geared specifically for the sciences. We need to re-write them for the arts.

ship, I created an annotated outline as an abstract for my thesis. During the second and third years, following more reading in the field, the topic was refined even more closely. This was represented by a shift in my thesis title. During my third year I presented a paper to our PG seminar, which sprang from work on one of the chapters. Again this became part of the refining process of my topic and methodology, and produced yet another change in the title.

Luckily for me these changes represented only a slight shift in focus and not a complete change in topic. I cannot quite imagine how I would have survived the devastation wreaked by a change in topic in the middle of my research. As I look back, it seems that it was all an identity crisis. This shifting of titles was equal to asking, 'Who am I (who will I be) in this world of biblical scholars?' As for my methodology, was I going to choose one and stick with it, pure and simple? Or was I going to be more eclectic and 'do it my way'? I think I have opted for the second choice. No wonder I have trouble discussing my methodology — it doesn't have a name.

Organization of Material

Besides methodology, the organisation of information is crucial. If you were to have looked at the notecards on my desk, you would have seen plainly the evidence of the three different times I have been a librarian. I had bibliography cards, book summaries and annotations, and quotes all colour coded. And it saved me a lot of energy to be so organised — at least I have tried to convince myself so. Each card was cross-referenced and dated and subject indexed. So I could shuffle them as I pleased and still maintain some sort of sanity. Maybe doing it on a computer would have been an improvement. The organisation of the material I read was the least of my problems. I just wish that the writing-up would have moved quicker than sludge.

Organisation of material was not a big problem for me, but finding the material in a form which was readable caused some trouble. If only I had known what German would be like. My first try at learning German was when I was overseas using Chinese to teach Hebrew. It was more than my poor brain could take and I had to give it up. I followed that with some self-study augmented by university night classes. Then during the summer of my second year of Ph.D. research, I took a month for a Ferienkurs in Thuringen, Germany. Even still, many painstaking hours are spent with dictionaries and grammar guide in one hand and text in the other. A colleague has had to use his third hand to hold his French dictionary and grammar as well as his German.

Supervision

If someone said I had to talk about supervision in this paper, I could probably give a whole treatise about supervisors and being a super-advisee. For the first three years of my work in the biblical studies department my supervisor was the chair of the department. He always had an open-door policy and was available to chat at any time about any aspect of postgraduate life. I wish I had realised what this meant during that first term. My work that first term set the tone and habits for the rest of what I have done in my research. I was quite intimidated by my supervisor in the very beginning, and found myself having to make so many shifts in what I thought biblical studies was about, that I was very shy about going in and spending time talking with my mentor. And gentleman that he is, he rarely pressed me for an audience, but rather waited until I was ready to see him. This meant that there were long lapses between our times together. His last year in the department before his retirement he was very busy and even out of the country for several periods of time. So, the opportunities to see him were limited. At that point in my work I found that I needed to see him more often just to be sure that I was not straying too far afield.

The purposes of supervision are laid out in a university published handbook, titled *Notes of Guidance for Research Students and Supervisors*. I am also sure that the topic was discussed or presented in the induction course. But somehow by the second and third semester of research all those introductory remarks seem to get forgotten and the handbook gets lost or shelved. A friend has said of supervisors: 'You can't find them, they are on pilgrimage to Jerusalem'; or, 'You find them, and they don't have time.' Busy people, these supervisors; you would think that their sole purpose in life was to take care of their PG students. And, when is following a lead given by a supervisor more than a suggestion? Someone has said, 'I came here to do my Ph.D., not my supervisor's'.

As a disclaimer, I must say that my own supervisor gave me all the credit for agreeing that my topic would be a good one to follow. I asked for his help from the beginning. I still shake my head in wonder at choosing Jeremiah as a basic text.

Communication

Communication is something that has to be pursued. I am more and more of the belief that it does not just happen. I thought I understood the English language before I came here. I also thought that I understood what people meant by what they said and did not say. Where I come from, the most polite way to tell someone that you do not like what they did is to say not a word about it. I had the impression that the British were very polite people. So, when critiques regarding my papers were not countered by what was good about it, I got worried; 'He doesn't like it!', 'It is a horrible paper!', etc. I have friends who had to beg their supervisors to say something nice about their work.

I have found myself in the position, as have many of my fellow students, skulking about the halls avoiding my supervisor for fear that he would ask, 'How is the work going?' This question elicits reactions of guilt, fear, and shame. Someone mentioned anger as a response to such a simple question. The mixing and harmonising of personalities (or lack of harmony) can have a significant effect on how research progresses. What happens when the supervisor and advisee cannot see eye to eye, and it all goes terribly wrong? Another question asked was, 'Do women experience supervision differently from men?' I am a woman in higher education, which is not as rare as it used to be, but still I am a minority in the field. Do I react differently to supervision from my male colleagues?

The Life

What about 'The Life' of a Ph.D. student? Before I started this, I thought, 'What a life! Study all day. No one else running my schedule. All that is missing is the sun and the beaches'. Little did I know. No one could have told me how hard it was going to be.

Adjustments

I was not prepared for the adjustments that I would have to make. I did my undergraduate and master's work in Christian institutions. The motto for both was 'faith integrated with learning'. Theology is not openly encouraged where I did my research. But it is more than just the system of education that is different. I have crossed culture as well as 'crossed institutions'. For my Arts degrees, I came out of eight years of American higher education with a very broad base of subjects studied, as compared to the British system where students begin to focus specifically in their fields from national examinations taken at the ages of sixteen or eighteen. The first six months I wandered about in a dazed confusion. It took at least another six months, maybe a year, before I felt like I knew what was going on. I gradually began to feel that I was catching up.

How does one count the cost? Time, money, emotional and spiritual elements all make it add up to a very expensive venture. Being self-financed has meant that I had to work my way through. The time that I had to spend in preparing to teach or tutor classes, do secretarial work, etc. sapped my energy and ate into the time that I 'should' have been using to work on my research. I was more optimistic about finances than maybe I should have been. I was working with a nebulous time line. I watched my deadlines get gobbled up by the calendar and spat out onto my plate of despair. The university set a deadline, my passport and visa set deadlines, my supervisor expected some work, and it all worked out to an emotional and psychological roller-coaster ride. There were long stretches that I could not see any progress in my work. Somehow the piles of note cards on the corner of my desk did not count for much in the way toward a thesis. Often I found myself asking, 'Is all this work worth it?' or, 'What is the relationship between this work and the real world?' Even as I was writing it up, I wondered if it was Ph.D. quality work. For this confirmation and critique, I was completely dependent on my supervisor. The horror stories of individuals who have worked for a spate of time on Ph.D. research and wrote it up and in the end came out with an M.Phil. or less were my nightmares. On the other hand, each time someone completed, then a ray of hope flooded in and the motivators started to work again.

Socializing and Spirituality

Then add to this the attempt to maintain a social life. It can be great fun to spend time with friends. Time is a precious commodity when deadlines loom in the near and distant future. Even in my master's work I was jealous of the married men in my course. They would rush into class with an assignment at the last minute and make a side comment, 'My wife typed the last word just as I left the house'. I have wondered where I could rent one of these 'wives'; someone to do my cooking, cleaning, and typing. But, in reality I am glad that I had not had to drag a husband (or beau) through all of my ups and downs.

It seems to me that a community context is crucial regarding the issues of psyche, emotions, and spirit. Ph.D. work by nature is very isolating and without community to be accountable to (and with) I can see where an individual would be even more at risk for the roller-coaster ride. I am grateful to my church for providing a refuge for me; and for those friends who wept with me over the phone and who provided the 'kick in the seat' when I needed it.

All of this has also taken a spiritual toll. Is it because my department is not a theology department or a Christian institution? Is it because the Bible is treated more often as a piece of literature or history? It may be, but I think that there is also something inherently stressful to faith when the Word goes under the scalpel. The Word can stand the surgery better than we can, sometimes. A brother from an eastern tradition has remarked that if faith rests in God rather than exclusively on the Word, then the trauma of the surgery may well be lessened. Maintaining a balanced spiritual walk demanded creativity and perseverance.

Cautions and Warnings

In the light of these reflections, I would certainly caution prospective Ph.D. students to take a reality check before starting. Is your sanity worth it? Do not start this kind of research just because it sounds like a good idea. Count the cost very carefully. It will be expensive in many more ways than you can imagine. Do your research before you start.

To first-year PGs, I say, read the step-by-step guide and the *Notes of Guidance for Research Students and Supervisors.* Set yourself a schedule to read them at least twice a year. Get organised from the beginning. Learn from your colleagues, what works for them and what mistakes they have made. Remember that bad habits are hard to break. Good habits take a lot of hard work to establish. Ph.D. research is not like anything that you have ever done and you will need to maintain vigilance. It will take longer than you expect, so, prepare yourself for a long haul. Get involved in a community which will feed you and will help you to stick with it. Try to find a place in that community where you can exercise your gifts and talents and be yourself; you will need it to maintain balance and perspective.

To the more seasoned player, I say, 'Keep the faith'. Continue to assess your work in the light of your original goals and purposes, not on how you are feeling now. Be assertive about getting the encouragement you need, about readjusting your priorities, about anything that will help to get you through this. Be ruthless with yourself, but remember you are only human and you too need rest, relaxation, and reality checks. Take your rest and relaxation seriously. We do not need any more basket cases standing in the dole queue. Read the handbook for research students and supervisors again — and talk it over with your supervisor.

To supervisors (and would-be supervisors), I say, thank you for investing yourselves in us. Sometimes we are very fragile; sometimes very stubborn; and sometimes we have lost our perspective and need to be reminded of where we are going and that it is worth it. We need your correctives and your encouragement. We need your help to see what comes first (such as language study early on) and second and third and when to quit. Remember that we may be intimidated by your expertise, the enormity of the project, and the vast amount of material that looms before us. Help us to make reality checks and to work through the depression that descends upon us as a consequence. Remind us to read the step-by-step guide for Ph.D. research and the *Notes of Guidance for Research Students and Supervisors* and point out to us where we can and need to follow them. Some of us need a lot of hands-on and some of us need lots of room to do our work best; we know that often your sensitivity will be/is stretched to the limit. Without you, our Ph.D. research would be nigh unto impossible. Again thank you for all that you have and will do to help us get to and through that viva (and for that reference for the perfect job). As a last note, a friend's comment is worth repeating: 'Life is more than a Ph.D.'[2]

2. Thanks are due to several friends for reading and making valuable critiques and comments on the contents of this paper, especially to K. Heim, R. A. Reese, R. Idestrom, and J. Jarick.

From Scholar to Student: Supervising Old Testament Ph.D. Students

H. G. M. WILLIAMSON

Hugh Williamson was reader at Cambridge before moving to Oxford as Regius professor of Hebrew. His experience of supervising graduate students is limited to these places, and he does not claim his approach is a blueprint for everywhere. These are some reflections on what he tries to put into practise as a supervisor.

In facing this topic I have asked the question (1) what is distinctive about supervising the Old Testament as opposed to supervising, for example, Reformation history or Shakespeare's plays; (2) is there anything from a distinctive evangelical perspective, that is, is the evangelical supervisor inherently better or worse than any other? I have not come up with any answers to those two points in specific terms. So what I say would apply to anybody who is confronted with the task of supervising graduates.

There is one exception which is both trivial and yet tremendously important — my hope that I carry my Christian concern for people over into my graduate supervision, just as I try to love my neighbour in every context. I think this is an important point. Others doing research have written of some of the horror stories as well as some of the good things from the other side of the fence. Of course, I was a graduate student myself once, so it is not totally unknown to me what it is like, but as a Christian I want to affirm that each student is an individual and that each one is different and has different needs. This means that I must work with each person's situation sympathetically.

Number of Ph.D. students

This specifically Christian perspective has one practical consequence for the supervision of Ph.D. students as opposed to taught graduate courses which are more an extension of the undergraduate work: when it comes to supervising those engaged in research for a doctorate, if I am to do it properly and ultimately to the glory of God, it is very important not to have too many graduate students at one time. I know of some who have numbers reaching into double figures. At one stage I had seven graduate students and I thought I could manage that. 'What's the problem,' I thought, 'all these lazy people say they can't cope but of course I can manage'. I did manage, but what happened was that every time a student gave me a piece of work to read, I would read it and just think, 'That's got that clear, now I can get on with something of my own'. Then the next piece of work arrived! Soon it reached the stage where I began to resent my students handing in work and I wished they would stop writing!

Clearly that is a hopeless position to be in and I learnt then that we had an informal rule in our faculty that six was a maximum. I see the wisdom of that rule and, in fact, one could argue that even six is too many, although I think one could manage up to that. To deal with each student in the way that they deserve, the supervisor should not take on too many graduate students.

Accessibility

The other obvious point that should arise out of Christian concern for everybody, including graduate students, is that the supervisor should be reasonably accessible. Now what supervisors understand as accessible may be rather different from the students' perception. They may think they are accessible if they see a student once a fortnight — that's pretty generous with their very important time — but remember that many graduate students are probably working in relative isolation; that does not mean they do not have friends and so on, but that most of the time they work alone. Then they produce a piece of work which you are going to discuss with them for two hours, or however long, and for that person that couple of hours, which may be once a month or perhaps once every other month, is absolutely the highlight, academically and intellectually speaking, of life. Two months builds up to it and the next week falls away from it, whereas for the supervisor it is just two hours on a particular afternoon before seeing somebody else for two hours on another afternoon. It is very important that the supervisor gives the impression that this is really terribly important now; this is what the student has produced and the supervisor is engaging with it seriously; the student has invested time in it and the supervisor should indicate that he/she wants to respond in like kind. So it is not just that one is accessible in terms of making oneself available, but that, however often that needs to be, it is concentrated attention and real time which takes the other person seriously. These are general reflections — obviously others besides Christians would do that, but supervisors should regard it as part of their Christian commitment.

Chronology

There is a chronological order of things which comes up from time to time. The first contact one generally has with a student is they write and say, 'Somebody has suggested I should come and pursue a doctorate with you, will you please suggest a topic'. I will never suggest a topic, if I can avoid it. In fact I do avoid it. I will not choose students' topics for them and I suggest that it is always unwise for supervisors to choose a dissertation topic. There are several reasons for this. One is that it can be grossly abused: I as a supervisor can get a graduate student to do all the bits of my research that I am not interested in, and that is quite wrong. It is different in the sciences where people have research teams and where for funding reasons they have to work on their own projects. In the humanities generally, and in the Old Testament, that is not the case. I can think of one very well known American supervisor who has supervised successfully over a hundred Ph.D.'s who uses this method. What happens is the students take their supervisor's theories and perhaps develop them a little, or tidy up a corner here or there, and then they start to combine his theories. If you read their bibliographies, all they tend to do is to cite his works and the work of his students, usually unpublished seminar papers, and the whole thing gets so introspective that they do not realise there is a world out there that actually sees the Old Testament from a slightly different point of view! So I think it is bad for the supervisor to choose the topic of the dissertation, but, more importantly, I think it is bad because at the end of the day the graduate student is going to spend three years living with this topic day and night, if I have my way! It is therefore terribly important that it should be something that the student is interested in and thinks is worthwhile: that can really only come by the students themselves choosing. Initially they may choose a general area and then narrow it down, or they may take an area and then move on.

Obviously people do not always stick with the topic they start with. In fact, I have very rarely met anyone who has submitted a thesis under the same title as on the original application form. I had one, and he wrote to me a few weeks ago and said, 'There you are, I'm the first one who has done it', but it is very rare.

Choosing a Topic

It is most important for motivation that the students make the choice of topic. Naturally I would advise them about that choice. They are right to ask, 'I'm interested in this field, do you think there is a topic here?' and I may say, 'Well actually somebody has just written a definitive monograph on it, and you might look at that before you decide you want to go ahead or you might want to change it'. It is also appropriate for a supervisor to discuss how one would approach the topic, but the choice of a topic ought to be made by the student. Also a student's choice of topic may help a supervisor to decide whether to accept the student: it gives a much better idea of whether the person is ready for research and has actually read enough to realise that there is a problem.

Assuming that the person has chosen a topic and he/she turns up on 1st October and sits down and says, 'I'm X and I'm your graduate student', What do you do, how do you get started? I do not know how

125

different people handle this. I suppose most of us copy our supervisors! What I was taught was actually very helpful. I wanted to work on the book of Chronicles. My supervisor said, 'There are important books on Chronicles like von Rad and Noth and so on, go away and read them and respond to them'. I found that extremely helpful. So if a person has no better idea on how to start, I recommend they read a monograph and write a review. This may take a week or so because they may need to read around to hone in on it. It is also a manageable-sized task to write five or ten pages, not just describing the book but evaluating it and probing it. This is the easiest way for people to start, to take a classic text, or an article, and to work on it. It gets them into the subject and into the primary sources, because obviously it is against the primary sources that they must assess the book. It also leads them into some of the most important secondary literature without them having to sit down in a vacuum and say, 'What is my first bright idea this morning?' It is a very focused task which a good undergraduate moving into graduate work should be ready to manage, and means that I can see the student fortnightly, which is what I like to do at least for the first term, each time with a manageable-sized piece of work, of five to ten pages.

Becoming Focused

Thereafter the thesis begins to emerge as the topic becomes focused, but even at this stage it is still advisable to split the task up into manageable-sized chunks. If somebody turns in a paper to discuss, and I go through it and then say, 'Right, now what are you going to do next?' and they say, 'I'm going to write a three-hundred-page monograph', I say, 'No you're not, you're going to write chapter one, part one, and I want to see that'. Throughout the period of research it is important to divide the task up in a way that gives a series of specific goals. Obviously when you reach the end of the first year and enter the second year it may well be a goal which is going to take a month or two months to achieve, as by this stage you are into the engine room of the research project, but it still needs to be an achievable goal that can be written up in preliminary form.

Let me illustrate what can go wrong, if a supervisor allows a student too much freedom. One of my earliest research students did fine for the first year. Then towards the end of the summer term he said to me, 'Now this seems to be leading me to study this matter', so I said, 'That's fine'. And every time I met him he said everything was all right. Eventually six months later he gave me a hundred pages. So I settled down to study this hundred pages and found the fatal flaw on page two, which in my opinion threw the rest of the ninety-eight pages out of joint! We then spent a very sticky three or four hours working on this and trying to salvage something, and discussing where to go next. Happily the thesis did go somewhere else and it was very successful. It has been published now and he is teaching in a university, and it is all very satisfactory. But I blame myself for the fact that he wasted a lot of time because I let him go too far. It should have been possible for me to have stopped him earlier. So nowadays I will not let anybody go that long: they must give me something, even if it is only an outline, more frequently than every six months! So let us look for manageable-sized topics that lead to an achievable goal.

When work is given to me I try to turn it round in a week. Now it is not always possible as you will appreciate, but I set myself that target. If somebody gives you one hundred and fifty pages of dense stuff and you are in the middle of exams you're stumped. But giving manageable-sized hunks should make it possible. I think a quick response is important because students have invested a lot of work in it and they are very anxious to know how you are going to respond and I do not think it is right to keep them waiting for six weeks or so. Obviously the supervisor's comments are important. Comment on anything and everything. In discussion of the piece as a whole, as well as going through the points one by one, I look for the expected follow-up: where does this lead to, what is the next step?

To Publish or Not to Publish

One question that a lot of students raise at this point is, 'Should I publish this as an article?' They think it may be a good challenge. My own experience as a research student taught me a very interesting lesson. A week after I began I gave in a book review and my supervisor said, 'A very interesting idea here, I think you should write this up as a short note'. So I wrote it up as a short note (it was a little textual point), and he said, 'I think you should send this off and publish it'. So within ten days one had a little plug and I thought that was great. Then I gave him what I thought was far superior work, but he never mentioned publishing again! This went on and on and on and he never ever suggested anything to do with publication. Afterwards I learned why. I asked him and he said, 'If you publish all your research as you go along in the form of articles, you've then not got a book at the end of it; and it's far, far better if you're talking of career prospects to have a book published; a book is worth any number of articles, because a book gets reviewed and a book gets noticed. People notice the name on a book. If you then write an article, they say, 'That's so-and-so, he wrote a book on X'. You can write half a dozen articles in all the best journals and people don't connect them. An article in *JBL* and one in *ZAW* and one in *VT* and people don't realise that you are the same person. You make no impact. But one book, followed with articles, makes all the difference, so if a person is doing work that looks as though it's coming together, I would strongly urge people not to publish as they go along but to wait till they can write a book.

The Nature of a Ph.D.

One needs to keep a realistic goal in view, especially in this country in these days. The days when one's Ph.D. was one's life statement to the world and the universe are gone. A Ph.D. is partly a training exercise: it can be seen as preparing for a lifetime in research, not as the final word on everything. Of course, it is going to be as good as anybody can make it and it will cover all the secondary literature, but one ought to encourage students to be realistic and take a topic and work at it, complete it and hopefully publish it. This is something that we are increasingly conscious of in this country because of time constraints.

Overcoming a 'Blockage'

What is the supervisor's responsibility when the person gets stuck? This is a real problem for most research students at some time. It is not that they have not a topic; it is not that they have not faced problems before; but they somehow just run out of steam for a period at the end of the second year and cannot see the way forward; they get totally phased out, hung up, and stuck. The supervisor is usually aware of the problem, even if students have not told him, because active material is not forthcoming and they are fiddling around: they have gone off to learn German or something. The only way the supervisor can help — of course ultimately it is something the student has got to work through herself or himself — is to set even a very small task and say, 'Let's forget that problem, there was that textual note that you never quite finished off here'. Find a little job, a very small one. 'Look, there's a recent article just appeared that's relevant. Go and read that and tell me what you think of it'. This way they can start again with a very small job and perhaps then they can find the bigger things again.

Attending Seminars?

Should a supervisor require attendance at seminars, on other courses that are being offered in the department, or someone else's department, or indeed on courses on teaching? There are no rules here. It is very helpful for graduate students to do something besides their doctorate. They are probably having to do something extra, if they have not learnt French or German before they started research. These languages must be known. It is also helpful to go to other teachers, especially in a larger university whatever their approach is, and to attend relevant seminars and guest lectures. Classes on the Hebrew text of the Old Testament can also be very valuable. Where there is opportunity, it is useful to do some teaching, but it is not necessary for everybody.

A Degree or a Job?

The last job of the supervisor is not to get students their degree; it is to secure them a job. That actually is becoming an increasing nightmare. It is not the supervisor's business to find a job for a person, but I do regard it as part of my responsibility to support students as they apply for jobs, even though in this age, when everybody applies for everything, I typically end up in the course of a year writing ten references for the same student. If you have several of them, you are writing two or three letters a week, and that is quite a lot of work! This is especially so as each reference ought to be tailored to the dissertation and to the position applied for. One person is going to apply for a job in a Bible college, a very evangelical base, and the next interview is at a university in this country and then somewhere in the States. Each place has its quirks, so each reference has to be angled. I regard writing references as important, and I appreciate it when the student asks before giving my name as a referee. Although I would never say no, I am annoyed when I am inundated with requests for somebody who has never even bothered to ask.

Teaching the Old Testament in the Context of Islam

IDA GLASER

Since 1992 Ida Glaser has been responsible for 'Crosslinks' work among people of other faiths in the U.K. She is currently seconded to Crowther Hall, the training college of the Church Missionary Society in Birmingham. Her dissertation, 'An Experiment in Contextual Comparative Hermeneutics,' read the early chapters of Genesis alongside parallel Quranic material.

What Are We Talking About?

To teach the Old Testament in the context of Islam, we must read the Old Testament in the context of Islam. If this seems so obvious as to be tautologous, let us reflect that it has not often been the way in which evangelicals have contextualised their theology. More commonly, they have followed the model developed by such writers as Nida[1] in the context of Bible translation.

The model is described by Hesselgrave and Rommen.[2] The Bible is seen as comprising supracultural (divine) and cultural (human) ele-

---

1. E. A. Nida, *Message and Mission* (San Francisco: Harper & Row, 1960).
2. D. J. Hesselgrave and E. Rommen, *Contextualization: Meanings, Methods and Models* (Grand Rapids: Baker, 1989).

ments. The hermeneutic task when moving to a new culture involves first reading the Bible in one's own culture and then discerning supracultural truth through a process of de-contextualisation. This is then re-contextualised into forms appropriate to the receiving culture. That is, the truth discerned through one culture is translated for another.

Such a model has two major problems. First, while the Bible undoubtedly contains both divine and human elements, I would argue that it is not possible to separate the two. It is a Muslim and not a Christian understanding of revelation that suggests that human elements are not divine and *vice versa*.[3] As the living Word, the Lord Jesus Christ, is indivisibly one hundred per cent human and one hundred per cent divine, so the written Word, the Bible, is indivisibly one hundred per cent human and one hundred per cent divine. God revealed is in culture, and is not just expressing a supracultural self in limited cultural form. If this is so, any attempt to abstract 'supracultural' truth necessarily reduces the Scriptures. While it may sometimes be useful to abstract and translate propositions, this cannot be a satisfactory way of teaching the Old Testament.

Second, the aim of teaching the Old Testament is not that students should understand it as does the teacher, but that students should themselves develop reading competence. The translation model is likely to teach them that they need first to become skilled in the teacher's cultural (usually western) method of reading and then to become skilled in translating into their own culture. Apart from being unnecessarily burdensome, such a pattern can reduce the students' understanding of the Bible and thus impoverish the church. The task of becoming skilled in western hermeneutics can be so onerous that the translation step is omitted, thus impoverishing the church in the students' culture. More seriously, important insights from that culture can be lost to the rest of the world.

For the Old Testament teacher, this has serious implications. It suggests that the task is not to replace the student's world view with that of western academia, but to help the student so to learn from others' work that he or she can read competently within his or her own culture — which may well be nearer to Old Testament cultures than is that of

---

3. See I. J. Glaser, 'Towards a Mutual Understanding of Christian and Islamic Concepts of Revelation', in *Themelios* (1982), pp. 16-22.

the teacher. The teacher's expectation will then be that students from different backgrounds will be important teaching and learning resources — for the teacher as well as for the taught.

Example

Twentieth-century western Christians may have to work hard to grasp the impact of God's commandment to Hosea to marry a prostitute[4] and then to take her back again. We have to consider the male-female dynamic of biblical times, and to remind ourselves that our current tolerance of extra-marital sex is not a universal phenomenon. We then ask ourselves what Hosea's actions would have meant to Israel.

To teach all this in an Islamic context might obscure the point. In common with many other non-western cultures, most Islamic cultures are centred on shame rather than guilt, and family honour is bound up in female purity.[5] Deliberately to marry a woman who is not a virgin or openly to take back an adulterous wife can result in reprobation not only for oneself but also for one's family. The westerner may need to learn from the non-westerner that God was not only asking the prophet to be hurt, but, more awfully, to be publicly dishonoured; and in taking Israel back God is not only accepting the hurt of their rebellion but exposing himself to dishonour. He is doing something that might actually be seen as being wrong.

This is further highlighted in Islamic contexts by reflection on the role of Muhammad's wives. As well as cementing various alliances, their relationship with the prophet functions as exemplar, and the maintenance of the prophet's honour through their behaviour is paramount. The following story about A'ishah,[6] Muhammad's favourite wife, makes the point by contrast:

> Muhammad's wives used to draw lots to decide who should accompany him on journeys. The lot fell on A'ishah during one of the

4. Or someone who was going to become a prostitute.
5. See B. Musk, *Touching the Soul of Islam* (Crowborough: Monarch, 1995), chs. 2-4.
6. This story is told in the hadith of Al-Bukhari and referred to in Qur'an 23: 11ff. See also B. Musk, *Touching the Soul of Islam*, pp. 77-79.

battles, and she had joined the army travelling inside a *howdah* on the back of a camel so that none but Muhammad should see her. At the end of the battle, she went away from the camp to relieve herself, and, on returning, found that she had lost a necklace. While she was retrieving it, the *howdah*, presumed to contain her, was put on the camel and everyone left for home. A'ishah sat down in the place where she had been staying and went to sleep.

Continuing the story in her own words: 'Safwan bin Al-Mu' attal As-Sulam Adh-Dhakwani was behind the army. When he reached my place in the morning, he saw the figure of a sleeping person and he recognised me as he had seen me before the order of compulsory veiling was prescribed. So I woke up when he recited Istirja'[7] (Qur'an 2:156). As soon as he recognised me, I veiled my face with my head cover at once, and, by Allah, we did not speak a single word, and I did not hear him saying any word besides his Istirja'. He dismounted from his camel and made it kneel down, putting his leg on its front legs and then I got up and rode on it. Then he set out leading the camel that was carrying me till we overtook the army in the extreme heat of midday while they were at a halt.'

Because A'ishah had spent time alone with the soldier, the rumour spread that they had made love. Muhammad was upset, and told A'ishah to stay in her parents' house while he decided whether the rumour was true. A'ishah was so upset that she wept day and night until, a month later, Muhammad received the revelation that declared her innocence and the punishment for slander (Qur'an 24:11-23). She could then be taken back.

To deny that we can abstract supranatural truth from the Bible without reducing it is not to relativise the Bible. Rather, it is to take the Bible in the actual form in which it has been given as absolute, and to refuse to equate biblical revelation with any particular reading of it. That is, it is the hermeneutic and not the text that is relativised.

This is not to say that any hermeneutic will do, and that all conceivable interpretations are equally valid: any reading from within any context needs to be checked. A game analogy is helpful here:

The Scripture itself imposes rules for reading: the Old Testament cannot be interpreted outside the possible meanings of the Hebrew text; if we

---

7. *I.e.*, a verse recited on seeing someone dead.

accept that the Scripture is God-given, we must read the final form of the text whatever its provenance; if we accept the canon, any particular text must be interpreted in the light of the rest of the Bible; and so on. In the above example, we would need to ask whether the insights from the Islamic context are consistent with Old Testament thinking about marriage and honour, and whether ideas about God bearing human shame can be found elsewhere in the Bible. We would also need to check on the consistency of any insights with the rest of Hosea.

The history of interpretation provides tools for reading: these range from the New Testament's handling of Messianic prophecy through the patristic uses of allegory and the reformation key of Justification faith to western critical studies and liberation theologies.

Within the constraints of the rules and using a choice of tools, it is possible to play a variety of games and even to develop new tools. The games played in late twentieth-century Islamic contexts will not be the same as those played in, for example, nineteenth-century Enlightenment contexts. Different games will produce different insights, which, if the rules are followed, will be complementary and will together give a rounded understanding of the text. The following explores something of how this can work out in various Islamic contexts.

The Comparative 'Game'

When one is perfectly familiar with a religious symbol from one's own tradition and personal experience, and when one finds this symbol in another tradition, more rather than less effort will be required to penetrate behind the face of the symbol to grasp what it means to the other.

So writes C. J. Adams[8] in a paper entitled, 'Islam and Christianity: the opposition of similarities'. Islam and Christianity do indeed appear similar. They share such themes as monotheism, providence, prophethood, revelation, sin, judgement, covenant, and Scripture. But each

---

8. In R. M. Savory and D. A. Agius (eds.), *Logos Islamikos* (Toronto: Pontifical Institute of Medieval Studies, 1984), p. 289.

135

of these words masks differences in meanings. As Muslims hear about Christianity and Christians about Islam, it is inevitable that each will at least begin by assigning their own meanings to the other's words. As Adams suggests, much effort is required if effective communication is to take place. Reading the Old Testament in comparison with Islamic material is a possible place to start.

For the past thousand years of Christian–Muslim conversation, discussion has consistently centred on the Trinity, the divinity of Christ, the atonement, and the reliability of the Bible. All these have a New Testament focus, and debates have had an unfortunate tendency to go over centuries-old ground and generate more heat than light. One of the reasons for this is that the two sides use similar words with different meanings.

The Old Testament offers resources for breaking the impasse, since it is thence that many Christian words derive their meanings. Further, it contains many stories that are known to Islam, either through the Qur'an or through the *isra iliyyat* (traditional knowledge gained from Jewish and Christian sources).

This brings us again to Adams' observation, but now the shared symbols are people and events rather than words. Apparently similar stories display subtle variations that betray differences in meaning: the Qur'anic and biblical narratives develop two different world views.

In that the Qur'an claims complete divine authority, Muslims accept its versions as the true ones, and either harmonise them with the Bible or question the biblical text. Insofar as harmonisation is impossible, therefore, the versions of the stories are in competition. However, discussion of stories is more fun and less confrontational than polemic about doctrine, and discussion within the framework of the stories rather than argument about abstractions from them can move the debate to symbolic ground where at least the debaters can learn to listen to each other. Differences in meaning can then be discerned through differences in stories rather than arguments over words, and understanding can grow even if the differences are not made explicit.

Thus an important 'game' for reading, and therefore for teaching, the Old Testament in the context of Islam, is that of comparison. The Old Testament is to be read and taught with reference to parallel Islamic material and Islamic thought and culture, thus both developing mutual understanding and highlighting aspects of each system over against the other.

'Games' Provoked by the Study of Islam

The study of Islam can (and should) send students to the Old Testament for several reasons. First, we can only understand another faith in the light of our own. This means that one of the best ways of understanding Islamic thinking is to compare it with our own thinking; and there are many aspects of Islam that relate more obviously to the Old Testament than to the New.

In particular, the call and career of Muhammad suggest Old Testament comparisons. In teaching Islam, I ask students to read the calls of the Old Testament prophets, and to see where there are parallels and where differences with the call of Muhammad. We can also reflect on how Muhammad's career as law-giver, conqueror, and statesman might be compared with those of Moses, Joshua, and David.

This raises questions about the nature of prophethood, and whether it is possible to be chronologically A.D. but functionally B.C. It also underlines the importance of biblical views of covenant and the place of Israel, and indicates fundamental differences in Islamic and Christian views of human beings and how they relate to God.

The latter is particularly evident in the Adam stories. I sometimes give groups the simple exercise of reading the Islamic version[9] and asking them to note differences from the biblical version. It is interesting that students tend to focus on the details of the 'fall', or rather on the lack of it in the Qur'anic versions. They may not notice that the Qur'anic stories are not about the 'fall' at all, but about the status of human beings relative to the other created orders, and about the fall and activities of Satan. In parallel, I have sometimes found that Muslims reading the Bible focus on small details and do not seem to appreciate the thrust of the stories.[10]

---

9. We focus on Surah II:30-39, but may also refer to VII:11-25, XV:26-44, and XX:115-24.

10. A classic Old Testament example is a reading of Genesis 1–3 that resulted in a discussion about what kind of fruit was forbidden and whether it was Satan

Second, the study of Islam stimulates questions for the Old Testament. For example, the establishment of the Islamic community at Medina and the foundational battles against the Meccans raise questions about the relationship between faith and community and about the place of physical warfare. The obvious place to look at these questions is in the establishment of Israel. Thus studying Islam can raise students' interest in the book of Joshua, and provoke the question of why such conquests are not seen as paradigmatic for Christians while they are for Muslims.

Sometimes, the questions that arise surprise me. One Chinese student became fascinated by the book of Job over against Islam, seeing parallels and differences in its understanding of Satan, asking questions about whether the answer from the whirlwind is essentially Islamic, and wondering whether the comforters are like some Muslims.

Third, Muslim apologists sometimes use the Old Testament. As mentioned above, most Muslim–Christian debate uses the New Testament, but there are several areas that turn us to the Old.

a. Most Muslims believe that all prophets are basically sinless. They can make minor mistakes, but not commit major sins. Old Testament accounts of prophetic lapses are therefore cited as proof of biblical corruption.

It is simply shocking to see that the Bible attributes deceit and lies to Abraham, cheating and treachery to Isaac and Jacob, adultery to David, incest to Lot, idol-worship to Aaron, apostasy to Solomon, and inhuman brutalities to Moses and Joshua, and at the same time calls them men after God's heart, pointing unceasingly perhaps to the (sic) defect in God himself for approving nefarious and heinous practices.[11]

b. The Qur'an teaches that Muhammad was foretold by a Jewish witness (XLVI:10) and by Jesus (LXI:6). The former is usually taken to refer to the 'prophet like Moses' in Deuteronomy 18:18, and

or a snake that tempted Eve. From the New Testament, there is the one point that worried a Muslim after a presentation of the Easter story — how could such a great prophet drink wine?

11. Dust cover of A. M. R. Muhajir, *Lessons from the Stories of the Qur'an* (Lahore: Sh. Muhammad Ashrafi, 1965).

invites consideration of the meaning of 'like Moses'.[12] Some Muslims also cite Song of Solomon 5:16, where they insist that *mahmadim* (usually translated 'desirable' or 'lovely') is a name, so that the lover of the Song is Muhammad.

c. Muslim debates about the Bible are generally based on the assumption that all God-given books should be like the Qur'an. The variety of Old Testament literature can offer an even greater challenge to Christians than that of the New Testament in this context; but an appreciation of Old Testament revelation can also give a good foundation for being secure in a Bible that is itself and NOT like the Qur'an.

d. Islamic versions of Old Testament stories can function as biblical interpretation. An unusual example is the *Mohomedan Commentary on the Holy Bible*[13] which uses Qur'anic and other Islamic material as a comment on Genesis 1–11, and thus interprets Genesis as an Islamic text. Current apologists do not take the Bible so seriously, but do interpret it as a book like the Qur'an and having the same message as the Qur'an. This can challenge students to check received interpretations and find out whether the text can support Islamic meanings.

Finally, realization of the differences between Christianity and Islam can lead to an increased awareness of the need for Old Testament foundations. In particular, the context of mission should lead to an understanding of the Old Testament as a key resource. Many Muslims may be best introduced to the Bible through the Psalms, which are mentioned in the Qur'an, or through Genesis, which gives a coherent account of stories they have heard only in part.

Students who want to minister to Muslims are, then, likely to look to the Old Testament as an important resource for evangelism. They will want to read it as it might address itself to Islamic thinking, and to learn to tell its stories effectively into Islamic cultures. Such issues as

12. The latter is taken to refer to the paraclete of John 14 and 16. See, for example, the note on this verse in Yusuf Ah, *The Holy Qur'an. Text, Translation and Commentary* (Jeddah: Islamic Education Centre, 1946). The verse gives an alternative name for Muhammad: Ahmad, which means 'the praised'. Ali and others claim that this is a translation of the Greek *periclutos*, of which *paracletos* is a corruption.

13. Sir Syed Ahmad Khan (Ghazeepore, 1862).

the above are likely to determine their 'games' for reading Scripture: it is for teachers of the Old Testament in such contexts to explain the rules and offer tools for effective reading.

Teaching the Old Testament as Mission to Muslims

In order for the gospel to make sense, biblical ideas of creation, revelation, responsibility, sin, righteousness, and justice need to be understood. Two examples indicate the importance of the Old Testament in presenting such ideas in Islamic situations.

West Africa

One missionary[14] reports on two years of teaching the Bible to a group of Muslim men at their request. His starting point in choosing a teaching approach was Luke 24:13-32, the road to Emmaus. His Muslim friends shared with Jesus' disciples a belief in one God, and in Jesus as a prophet. As the Muslims did not believe in the divinity of Christ, so the disciples did not realise it. As the Muslims believed that Jesus did not die, and that this would have been a defeat of God's prophet, so the disciples believed that Jesus should not have been defeated in crucifixion.

He noted how Jesus dealt with the situation, by starting from the beginning and opening up the Scriptures, and did the same with his Muslim study group. They worked their way in some detail through Genesis and Exodus, and then more briefly through the rest of Old Testament history, with a special focus on Jonah. They then worked through the gospel story until they reached the Emmaus road passage.

The result was that several men accepted the message. The missionary reports that there were no difficult confrontations, that where there was contradiction with Islam the men accepted the Bible, and that one man said that, if they had started with the Gospels, he probably would not have believed it, but since they started with Genesis and laid the foundation he had to believe it. Such results do not necessarily follow the method, but they are interesting.

14. Source protected.

United Kingdom

I have (quite independently) followed a similar principle in my teaching of Muslim children in an inner-city area, although not so systematically. That the children are minors with no pretensions to Christianity, and that relationships with their families are of first importance, places restrictions on ministry. I have decided never to push Christian words into Muslim mouths, so that we have been restricted in ways of praying and in the choice of songs during our story sessions. I have also decided not to exhort children to believe what I believe, so we have aimed to let stories speak for themselves rather than telling the children what they should learn from them.

However, the teaching has borne in mind the parallel Islamic stories, and the ways of thinking that the Muslim children might bring to their learning. We have prayed and worked towards building their understanding of biblical ideas. Experience suggests that the Bible stories challenge their thinking on important points, and move them towards an understanding of the fallenness of human beings and the grace of God. We pray that this foundation will enable some to respond to Christ as they grow up.

Example

In telling the story of Babel, I had in mind the parallel Qur'anic passage (XVI:26), in which people build a tower against God and it falls on them and kills them.[15] I therefore told the story the week after telling of the flood and Noachic covenant. I reminded the children about the flood, and then told them about the people of Babel: how they were not obeying God's command to scatter, and how they were building to make their own name and not to honour God's name. Then I asked, 'What do you think God did about it?' The answer was immediate: 'Sent another flood!' This gave opportunity to highlight the implica-

15. There are also parallels in the traditional stories about Namrud (Nimrod), who is thought to have been the king who opposed Abraham in II:258 and XXI:68-71. He quite literally challenged God by building a vulture-powered flying machine and firing an arrow into heaven from it, and by mustering a large army and issuing a challenge to God to fight him.

tions of the covenant and God's commitment to humanity despite its rebellion. It also raised the question of how God might deal with sin if he doesn't destroy the sinners.

Over against Islam, these are two key 'opposed similarities': 'Covenant' in the Qur'an refers not to a relationship in which God commits himself to human beings, but to an agreement in which God commands and humans recognise their duty to obey.

The flood in the Qur'an is not a never-to-be-repeated destruction, but a paradigm judgement. It is the first of a series of stories with a pattern of wickedness/prophetic warning/destruction of unbelievers/vindication of prophet and believers. This represents the way in which God deals with humanity throughout history.

Thus, in the Islamic context, the apparently simple exercise of telling a well-known Bible story requires a re-reading that can lead to new appreciations of the text. Teaching the Old Testament to Muslim children adds a new dimension to the hermeneutic process, as the stories are allowed to enter into dialogue with Islamic versions as mediated through the children's understandings.

Does It Matter?

While writing this, I read a paper from the 1994 Tyndale Fellowship conference,[16] and was struck by this question, 'Is anyone listening?' and the suggestion that the Old Testament might be key to the re-evangelism of the western world. I also noticed the footnote on the Muslim world[17] as the author wonders 'if story exegesis might not be the key to help yet others hear, who at this point seem resistant to the Christian faith'.

I want to answer, 'Yes!' Most Muslims are already listening to versions of much of our biblical story. By telling them the Old Testament, we are not only inviting them into our story, but also entering into theirs. This presents us with a unique opportunity, but also with a unique challenge. Religions related to Hinduism have stories that deal

16. C. Armerding in P. E. Satterthwaite and D. F. Wright (eds.), *A Pathway into the Holy Scripture* (Grand Rapids: Eerdmans, 1994), pp. 31-49.
17. N. 34, p. 48.

with similar human issues to those in the Bible, but they are obviously different stories. Jews have different interpretations of the biblical stories, but hold to the Bible as norm. It is only Islam that has different versions of the same stories, and invites a dialogue between competing narrative worlds.

The question is, can we go beyond the re-telling of our traditional western interpretations into Islamic contexts, and re-read our Scriptures so that they can speak directly to Muslim people? Can we follow the rules imposed by Scripture itself while we ask new questions? Can we adapt the old tools and develop new ones for new 'games' in new situations?

For the teacher of the Old Testament, the challenge is even deeper, since the task is to teach in such a way that students will be able to read competently in new contexts: not to initiate students into our own academic 'game', but to equip them to choose and play the appropriate 'games' wherever God may send them.

And this matters for us all. It is not only that cultures change and we need constantly to adapt: it is also that Islam is part of our world, and is going to remain so for the foreseeable future. The Old Testament is not only foundational to Judaism and Christianity and therefore to cultures based on them: it is also foundational to Islam. But it is foundational in a different way. The Old Testament basis has been filtered through Rabbinic teaching and then through Muhammad and the early Muslims, so that, as asserted in section 2, the very similarities obscure profound differences in world view.

If it is urgent to national and international relationships as well as to mission that Christians understand Muslims, then it is urgent that these profound differences be explored. Reading the Old Testament in the context of Islam is a fruitful way of doing this. Old Testament scholars and teachers could, if they would, have much to offer our strife-ridden world.

Perspectives on Teaching the Old Testament from the Two-Thirds World

M. DANIEL CARROLL R.

M. Daniel Carroll R., professor of Old Testament at Denver Seminary, was for fifteen years Lecturer in Old Testament at El Seminario Teológico Centroamericano in Guatemala City, Guatemala. From 1992-1995 he was a regional Vice-President, and he continues as a member of the accreditation commission of A.E.T.A.L. (Asociación Evangélica de Educación Teológica en América Latina), an association of evangelical institutions in Latin America with over one hundred affiliated Bible institutes and seminaries.

Those who live and minister in the Two-Thirds World not only face a unique set of logistical circumstances in education, but also can contribute new insights and perspectives into the study of the biblical text itself. Other essays in this book are each dedicated to specific aspects of teaching the Old Testament in more developed regions of the globe (North America, Europe, Australia), but what follows might help readers to globalize their appreciation of biblical studies. My experience is in Latin America, but I suspect that many of the educational realities of that continent would also be true of Africa and Asia. This essay is divided into three main sections: (1) the educational context of Two-Thirds World Old Testament studies; (2) the necessity of their contextualization; and (3) observations on relating First and Two-Thirds World Old Testament studies.

The Educational Context for Teaching the Old Testament in the Two-Thirds World

Any discussion of teaching the Old Testament within Two-Thirds World institutions must first be placed within the broader framework of certain fundamental traits of secular education in general that also are reflected in evangelical theological education. Two characteristics merit special mention.

The Focus on the Pragmatic and Demographics

Higher education in Latin America is often geared primarily to the training of professionals for careers in the market place or for the government bureaucracy. The interest is more in career advancement and social utility than in innovative research. Moreover, throughout the Americas there also flows a deep commitment to the democratizing of education — that is, of putting education within the reach of the masses.[1] Accordingly, recent decades have witnessed the establishing of new vocational schools, shorter degree training courses, a variety of different continuing education programs, and extension sites for both public and private universities. In other words, the vision of education is centred on the practical and on extending the demographic base.

These two concerns, the pragmatic and the demographic, also find a particular echo within the evangelical community. To begin with, evangelical institutions of theological education usually have a very practical mindset. They understand their purpose as equipping for the ministry, and, therefore, there can be great emphasis on evangelism and church planting. At its best, this orientation provides an inherent vibrancy for education and helps maintain links with the churches. Students and instructors are involved in local congregations, and national staff often also have a pastoral ministry in addition to their teaching or administrative roles.

---

1. This will continue to be a daunting challenge for the foreseeable future, especially in light of census reports which indicate that perhaps half the population in Latin America is under the age of twenty-five. In many countries the educational level of the general public is very low, with few finishing secondary education and only a miniscule percentage ever even beginning university level education.

As is the case in much of the Two-Thirds World, the growth of the evangelical church in Latin America over the last couple of decades has been phenomenal. This growth has resulted as well in the explosion in the number of new training institutions. In addition to those founded and sponsored by mission agencies and the historic international denominations, national pentecostal and neo-pentecostal groups have begun to get involved in theological education. This move to meet the needs of evangelical demographics, however, is designed not only to train pastors and professional church and parachurch workers, but also to reach the laity. The educational landscape continues to have more traditional residential study programs, but is now marked as well by the increase in extension programs, distance learning, and evening and weekend courses.

The impact of these various factors on teaching the Old Testament can be quite positive. The educational and ecclesial context is a continual impetus to make biblical studies pertinent to everyday life. There is little time for pursuing technical minutiae or researching ephemeral issues. Also, the constant contact with the laity, both in the classroom and the local church, can force teachers of the Old Testament to work on communication skills in order to be able to transmit their material in a way that all kinds of people from different social and educational backgrounds can understand. Teaching in the classroom truly is a full-time job, and course relevancy and pedagogy become key factors in evaluating teacher performance.

On the campus of the seminary in Guatemala City, where I taught from 1982 until the spring of 1996, I have had the experience of teaching a pastors' continuing education course on Old Testament social ethics at secondary level, a bachelors level Old Testament survey course for our pastoral training program, and a masters Hebrew exegesis class — all within the same week! This sort of breadth, with its diversity of audiences and kinds of interaction, can invigorate the teaching of the Old Testament and keeps one accountable to the whole body of Christ. Interestingly, this engagement with life poses a striking contrast to the recent call of alarm in North America concerning the apparent gulf between seminary education and practical pastoral training and church life.[2]

2. This is not to say that institution-church relations are not a topic of debate in Latin America. The recent triennial assembly of A.E.T.A.L. in September, 1995,

At the same time, the proliferation of institutions and programs can, in some cases, be a trend to watch with caution. On the one hand, with such an increase in the number of educational opportunities on offer, consistent quality control can be difficult to establish. What should be the entrance and graduation requirements for each level, and how can these degrees be coordinated in terms of credit transfers? The reality is that currently a variety of institutions can offer the same degree, yet with very disparate academic demands on the students and personnel.

On the other hand, the tendency to the practical and the sheer amount of actual teaching activity can slide the teacher and the institution alike into an activism which neglects serious class preparation and ignores research. Time for investigation and writing in the Two-Thirds World more often than not ultimately depends on a personal commitment to work extra hours on one's own time, as job descriptions allow little or no possibility for scholarly endeavour. The sheer quantity of teaching, then, though constructive in some ways, can be counter-productive in others.

Limitations in Physical Resources

Education in Latin America seems to be continually in a state of economic crisis. This financial pinch pertains to student and institution alike. From the students' perspective, only a few can aspire to dedicate themselves solely to study. The vast majority of students in higher education have to work, and so the pursuit of a degree must be relegated to free times at night or on weekends.

For many different reasons, which can be very context-specific (such as foreign debt, natural disasters, bureaucratic graft, civil war), the government as well contends with a lack of funding. The repercussions of this state of affairs are felt in various areas. For example, the hiring of full-time faculty is almost impossible, even in the private sector, so teachers usually also have to hold another job in order to be able to support themselves and their families. This economic reality,

---

whose theme was 'El Diálogo del Milenio' (The Dialogue of the Millennium), provided a venue for the interchange between theologians, institution administrators, and pastors.

therefore, is yet another factor, beyond the pragmatic and the demographic, in the emergence of new delivery systems. The maintenance and improvement of the physical infrastructure are also adversely affected by this lack of resources, libraries suffer, and Latin American institutions struggle to be able to take full advantage of the new dimensions of the computer age for the classroom and academic administration.

Theological institutions also function under financial constraints, again both from the student side of things and because of the pressures felt by the funding sources. In this case, of course, the latter would refer to the financial capacities of national donors and the mission and denominational sponsors. As in the secular arena, the economic circumstances have a ripple effect within the educational enterprise.

Most classes are given in the evenings, and increasingly more are appearing in Saturday formats. Often only missionary personnel have the luxury of being able to focus primarily on their teaching, whereas national staff may have a pastorate and give lectures in other institutions over and beyond their regular teaching obligations in order to make a decent living wage. These limitations can determine in large degree the time available for research and publication and so define who can write among the faculty.

Another consequence of these economic strictures is the growing electronic gap between the First and Two-Thirds Worlds. It can be difficult to find secretarial help that is computer literate, and while more developed countries continue to advertise the latest achievements in e-mail and the internet, Two-Thirds World theological institutions struggle just to keep their faxes working and wait with frustration for the national phone systems to reach the capacity to allow students and scholars to participate in the global exchange of information.

Intimately related to this lack of resources is the difficult library situation. Libraries must wrestle with strict restrictions on acquiring new titles on a regular basis and subscribing to academic and pastoral journals. Complicating this handicap is the inefficiency and corruption in the national postal systems. Book orders might take many months (and even years!) to arrive or might be lost (or stolen) in the customs houses. Still another limiting factor is the actual amount of quality academic books available in the national language. This is not so much a problem with English, but the situation is different with Spanish,

Portuguese, and French. Not a great number of evangelical academic titles have been produced by Latin Americans; those that are available often are simply translations of works in English. Many technical texts are produced by Roman Catholic faculties in Spain and so must be ordered out of Europe, or are liberationist works.

The result of these stark material and financial realities is that a theological institution can find itself forced to limit itself to the preparation of ministerial professionals and to providing instruction to committed laity — not only as a response to the practical impulses of the context, but also because there might not be adequate resources for more credible academic efforts. This first impression, however, would not do justice to the more comprehensive picture of how evangelical theological education is responding to the on-going economic crisis.

There are many laudable efforts being made to remedy the seeming dearth of solid academic scholarship which are worthy of mention. Those evangelicals teaching Old Testament, for instance, can now find publishing possibilities through such journals as *Kairós, Boletín Teológico,* and *Vox Scripturae*.[3] New commentary projects are appearing, like the 'Mundo Hispano'[4] series that is a mid-level effort with sermon helps; 'Nueva Creación'[5] comes from a quality Spanish language arm of a North American publisher that is publishing both translations of significant English works (for example, some titles of the NICOT and NICNT series) as well as original work by Latin Americans. A.E.T.A.L., an association of evangelical institutions on the continent, has begun to try to develop a network of teachers and scholars in different fields to facilitate communication and interchange, and other regional associations also regularly sponsor consultations and workshops.

The economic situation, however, also can have a positive formative influence in shaping values in education, which would emphasize the healthy focus on the practical mentioned earlier although from another angle. On the one hand, Old Testament teachers must ask themselves why they might write on a particular topic. What is its value, not simply in royalties or in terms of professional prestige, but rather for

---

3. *Kairós* is published by El Seminario Teológico Centroamericano; *Boletín Teológico* by the Latin American Theological Fraternity; *Vox Scripturae* by A.E.T.A.L.
4. Baptist Spanish Publishing House.
5. Eerdmans Publishing Company, Grand Rapids, MI.

the classroom and for the Latin American church? There is little room for the simply 'interesting' or the 'exotic'. Research must be responsible, because the financial limitations and time constraints are too great. On the other hand, these circumstances can reorient how one evaluates available resources. Libraries must now think in terms of accessibility and actual use, and not just of the quantity of titles in the stacks. A distinction must be made between constructive research within the language abilities and cultural concerns of students and staff and the temptation to keep up with the latest Western theological fad or debate.[6]

The Contextualization of Old Testament Studies

Oftentimes those in the First World identify contextualized biblical studies in the Two-Thirds World with liberationist approaches. This is not surprising, because publishing houses such as Orbis Books and SCM Press have dominated the English-speaking market, and their releases have shaped in large measure the perception of the theological and ecclesial scene in developing countries. The most well-known names of Latin American liberationist Old Testament scholarship within the First World probably would be J. S. Croatto, G. V. Pixley, and E. Tamez.

Those of us who live in Latin America, however, have always known that these ways of looking at church life and doing biblical studies have represented only a small minority of the Christian populace (Roman Catholic and Protestant), a fact that liberationists themselves are admitting in recent literature that reflects on the failure of liberationist hopes in our countries.[7] And yet, although liberation the-

6. Some accreditation agencies in the Two-Thirds World also now factor in to library requirements the relative nature of the production of theological literature in the national language. For example, English-speaking institutions would have greater requirements for the number of titles in the library than Spanish-speaking ones. Several Latin American institutions require English for higher degree programs, so in these cases one should expect English titles in the libraries.

7. Note, *e.g.*, P. Berryman, *Stubborn Hope: Religion, Politics, and Revolution in Central America* (Maryknoll: Orbis Books/New York: The New Press, 1994); idem, *Religion in the Megacity: Catholic and Protestant Portraits from Latin America* (Maryknoll: Orbis Books, 1996).

ology actually has been a peripheral movement with little popular following, on our continent it has served the positive function of forcing the spectrum of Christian churches to consider seriously, and not in a few instances for the first time, the grave political and economic issues of our societies, the social context and commitments of the interpreter, and the importance of praxis.

In contrast to liberationist groups the evangelical church, as was pointed out earlier, has been growing rapidly and now numbers in the millions. It is impossible to expect that this widespread and very heterogeneous phenomenon would offer a consistent approach to the Bible. What one commonly finds in the bookstores and theological institutions in the area of Old Testament studies are translations of First World (usually North American) popular style books on biblical characters and themes, standard texts (*e.g.,* introductions, histories of Israel), and lay-level commentaries. These in no way should be rejected out of hand as foreign imports or theological impositions; rather, they can represent helpful contributions of the body of Christ from other parts of the globe. But, because our socio-cultural world does influence the lenses with which we read the Old Testament, the Two-Thirds World can see different things within the sacred text. Perhaps to a degree these insights are born out of our contexts of war, rural agricultural economies, and extended families that mirror some aspects of the life pictured in the Bible that sometimes are no longer true of the West.

The challenge that lies before the Latin American evangelical church is to continue to develop its own Old Testament literature in order to complement First World studies. This literature should speak to the issues of our world from our own cultural and religious perspectives: in other words, it must be grounded in solid evangelical convictions and explore as well the relevance of context in the hermeneutical task. At this juncture of Latin American history some pressing concerns requiring careful interaction with the sacred text include poverty, national reconstruction and the fate of refugees after the termination of civil war, the status and rights of women within a *machista* culture, and issues of racism and religious pluralism against the background of the emergence of indigenous rights movements (in Guatemala, of the Maya).

This challenge to respond creatively from the biblical text will demand the training both of contextually sensitive Old Testament teachers for theological education programmes at all levels and of capable scholars committed to doing research and publishing for Latin American needs. The tendency to focus on the practical should be informed by sound biblical studies engaged with life on the ground, in all of its richness, variety, and complexity. Some publication trends and the themes chosen for dialogue by the various institutional and professional associations are a sign that there is interest in pursuing this important goal. On the whole, however, evangelical institutions have only just begun to consider the many possible implications of this orientation for directions of course work and the elaboration of curricula.

Relating the Two-Thirds and First Worlds in the Teaching of the Old Testament

The Importance of Mature Mutual Appreciation

I use the phrase 'mature mutual appreciation' in the title of this section, because the perceptions in theological education of the First World towards the Two-Thirds World and vice versa sometimes are unhealthy and short-sighted. These erroneous perspectives have historical, institutional, and social roots.

Students and national staff in Two-Thirds World institutions can exhibit a bit of an inferiority complex toward the West. This can be traced back in part to a mindset fostered during their theological training. A significant percentage of these theological institutions were founded by European and North American mission agencies, and missionary personnel in the past tended to dominate administration and do the bulk of the teaching. (This situation is still operative today in some centres.) It was natural that missionaries reproduced the systems and curricula of their own education.

For some of these leaders academic excellence was (and still can be) represented ultimately by a few select historically prestigious institutions (*e.g.*, Oxford, Cambridge, Princeton) or by well-known independent and denominational seminaries of their home countries. What was communicated consciously or unwittingly to promising national leaders who might aspire to higher degrees was that these institutions 'back home' were the pinnacles of learning. The constraints in physical resources on Two-Thirds World campuses, as well as the view of their own societies in general that Latin America was woefully underdeveloped, reinforced the feeling that First World students were sharper, Western faculty more scholarly, and First World institutions the undisputed capitals of theological and biblical studies. As degree programs continue to evolve and as Latin American evangelicals persist in the on-going task of raising up contextualized teachers and publishing their own scholarly material, this sense of being second-class citizens within the world-wide discourse of biblical studies is being replaced by the growing conviction that the Two-Thirds World has important contributions to make to fresh understandings of the Scripture.

Unfortunately, this process can be hindered by an inverse attitude in First World scholars, the feeling that West truly is best. On several occasions I have had to face the prejudice that, although the Two-Thirds World might be able to offer 'interesting' readings of the Old Testament, the 'really serious' academic work is done in North America and Europe.[8] This disposition can be transmitted in several ways. For example, students studying in First World institutions learn early on from teachers and thesis advisors that they must deal with the text full stop, and not delve into contextual issues. The result is that research in evangelical First World seminaries by foreign students often is limited to background concerns and to the theological parameters of the teacher.

This reality was brought home afresh at some recent meetings. At a lunch during the early stages of the conference I asked a Two-Thirds World student doing a Ph.D. in Old Testament at a British university what was the topic of his research. I sensed a number of exciting possibilities for connecting his research to his native context but surprisingly got little reaction. As the meetings continued, however, and

---

8. For an example of rare openness exhibited by the North American evangelical biblical scholarly community, see the contributions of C. Blomberg: 'Implications of Globalization for Biblical Understanding', in A. Frazer Evans, R. A. Evans, and D. A. Roozen (eds.), *The Globalization of Theological Education* (Maryknoll: Orbis Books, 1993), pp. 213-28; idem, 'Critical Issues in New Testament Studies for Evangelicals Today', in P. E. Satterthwaite, D. F. Wright (eds.), *A Pathway into the Holy Scripture* (Grand Rapids: Eerdmans, 1994), pp. 51-79 (especially, pp. 65-69).

as several of us spoke up, he began to join in the critique of First World studies. I approached him once more and asked him for the reasons for the change. What he said to me could be replicated in many different centres of Western theological education: he had kept silent until he had felt that it would be safe to speak out along with others who would echo his feelings; he told me that in one of his first essays he had mentioned in a footnote how his research could dovetail with issues of his context — the advisor's response in the margin: the text does not talk about that! Since that time, he told me, he had learned the rules of the game for securing a degree and buried certain concerns until his return to the Two-Thirds World.

Similar obstacles are faced by missionaries teaching in the Two-Thirds World who have become animated by the new vistas opened to them by the possibilities of contextualizing their biblical studies. A few months ago at a meeting in a Central American country I had a conversation with a missionary who was working on a Ph.D. in Old Testament at a prominent seminary in the United States. When he shared with me his ideas for his thesis topic, I asked if he had considered how he might relate his research to Latin American needs. His answer was sadly all too familiar: his professors were not interested in those issues and could not see them in the text; his work would have to develop along more traditional lines.

In both instances these students still held deep contextual convictions within their inner being. Their attitudes, however, are not always typical. Missionary personnel can come with pre-packaged notes and set ideas and can seem oblivious to the different setting in which they now minister. Moreover, all too often Two-Thirds World students studying in the West will absorb the perspectives of their educational environment, begin to devalue the perspectives and theological needs of their national churches, and accept the First World agenda. If they return to their home countries to teach in theological institutions, sometimes a 'detoxifying' process is required in order that they might get reacquainted with Latin American everyday life and recommit themselves to teaching the biblical text to deal with our issues and not to please a Western professor and that First World scholarly guild. They must learn anew to read the Scripture with Latin eyes.

In addition to having to deal with this negative view of the relevance of Two-Thirds World concern and approaches to academic biblical studies, evangelicals from Latin America, who are aware of the richness of their traditions in their countries and are pursuing a degree in Old Testament in the First World, can feel frustrated by at least two other related factors. On the one hand, what little biblical scholars in the First World do know of Latin America is usually circumscribed by a few translated liberationist theological publications; there is no acquaintance with the variety of different liberationist types of textual study (from the classical source-critical methods to the newer sociological approaches), let alone with evangelical work. On the other hand, the languages of choice of First World academics are French and German. In other words, the wealth of Old Testament studies coming out of Spain and Latin America is automatically eliminated from consideration for research. Students can neither read scholars from their context nor discuss them with their teachers. From the very start, they are locked in linguistically and limited to a predetermined set of foreign issues and sources.

Both Worlds should be aware of these complex academic realities. What is called for is a new set of attitudes by all, a mature mutual appreciation of strengths and weaknesses, and the humble admission of the particular shortcomings of each side of the cultural divide.

Suggestions for Implementing Constructive Dialogue

In this closing section I would like to mention briefly out of my own experience a few positive efforts at cross-pollination between the First and Two-Thirds Worlds. To be sure, there are many other avenues to be explored, but perhaps the following thoughts will stimulate new and creative means of fruitful interchange.

Probably the easiest first step is to assign biblical studies from the Two-Thirds World as readings for a particular class. In the case of Latin America, there is a growing range of material available in English by liberationist scholars and evangelicals. At the beginning the First World teacher may be aware of only a few titles, but the effort to investigate for more sources or to contact Two-Thirds World colleagues for suggestions will be a stretching exercise. Attitude is important, though. It is one thing to assign readings for novelty's sake or to use them simply to point out perceived weaknesses; it is quite another to truly interact with ideas from other peoples and places.

A second suggestion comes from an experiment that proved a great success at the seminary in Guatemala where I was teaching. Our institution offered a two-week intensive course on hermeneutics and contextualization in conjunction with a U.S. seminary. This North American seminary allowed their students to pay our tuition fee (minimal in comparison with U.S. charges), with the bulk of their expenses going to airfare, and then transfer the credits; the total expenditure by the North American students was roughly equivalent to what they would have paid for a course in their seminary. North American and Latin students took the course together, and I shared the teaching with a North American professor and also served as his translator. It was, in other words, a bilingual and bicultural experience — both for the students and the teachers. Both groups were forced to work at communicating across language barriers, theological traditions, and cultural differences. Students went to local churches together and were encouraged to spend as much informal time as possible with each other. Contextualization theory thus became a lived and shared reality that now made concrete sense both in the classroom and in worship.

Another possibility would be to invite a professor from the Two-Thirds World to teach a short course or to lecture for a term. I had the privilege a couple of years ago of teaching my Old Testament social ethics course at a seminary in Canada. The classroom time was mutually stimulating: students could hear how social issues take on particular characteristics in Latin America, while I learned from Canadian evangelical perspectives. My stay was fascinating for me culturally, too. I was there in mid-February, and the deep snow and sub-freezing temperatures were a shock to my Central American system; but I went to my first ice hockey match, met some Mounties, and worshipped at a denominational church different from my own evangelical background. Sitting with faculty and students over meals, studying the seminary catalogue, and browsing through the library shelves and journal section also broadened my understanding of evangelical education. A similar experience at a British university, where I taught for a term, expanded my vistas in other directions.

Of course, this kind of invitation can work the other way, with First World professors going to the Two-Thirds World. The financial realities of the latter, however, might require that First World teachers secure their own travel funds. If such an arrangement can be made,

156

once again the issue of attitudes becomes paramount. The First World professor must consider the experience more than just a short-term missionary excursion, where tourist activity is just as important as the classroom and where there is little or no commitment to learning from Two-Thirds World students and faculty. That is, the impact for the First World professor must go beyond the photo album to a new biblical and theological awareness of other ways of looking at Christian faith and the Scripture.

Finally, a related activity would be a faculty exchange, in which one from each context picks up the classes of the other for a specified time. One spring I did this with an Old Testament professor at a U.S. seminary. I took up his Old Testament survey course and Hebrew elective on Joshua in mid-term for two weeks, while he travelled to Guatemala to handle an Old Testament survey and my Hebrew elective on Amos. Each of us also had a chapel series. Once more, the experience for all parties was extremely positive. This North American professor is travelling again to Guatemala to give a short module on the exposition of an Old Testament book and has been asked to entertain the possibility of being considered for adjunct status.

There is so much to learn and share in a host of areas. Though the First and Two-Thirds Worlds are different in many ways, each can contribute to the development of Old Testament studies. It is my hope that this short essay might stimulate Old Testament teachers and scholars from around the globe to expand their cultural and academic horizons with graciousness and with the common goal of growing in the knowledge of the Scripture.

COMMUNICATION

Studying the Original Texts: Effective Learning and Teaching of Biblical Hebrew[1]

DAVID W. BAKER

David Baker is professor of Old Testament at Ashland Theological Seminary in Ohio. Here he reflects on the difficulties students face in learning Hebrew and how an inductive approach to teaching the language can overcome them.

In his Oxford inaugural address upon appointment to the Regius Chair of Hebrew, Professor H. G. M. Williamson addressed the place of 'Ancient Hebrew in a Modern University'.[2] A surprising and related problem that faces many of us could be entitled 'Ancient Hebrew in a Modern Seminary'. This is a surprising problem since it would be expected that, if the teaching and learning of Hebrew would find a home anywhere, it would be in this seminary environment. That this expectation is not self-evidently true is demonstrated, in North America at any rate, by the preponderance of seminaries which have done away with any language requirements, or at most only require Greek. Few indeed require sufficient contact with the language as to even approach

1. The oral nature of the original presentation has not been altered for publication.
2. H. G. M. Williamson, 'Ancient Hebrew in a Modern University', *JJS* 44 (1993), pp. 167-75.

some measure of facility in its use. I must admit that this includes my own institution which, upon my arrival nine years ago, required but one quarter of Hebrew and three of Greek, and even now only demands two quarters in each language, with a third quarter in the one of the student's choice. Even at this less than acceptable minimum, students are dissatisfied — 'Why do we need to take it at all?'[3]

Those of us who have reached some measure of competence in Hebrew and are now attempting to pass that skill on to our students are aware that the problem is not with the language itself but with the less-than-adequate exposure to it. In my first teaching experience in which we offered an intensive, six-week immersion course in Hebrew, I discovered to my chagrin that one student, who just barely made it through the course with a passing grade, had been sent by his institution in order that he might teach the course himself two weeks later. Time, not some teaching gimmick or learning tool, is what is really needed, and time is what the student does not have and what the institution, with its already overloaded curriculum, is not able to provide. Our most immediate problem as teachers is not 'How do we make more Hebrew required for our degree?', though that might be a laudable long-term project toward which to work, but rather 'How do we use the time which we now have to the best advantage of the students, whom we teach in the situations where they will be called upon to use the language?'

It is to the last verb in the preceding paragraph that special attention must be given. In order to keep the interest of the student, not to cause her to resent the language or teacher after the course is completed, and to treat our pedagogical task with integrity, we at seminaries and Bible colleges must realize that we cannot adequately teach mastery of the language in the time at our disposal, but we can and must teach and model how to use it to the level learned in preaching and teaching. Learning Hebrew for learning's sake is not an acceptable option to most of today's students, if it were ever such. In our pragmatic age, even the learning of Hebrew must be seen to have pragmatic value, and it is not

3. On the questioning, language learning, and Bible study more widely, as well as other elements of anti-intellectualism more generally, see S. J. Hafemann, 'Seminary, Subjectivity, and the Centrality of Scripture: Reflections on the Current Crisis in Evangelical Seminary Education', *JETS* 31 (1988), pp. 129-44, and recent works by Wells, Noll, and Marsden.

sufficient for this purpose to be able to do well in some examination unless it is clearly demonstrated and understood that there is a real use for the discipline after the examination has been completed.

This is very difficult to accept for those of us who have struggled ourselves toward language mastery, and have grown to love its complexities and subtleties. How much the student is missing because he does not have it all! This is true, but we need to be reminded that, if the 'all' is unattainable in the time allocated, competence and enjoyment of the part which we are able to impart are much to be preferred over opting for nothing at all. Perhaps the small sip will show enough of the delicacy of the drink to convince that further quaffs will not only be beneficial, but enjoyable. We need by any means possible to assist in getting the students intoxicated by their very first sips.

First Steps

Starting a new project is always daunting, especially if it is something with which one has had no previous experience, or, even worse, if any previous experience has been negative. This is too often the case with language learning. Students are not shy about saying, 'I took German for three years in high school, and the only thing I can remember is "Ich kann nicht Deutsch sprechen"'. They sound like they are daring us to make the new language experience any different for them, and this is the gauntlet which we must enthusiastically take up. We must want and strive to make this experience indeed a different one. We, as well as they, want them to succeed.

A seemingly insurmountable barrier arises, however, the first time the student opens the textbook and sees that, unlike previous experiences with German, Latin, or French, this time there is *nothing* recognisable. In Hebrew all things are made new. In Hebrew we are now back into our pre-school days, before we could even recognize any letters. Whether it was a pedagogically sound thing to do, I have on the first day of class issued each student with an extra-wide lined piece of writing paper in a bright colour much as one uses in kindergarten. This was to light-heartedly remind them where they are in relation to Hebrew. (I have yet to issue coloured crayons as well!)

Prior to this, however, I attempt to address some of their apprehension by beginning to demystify the consonants and vowels. To do this, I have made a set of reading exercises with an audio tape. I start with monosyllabic, consonant-vowel combinations, which are written down and I read them aloud, giving enough time for the student to repeat after me [la . . . la . . . ma . . . ma . . . la . . . ma . . . mal . . . mal . . . le . . . le . . . me . . . me . . . ma . . . me . . .]. They can thus at least begin to associate sounds which they use in English (or in my case, American) with signs with which they are totally unfamiliar. This gives them the reassurance that not all things are new — at least the sounds are familiar (until they encounter the *'ayin* and *heth!*). I provide this to pre-registered students about three weeks before the course begins, and urge them to listen to it three or four times before we meet. Students respond favourably to this aid.

Since all do not receive this material in time, I also have handouts for the first day, which we go over for at least part of the first class session. I try to make this as inductive as possible, presenting element by element the constituents of words with which they are already familiar (*e.g., 'shalom'*, 'Bethlehem', 'Jerusalem'), though also some unfamiliar words as well (*e.g., melek/malkah, seneh*). I here seek to introduce the student to every consonant and vowel form, including final forms and those where a *dagesh lene* makes a difference in modern Israeli pronunciation, which I seek to approximate in my teaching. This is, of course, a foundational and vital step since all else in the course is dependent on this recognition of the basic building blocks of the language.

Some students have no trouble with this step, while others find it more challenging. There is a test available which can provide some prediction as to whether this might be a problem. It is the Modern Language Aptitude Test, and is available through the Psychological Corporation.[4] Although designed for modern language learning, it is applicable in some of its sections to ancient or non-spoken languages as well. The test has been used for over thirty years by Professor George Landes and colleagues at Union Theological Seminary in New York to address three problem areas: (1) how to ascertain what my students'

---

4. 'Modern Language Aptitude Test', J. B. Carroll and S. M. Sapon, 1959, available through The Psychology Corporation, P.O. Box 839954, San Antonio, TX 78283-3954, Fax 800-232-1223.

language-learning difficulties might be at the earliest possible moment, and then how to deal with them effectively; (2) how to determine the language-learning aptitudes of my students, and on the basis of that knowledge, be able to predict how successful they might or might not be in mastering a biblical language; (3) how to assure students whose previous language-learning experience had been more negative than positive that this did not necessarily mean that their native ability at language learning was impaired, and thus encourage them to enrol in a biblical language course with some prospect of a favourable outcome.[5]

The first two sections of the test deal with auditory comprehension and sound-symbol association, and so are most useful for spoken languages. The third section is more directly related to our problem. Landes describes 'the third part of their test, "Spelling Clues", in which students are asked mentally to pronounce words that are spelled largely only with consonants . . . , which would sound like a familiar word whose definition was provided by a synonym to be selected from among five choices. This exercise, which was to be done very rapidly (fifty within five minutes), tested the student's ability to correlate sounds with meanings, and in my experience, the score attained was an excellent indicator of how well the student would be able to pronounce and translate Hebrew. In fact, it was on the basis of the scores from this part that I was able to predict in advance which students would be able to read Hebrew well and which would have more difficulty with this.'[6] Since I only recently heard of the test, I have not had the opportunity to use it myself.

In light of predicted or actual problems in this initial step of letter recognition, we have available extra tutorial assistance for students who ask for it. Each class has a student tutorial assistant who handles group tutorials. Since the problem at issue is most often best addressed one-to-one, we also try to have a larger group of tutors upon which to call for help. One source of these tutors is members of Eta Beta Rho, the National Honor Society of Students of Hebrew Language and Literature, which

---

5. G. M. Landes and S. L. Cook, 'Predicting the Successful Learning of Hebrew or Greek: Results from a Thirty-Year Study', a paper presented before the National Association of the Professors of Hebrew at their annual meeting in conjunction with the Society of Biblical Literature and American Academy of Religion at Chicago in November, 1994.

6. Landes and Cook, 'Predicting', pp. 4-6.

has a chapter at Ashland Seminary.[7] These tutors, who are requested to donate an hour per week of their time, not only get the satisfaction of helping others, but also reinforce their own understanding of Hebrew since they have to be able to articulate and explain concepts to someone else. They are available to the students throughout the course.

Even at this preliminary sign-recognition phase I introduce students to some of the phonetic rules which will become important to them later. The first time we encounter a phenomenon, I explain it and try to have a short phrase for them to hold on to, *e.g.*, for *dageshes*, 'no preceding vowel sound, *dagesh lene* or "light *dagesh*"; preceding vowel sound, *dagesh forte* or "heavy *dagesh*" '. These phrases are repeated each time we run across the phenomenon so the students are soon repeating them by rote. I stress at our first encounter that they do not have to memorize these rules the first, or even the fifth, time we run across them. They must understand the rule, but remembering them comes from the repetition. These 'rules' can also be cumulative, as when noting the two different types of *sheva*. As we run across them, I teach the rules for vocal *sheva* in the following order:

Rule 1 — Letter 1 (under the first letter of a word);
Rule 2 — Second of two (*shevas* in a row);
Rule 3 — Long vowel (immediately following a long vowel);
Rule 4 — *Dagesh* (under a letter having a *dagesh*).[8]

---

7. The Honor Society is under the auspices of the National Association of the Professors of Hebrew, and has as its stated purpose: 'To recognize outstanding attainments in the study of Hebrew language and literature, to stimulate study and research in this field, and to promote an understanding and appreciation of the culture of Israel'. There are currently some twenty chapters in Canada and the U.S. Information on forming a chapter, along with a sample constitution, is available from me as the Co-ordinator of the Society, 910 Center St., Ashland, OH 44805, USA.

8. This could also be a place to introduce the use of Hebrew letters as numbers, since the Hebrew letters and their order provide the useful mnemonic:

Aleph (= 1) — Under letter 1 of word;
Beth (= 2) — Second of two;
Gimel — After long (Gadol) vowel;
Daleth — Dagesh

One could also introduce the fifth rule, which is rare enough not usually to be met in an introductory course: He — Hashva'ah ('resemblance, comparison') — between two occurrences of the same letter.

When the students start to smile, or groan, at the umpteenth repetition ` of the same rule in the same words, I point out that the feeling is like that of recognition of an old friend, which is, after all, the ultimate goal for every aspect of learning a language: that in each nuance it may be experienced as an old friend. That which was recently so completely strange and foreign is now fitting like an old slipper.

At this stage I need to express my preference for a more inductive form of Hebrew pedagogy such as that used in the texts of Sawyer, Kittel, and, more idiosyncratically, LaSor, over a more deductive form such as found in the texts by Weingreen, Lambdin, Seow, or Kelley,[9] all of which, except the latter, I have used for teaching texts. This allows not only the psychological boost to the student of actually reading biblical sections from day one,[10] showing at least one practical benefit of studying Hebrew, because they can read some 'real Bible'. It allows the 'rules' to be presented as they are encountered, and as often as they are encountered, in a way which seems less threatening than having to attempt to master rules prior to encountering significant texts in which they are used.[11]

There are also some rules which need not be learned in an inductive approach, though they are often taught there anyway. For example, why should a student learn which letters can take a *dagesh lene*? If she learns when to recognize *lene* or *forte* through the lack of a preceding vowel sound, or its presence, why is it really necessary that the *begad kefat* letters be learned as a special group?

9. J. F. A. Sawyer, *A Modern Introduction to Biblical Hebrew* (Stocksfield: Oriel, 1976); B. P. Kittel, V. Hoffer, R. A. Wright, *Biblical Hebrew: A Text and Workbook* (New Haven: Yale, 1989); T. O. Lambdin, *Introduction to Biblical Hebrew* (New York: Scribners, 1971; London: DLT, 1973); W. S. LaSor, *Handbook of Biblical Hebrew* (Grand Rapids: Eerdmans, 1978); J. Weingreen, *A Practical Grammar for Classical Hebrew*, 2nd ed. (Oxford: Clarendon, 1959); C. L. Seow, *A Grammar for Biblical Hebrew* (Nashville: Abingdon, 1987); P. H. Kelley, *Biblical Hebrew: An Introductory Grammar* (Grand Rapids: Eerdmans, 1992), p. 11.

10. It is always refreshing to see students' responses after the first chapter in the Kittel text, which explains *vayo'mer YHWH*, when the authors note, 'You now know about 4% of the Hebrew Bible's vocabulary' (*op cit.*, p. 8).

11. This is admittedly an oversimplification of both approaches, and of the above textbooks, since most are various combinations of both approaches. This is also simply a personal preference, since studies mentioned below seem to indicate that there is no statistically significant difference in performance between students trained in either of the two styles. For an alternative method of teaching Hebrew, see the appropriate section in this volume by R. S. Hess.

Further Stages

My emphasis on the ability to use Hebrew being more important than knowing it in its minutest detail has led me to expect less memorization of forms than I had to master myself, or than I am at times satisfied with, though my students are kind enough to encourage me to try to overcome my obsessive-compulsive desire to enforce memorization of paradigm after paradigm. I teach them how to use a lexicon in about the fifth week of class, BDB being the lexicon of choice at the moment, but encourage them to look at the cross-references given there (explaining that the cross-reference abbreviation v. [vide] means 'you twit, you should be looking up this word under root X on p. Y).[12] After some practice, they get to be called names less and less frequently.

I do require vocabulary memorization, and test them on it weekly.[13] Though they can use the lexicon, even in ordinary test situations, memorization is to show them that a few moments learning a word can alleviate numerous times having to look up that same word. I suppose that a more strictly inductive method would have them look it up enough times that frustration drove them to memorize it on their own. Memorization is thus like giving the medicine which is good for them, even if they do not want to take it.[14] Grammar and translation tests are structured in such a way that a lexicon can be used to advantage to use a word previously learned which has slipped the student's memory, or one not yet encountered. If students attempt to use the dictionary to look up every word, not having memorized vocabulary at all, they will have to leave the majority of the work untranslated, since it is too long to look up every word.

12. I require the Hendrickson reprint of BDB (F. Brown, S. Driver, C. Briggs, *Brown-Driver-Briggs Hebrew-English Lexicon* [Peabody, MA: Hendrickson, 1979]) because it has not only the added features of Strong's numbers, cross-references to specific pages, and an index of words in Strong's order, but it is also significantly cheaper than the Oxford University Press edition. Another useable dictionary for the introductory levels is Karl Feyerabend, *Langenscheidt's Pocket Hebrew Dictionary to the Old Testament* (Munich: Langenscheidt, n.d.).

13. Kittel, the text I am currently using, goes through the most common 425 Hebrew words.

14. One year an adjunct professor, teaching Hebrew for the first time, did not require any vocabulary memorization. The better students found this totally unsatisfactory and made their consternation felt in no uncertain terms.

I also require memorizing three paradigms, though I am still unsure of the optimum minimum. They must learn the Qal perfect and imperfect for the strong verb. As we encounter each form in the reading, I also have them develop the paradigm for the pronominal suffixes on nouns and prepositions, either using the preposition *le* or the direct object indicator as the paradigm. By the time it is about half complete, I fill in the remaining slots for them and have them memorize it.

Rather than requiring a new paradigm for each new stem and/or weak form, I note modifications on the Qal for them to watch for. This is supplemented by what I call a 'Prefix vowel chart' which we complete as we encounter each new prefix/imperfect form. I provide four sheets of paper for this chart, each headed respectively 'A', 'I', 'O', and ':' [sheva]. I use the *'yod'* as the typical prefix, since it is the first we encounter in the text, and is also the most frequent in the Masoretic Text. I divide each sheet into as many vowels as there are for each heading class, *e.g.*, on the 'A' page I have sections lined off with pre-printed *yod-kamatz*, *yod-patah*, and *yod-hataf-patah*. As we encounter each new imperfect form, I have them enter a note under the appropriate consonant-vowel combination. The first verb we read is *vayo'mer*, so in the top section of the 'O' page, beside *yod-holem* I have them write 'Qal 1-*'alef*, so they can find assistance next time they encounter such a form.

Some prefix vowels will have several possible identifications, *e.g.*, Qal hollows and Hifil hollows share the same vowel, so other clues of stem identification which they learn (a Hifil will have a *heh* prefixed and/or an 'I' class vowel before the last root letter) can then come into play to provide sharper discrimination. I allow them to use the Prefix vowel chart (PVC) in exams, but frequency of use naturally weans them off it for the more common forms since they soon become familiar. The chart is particularly helpful when there is an elided radical or two.

Morphological Analysis

Especially toward the beginning of the learning process, I require students to approach logically each word, noting and explaining each consonant and vowel, moving from right to left in the word. Later it might be more productive to move from left to right, but the discipline of systematic analysis must be grasped. They are also encouraged to observe combinations which are unambiguous and morphologically rich. For example, a *vav* of any kind at the beginning of the word will most likely be some form of the conjunction. If it is in the combination *vav + patah + dagesh*, it can only be one thing, a *vav*-consecutive/conversive, and this unambiguous observation provides much useful information: (1) the word will be a verb, (2) it will be translated as a completed action, usually by an English past, (3) it is imperfect/prefix in form, (4) it will be preceded by 'and, but, then'. As soon as the student sees item 3, she should automatically reach for the PVC where further information will be available. The other unambiguous form is a final *tsere-yod* combination which can only be a masculine plural construct nominal.

As the course progresses, I urge the student to start morphological analysis from whichever end of the word has least immediate ambiguity. An initial *'heh'* has so many possible functions (definite article, interrogative, initial root letter, Hifil, Hofal, Hitpael, Nifal), that it is usually easier to start at the back of the word. The analysis process involves noting all possibilities for identification of a consonant or vowel, and eliminating as many as possible when the next identification is made. One analyzes the morphological elements toward the centre until a letter which is unambiguously a root letter is encountered, at which time analysis moves to the other end of the word. Thus, for many verbs, by the time the root letters are reached, the verb has been completely analyzed.

Study of Language Learning

Previously we mentioned the Modern Language Aptitude Test used with some success at Union Theological Seminary. Two parts of it not mentioned heretofore, but which have some value in predicting success in Hebrew, are sections concerning 'Words in Sentences', the understanding of syntax, and 'Paired Associates', testing rote memory, which is necessary for vocabulary learning. These can be useful for indicating possible or probable areas of concern, so the student may be forewarned and be ready to accept special tutelage in the problem areas.

At Ashland Theological Seminary over the last half decade we have been studying the outcomes of our Hebrew courses in the light of a number of variables.[15] Our research has therefore looked at the other end of the learning process than that at Union. We determined through questionnaire and the student's academic file the following elements: age, race, marital/family status (single, married, widowed, divorced, children at home, children away from home), denomination, current or intended occupation, previous occupation, previous language study, tutorial attendance, personality type (using the Myers-Briggs or Kiersey-Bates personality inventory), and grade point average. We then administered a common portion of the final exam for each class during this period (this portion was not returned to the student, so it could not be passed on to subsequent students). These were administered in the same way the teacher ordinarily gave exams, with the same tools available for student consultation which they were accustomed to use in taking tests. Through this we were able to determine the effects of differences in pedagogical approach in such areas as inductive versus deductive method and class meeting times and frequency (1 day a week in 3 hour sessions/2 times a week in 1.5 hour sessions both over 22 weeks; summer intensive, 5 hours a day for 5 weeks).

There were only two statistically significant factors determined from the study: (1) Those previously or currently involved in pastoral ministry did better than those who were not so involved, and (2) the lower end of the student grades got appreciably lower after students reached age forty. This corresponds to some of Union's findings. Since neither of these variables is one over which we are able to have much control, we tried to determine why these variables existed. We hypothesize that those in ministry are able to see an immediate and practical use for their language study and so motivate themselves toward study, a suggestion we made at the outset of this paper. It also looks like older folks have a harder time with rote memorization. The latter of these is also indicated through the MLAT.

The next step, which we will inaugurate soon, is to determine what may assist in these two problem areas. Tutors should continue to provide assistance, especially for our older students, as will some software programmes for review and drill. It is especially in this last area

15. Involved in the study have been Dr. Bill Arnold and Dr. David Weyrick (who has done the statistical analysis for our study).

where I solicit comments and suggestions from colleagues as to methods or tools which they and their students find beneficial not only for language learning, but also for retention and application.

One tool I have found of some use for this latter purpose is a work by Heinrich Bitzer which has brief daily readings in Hebrew and Greek.[16] I am preparing another such tool in which the pastor and student may spend some of their devotional time in the Hebrew and Greek texts,[17] so not only keeping their skills honed but, we hope, simultaneously deepening their walk with God, which is the ultimate goal of all study of God's Word.

16. H. Bitzer, *Light on the Path: Daily Readings in Hebrew and Greek,* vol. 1 (Grand Rapids: Baker, 1982).

17. This work, co-authored by Elaine Heath, will provide weekly excerpts from a devotional classic, daily readings from the Hebrew and Greek testaments, and a daily devotional thought and prayer. The first publication of it will be in electronic, computer format by Baker Book House (Baker Bytes) in conjunction with Logos Research Systems. The user may call up translations of the passages if necessary, as well as a morphological analysis of each word in the daily readings. A printed copy of the work will appear soon thereafter.

'Let the Wise Listen and Add to Their Learning': Modern Education and an Ancient Book

CLIVE LAWLESS

Clive Lawless is Professor of Educational Technology, Institute of Educational Technology at the Open University, the largest university in the U.K. Out of his experience of monitoring a wide variety of arts and science courses for their pedagogical integrity, he reviews the general principles of learning and applies them to some of the essays in this volume.

How Do People Learn?

'How do people learn?', 'What are the determinants of learning?', 'How can we facilitate learning?' — these are the questions on which this essay focuses with particular emphasis on 'Learning the Old Testament'. The stress is on learning rather than 'Educational Methods'. Learning is the end of teaching; educational methods are the means, or part of the means.

'How do people learn?' (and we must always remember that students are just people!). Theories which seek to explain learning have gone through three broad stages during the twentieth century. From the 1920s to 1950s behaviourist views were dominant, based on extrapolating lessons for human learning from rats performing tasks in mazes and pigeons pecking lights.[1] Behaviourist theories emphasized the development of stimulus response relationships as the foundation of learning and deliberately rejected any consideration of the intellectual processes involved. Such views have been superseded as they have been found inadequate to explain the complexities of human learning, beyond the most basic tasks. But their application to teaching has left a legacy of the effectiveness of carefully structuring information, or packaging it in pieces which learners could manage, of the value of analyzing students' responses to instruction and the important role of feedback in learning.

Within the past thirty or fifty years the emphasis in learning theory has turned to cognitive models.[2] Such models stress the importance of existing knowledge and the way it is organised into structures with associated skills as determinants of learning. Cognitive models stress the importance of the way in which information is processed in the mind by relating new information to existing knowledge and storing the resultant 'fused' information in memory. Although a more satisfying model of learning than behaviourism, in that it seeks to make clear the mental processes involved in learning, it is still rather mechanistic, being modelled on the ways in which computers handle information. Cognitive models of learning have been influential on teaching design with their stress on enabling students to link new knowledge with existing knowledge, in developing rich links between concepts to build up knowledge structures in such ways as they can be used for problem solving.

More recently constructivist views of learning have become influential. Human beings are seen as constantly seeking to develop meanings and to make sense of the information they receive from the environment and construct meaning by relating it to existing knowledge.[3] Though developed from cognitive models and sharing many of their features, the constructivist view takes into account the personal

1. E. L. Thorndike, *The Psychology of Arithmetic* (New York: Macmillan, 1922); B. F. Skinner, 'The Science of Learning and the Art of Teaching', *Harvard Educational Review* 24, 2 (1954), pp. 86-97.

2. R. E. Meyer, *The Promise of Cognitive Psychology* (San Francisco: W. H. Freeman, 1981).

3. R. Driver and V. Oldham, 'A Constructivist Approach to Curriculum Development in Science', *Studies in Science Education* 13 (1986), pp. 105-22.

and personality features of the individual such as intents, beliefs, and emotions.

From a biblical standpoint each of these models of learning has its faults. Behaviourism takes a mechanistic view of human beings, in which behaviour is conditioned by the environment. Cognitive and information processing views, if pushed too far, are similarly mechanistic. This emphasis is incompatible with the biblical view of men and women as being made in the likeness of God, as possessing decision-making capabilities and free will. The constructivist model allows for this to some extent, but there is a danger that it assumes a relativist view of truth. All constructions of meaning are personal and therefore, if this view is taken too far, can be seen as being of equal worth. Without delving into epistemological issues surrounding the question of the objectivity of knowledge, if we base our teaching on a constructivist position we need to be clear that we seek to enable students to construct meaning which is in accord with biblical truth.

What Are the Determinants of Learning?

Existing Knowledge

The most important single factor influencing learning is what the learner already knows. Ascertain this and teach him accordingly.[4]

True though this is, it is more than what a student 'knows', important though that is, but the whole package of relevant past experience that determines or influences learning. (Note that these questions represent arbitrary divisions between interrelated elements.) The most potent influence on what students, or anyone else for that matter, learn is what they bring to the learning situation. Learning involves taking in new information and striving to create new meaning. Learning in this sense is taking place all the time, but a 'learning situation' is a formal occasion usually at school, college or university, specifically designed to produce learning. Students bring their understanding of concepts and their re-

4. D. P. Ausubel, *Educational Psychology: A Cognitive View* (New York: Holt, Rhinehart and Winston, 1968).

lationships ('knowledge structures') and their cognitive skills into each learning situation. The importance of the influence of students' prior knowledge, or lack of it, is brought out in Gordon Wenham's chapter when he describes 'the broader range of students', 'by and large they are ignorant of the Old Testament and its contents' and he regrets their ignorance of Sarah and Rebekah, Rachel and Leah. Similarly Paul Barker highlights the 'widespread ignorance of the Old Testament' among his university students. Wenham brings out the importance of this: 'a student coming to the Bible for the first time cannot be expected to read the prophets on his own and make sense of it'. Prior knowledge, or lack of it, is crucial to what can be learned.

Research has shown that students who have done well in conventional examinations and tests often lack adequate structures to take on new knowledge and to use knowledge to solve problems.[5] My own research showed that students studying a popular and apparently successful unit in an Open University history of science course failed to develop concept structures based around the central concept of the section and their understanding of the links between concepts was, for some students, at a relatively low level.[6] There is always the danger for academics who are researching in their discipline and are involved with theoretical models of its structure, that we fail to realise that students may have difficulties in making a first entry into this discourse. What is needed is often a straightforward account of the structure and approach, possibly at a level that might be considered below higher education. For example, Paul Barker points out the usefulness of a basic text such as *How to Read the Bible for All Its Worth*[7] in enabling students to come to terms with the concept of biblical genres.

5. H. S. Becker, B. Geer, and E. C. Hughes, *Making the Grade: The Academic Side of College Life* (New York: Wiley, 1968); B. Johansson, F. Marton, and L. Svensson, 'An Approach to Describing Learning as Change between Qualitatively Different Conceptions', in L. H. T. West and A. L. Pines, *Cognitive Structure and Conceptual Change* (New York: Academic Press, 1985).

6. C. Lawless, 1994.

7. G. D. Fee and D. Stuart, *How to Read the Bible for All Its Worth* (London: Scripture Union, 1994).

General Learning Skills

Secondly students bring in a level of general study skills. Their ability to learn from texts, in lectures and from other media, their ability to make notes, to write assignments and reports are all important. I have no doubt that all of you set reading assignments, but I wonder if you are aware of their size (word count), their level of difficulty, how they relate to students' reading abilities, and therefore, how long it will take students to read them. Excessive workload is a major cause of students developing poor learning habits, leading to concentration on facts rather than meaning.[8]

Intents, Beliefs, and Emotions

If we take the constructivist position that the whole personality influences how and what we learn, the issue of purpose arises. 'Why am I taking this course?', 'Why am I studying this particular section or piece of work?' The question also arises whether work is valued for itself, for example, as against something that has to be done for assessment purposes only. An attitude that aims simply at surviving a course, getting as good a qualification as possible with minimum effort, will seriously affect the way that study is carried out! In an area such as Old Testament studies, personal belief and commitment will play a major part in influencing attitudes to and patterns of study. Richard Hess stresses the importance of the spiritual element in theological college study: '. . . the spiritual life of the lecturer and the students will have an inevitable impact on how the Old Testament is appropriated for ministry'. This is similarly brought out by Wenham's description of the attitudes of his students to the Old Testament as 'dubious of its value or interest'. Barker brings out a similar point in his comparison of students at theological college and at a secular university.

The influence of emotions can range from positive or negative reactions to members of staff and fellow students, to quite deep trauma from past educational experiences. For many, if not most, people school

8. E. Chambers, 'Work-Load and the Quality of Student Learning', *Studies in Higher Education* 17, 2 (1992), pp. 141-53.

has been a difficult experience, more marked by failure than success. Their impression of learning and their capacity to learn is distinctly negative. Even apparently well qualified and motivated students often harbour negative recollections of school, which influences their higher studies. Language learning experience can often be negative, for example, as David Baker points out. Hence the importance of motivating students, the need as Wenham puts it to 'to engage interest deeply' through looking at Old Testament marriage and family life and comparing them with ours.

Intellectual Development

Academic work at the higher education and theological college level requires a high degree of intellectual development. In a study lasting over twenty years at the Bureau of Study Counsel, Harvard University,[9] William Perry found that students' progress in improving their learning skills was largely dependent on what he described as the state of intellectual development they had reached. He identified nine dimensions from simple dualism (all situations and learning seen in terms of right or wrong answers) to commitment (acceptance of change and a readiness to make commitment and re-commitment). Perry's work is detailed and fascinating and I am hesitant about distilling it into a short summary. For practical purposes I will summarize it into three broad stages, *dualism* (simple right and wrong answers), *relativism* (acceptance of alternative views but with the proviso that the right one will be demonstrated), and *commitment* (accepting alternative views, judging or assessing them according to criteria, leading to a personal commitment). I suggest that many problems that students encounter in higher education are related to their level of intellectual development not being equal to the demands of a learning task.

This concept of intellectual development presents a challenge for those engaged in biblical studies. There is a starting point which R. Hess describes as '. . . a certain value and importance is placed on the Old Testament as a source of spiritual direction in all matters of faith and

9. W. G. Perry, *Forms of Intellectual and Ethical Development in the College Years* (New York: Holt, Rhinehart and Winston, 1970).

life'. Authority and truth are important issues. The concept of commitment remains important in seeking to enable students to come to a personal commitment to the Old Testament as 'a source of spiritual direction' rather than just accepting it because they have been told by someone else. Only if there is personal commitment based on thought and judgement can it mean anything.

Let me illustrate this from my own experience as a history tutor at Open University summer schools. Open University history courses are heavily based on students' use of primary source documents. Hence it is important for students right from the beginning of their studies to be able to identify primary sources, analyze them, and use them. Running seminars at summer school, roughly two thirds of the way through the foundation course, I have come across students who ask, 'why do we have to cope with all these primary sources, why doesn't the course tell us what the answer is; then we can learn it.' These students, a small minority it is true, appear not to have reached the level of intellectual development required to cope with alternative views and the importance of developing personal meaning.

Approach to Learning

These elements can be brought together in what has been identified as the learner's approach to learning.[10] In any learning situation students face tasks to carry out and problems to solve if they are to learn effectively. How they perform will depend not only on their having the necessary skills and information to perform the task, but on perceiving what knowledge and skills are relevant to a particular task. Ramsden describes the concept of the approach to learning as

> one of the most influential concepts to have emerged from research into teaching and learning in higher education during the last 15 years. . . . It is unquestionably a key concept in teaching and learning.[11]

10. F. Marton and R. Saljo, 'Approaches to Learning', in F. Marton, D. Hounsell, and N. Entwistle (eds.), *The Experience of Learning* (Edinburgh: Scottish Academic Press, 1984).

11. P. Ramsden, *Learning to Teach in Higher Education* (London: Routledge, 1992).

This research has identified two basic positions or approaches that students adopt to learning tasks, 'deep processing' and 'surface processing'. Broadly speaking 'deep processing' concentrates on meaning, and 'surface processing' concentrates on the form of the book, lecture, or other learning experience. The best way I can explain this is to illustrate this with quotations from students' responses to research carried out by my colleague, Professor Diana Laurillard.[12] See if you can identify which illustrate deep and which illustrate surface processing.

A Geography (essay preparation)

I read it very slowly, trying to concentrate on what it means, what the actual passage means. Obviously I've read the quotations a few times and I've got it in my mind what they mean. There's a lot of meaning behind it. You really have to get into it and take every passage, every sentence and try to really think, 'Well, what does this mean?' You mustn't regurgitate what David is saying, because that's not the idea of the exercise. I suppose it's really original ideas in this one, getting it all together.

B Computer studies (lecture notes, revision)

Learning this course is getting enough facts so that you can write something relevant in the exam. You've got enough information so you can write an essay on it. What I do is learn certain headings. In the exam I can go: 'Introduction' and I'll 'look' at the next heading, and I know what I've got to write about without really thinking about it really. I know the facts about it. I go to the next heading and regurgitate.

C Physics (exam revision)

Formulae. You just have to go into the exam with as many formulae as possible. So you must learn those parrot-fashion. And approaches to the way you write out problems, techniques involved in maths, I seem to remember these just sort of one day or two.

12. D. Laurillard, 'Learning from Problem-Solving', in Marton, Hounsell, and Entwistle (eds.), *The Experience of Learning*.

Deep Approach

Intention to understand. Student maintains structure of task

Focus on 'what is signified' (*e.g.*, the author's argument, or the concepts applicable to solving the problem).

Relate previous knowledge to new knowledge

Relate knowledge from different courses

Relate theoretical ideas to everyday experience

Relate and distinguish evidence and argument

Organise and structure content into a coherent whole

Internal emphasis — making reality more intelligible

Surface Approach

Intention only to complete task requirements. Student distorts structure of task

Focus on 'the signs' (*e.g.*, the words and sentences of the text, or unthinkingly on the formula needed to solve the problem)

Focus on unrelated parts of the task

Memorise information for assessments

Associate facts and concepts unreflectively

Fail to distinguish principles from examples

Treat the task as an external imposition

External emphasis: demands of assessments, knowledge cut off from everyday reality.

D Physics (practical work)

I'm trying to imagine what the experiment is talking about, in a physical sense, sort of get the picture of what it's about. This one says an ultra-violet lamp emits one watt of power; it says calculate the energy falling on a square centimetre per second. I'm just thinking of the light and the way it spreads out, so therefore I know it's the inverse square law.

E Engineering (problem solving)

I knew how I'd do it from looking at it; it practically tells you what equation to use. You just have to bash the numbers out. I

181

knew how to do it before I started so I didn't get anything out of it. There's not really any thinking. You just need to know what you need to solve the problem. I read through the relevant notes, but not much because you don't need to look at the system.

F Engineering (problem solving)

. It's an operation research exercise, a programme to find a minimum point on a curve. First I had to decide on the criteria of how to approach it, then drew a flow diagram, and checked through each stage. You have to think about it and understand it first. I used my knowledge of O.R. design of starting with one point, testing it and judging the next move. I try to work through logically. . . . I chose this problem because it was more applied, more realistic.

As you probably identified, A, D, and F demonstrate a deep approach and B, C, and E a surface approach. Ramsden contrasts the two approaches.[13]

Central to the deep approach is the building up of knowledge or conceptual structure. The problem in teaching is to move away from providing students with a structure to the position where they develop structures for themselves. Wenham's introductory course, 'Making Sense of the Old Testament', aims at doing just this, providing a structure for students to use as they build their knowledge.

While clearly deep processing is usually desirable, it is not always the most appropriate. Writing down and reading aloud monosyllabic consonant-vowel combinations in learning Hebrew, which David Baker describes, seems an excellent example where surface processing, even rote learning, is appropriate. Scientists have to learn formulae, but it is a detail in their learning; it does not represent the way they think!

How Can We Facilitate Learning?

At this stage I would like to make an apology and then withdraw it! I apologise for the fact that my paper was not ready in time to be circu-

13. P. Ramsden, *Learning to Teach*, p. 46.

lated with the other conference papers. But I withdraw that apology because when I received the papers I read them with a sense of excitement. It led me to restructure the paper. Indeed I wondered whether it was worth giving a paper at all. In an over-used cliché, I had a strong feeling of 'preaching to the converted'! The problem of giving what I call a 'cold' lecture, a lecture to a group who I did not know, fell away. My respect for what is being done has, I hope, been clear from the references I have made to the teaching described in the conference papers.

In looking at how learning can be facilitated, how students can be enabled to learn, I want to bring together the thrust of what I have been saying and focus on how it can work in practice. Firstly, though, I want to look in brief at what we conventionally regard as 'teaching'.

So far my focus has been on what students bring to the learning situation. This is extremely influential in determining how and what they learn; it is not, of course, the whole story. The other input into any formal learning situation is that from the teacher, whether direct in a face-to-face situation or indirect in a distance or open learning situation. As a teacher, what is your view of how learners learn? What is your view of your role? As Ramsden points out, 'To teach is to make an assumption about what and how the student learns'.[14]

First and most obvious is the role as conveyor of information. Many of you and I are called 'lecturers', so the assumption is that we teach by lecturing, haranguing large numbers of students in hour-long monologues! I recognise that this is a caricature! Nevertheless, I fear, the image and to some extent the reality persist. Such an approach sees students as sponges soaking up knowledge or to use a more modern analogy, as video cameras faithfully recording all that is placed before them!

A better model is to see the teacher's role as a facilitator of learning. In saying this I am aware that I am entering a minefield because this concept is often taken as meaning that children, usually in primary school, are left to their own devices, and it is contrasted with traditional teaching, which it is assumed was 'real teaching'. So let me make it clear that I in no way discount the importance of teaching subject matter in its own right and of ensuring that it is made available to students.

14. P. Ramsden, *Learning to Teach*, p. 6.

My position is knowledge oriented. Developing learning skills, which is my focus, can only take place when students are learning something.

Aims

Effective teaching should show clarity, coherence or consistency, and commitment. Starting with the aims for courses, most of us would include in our aims such statements to the effect that students are expected to be able to 'analyze critically', 'develop intellectual and imaginative powers', 'identify relationships', 'comprehend principles', 'demonstrate an enquiring and analytical approach'.

Such aims are the stuff of academic study, but the challenge is to be clear about what they mean, to be able to articulate what students will be doing when they are demonstrating these skills. The teacher's clarity about the aims of the course must be conveyed to the student. This surely is what Gordon Wenham is after when he has his students acting Old Testament ritual: he is clarifying to students what the aims of the course mean. High-sounding aims should be real and not just attractive wallpaper for the course.

Information

Traditionally the responsibility of the teacher is to provide information on the subject matter which students have to learn. I prefer the term 'making information available', since it does not pre-judge the method to be used. I make no apology for my opinion that the traditional formal lecture is not an efficient way of conveying information to students. It runs the risk of fulfilling the old adage of information going from the notes of the lecturer to the notes of the student without going through the head of either! This is not to decry the role of the well-structured, well-illustrated lecture in bringing together disparate aspects of knowledge or of providing an underlying explanation. Such lectures can have more effect if they are video-recorded and made available afterwards, as my son experienced when studying mechanical engineering at the University of Hertfordshire. The criteria would be the most effective way of giving students access to information, which could include audio-vision (sound and text/illustration) — a medium of which I am very fond because of its relatively low cost and ease of production. Books, of course, must play a large part as sources of information. Care is needed in prescribing reading because nothing is more destructive of deep processing, of learning for understanding, than excessive workload. For any reading assignment, as well as ensuring that the source is available, questions on how many words, level of difficulty, time it will take, need to be asked.

Above all information needs to be provided so that students can develop structures of the subject matter so that their learning is effective. There is a tension here between how much structure we give to students and how much we seek to enable students to develop their own personal structures. The importance of creating structure for learning cannot be over-emphasized. My own study of the Old Testament has been greatly enriched by the structural approach of such books as *Themes in Old Testament Theology*[15] and *Plot and Purpose in the Old Testament*.[16] Even broad themes can provide illumination on what can seem impenetrable to beginning students. A fine example comes from *The Faith of Israel*,[17] in the section on Leviticus: 'Two dominant threads run through the fabric of the book of Leviticus . . . the goal of holiness for Israel and the need for forgiveness'. The level and means by which this is done, will depend on the needs of particular groups of students but essentially it involves, as Hess concludes, 'a gradual development of difficulty in teaching and skills'. It is important for students to develop a coherent structure across the range of their studies.

As Hess puts it, '. . . the study of the Old Testament will inform and be informed by other disciplines', and Barker points out, '. . . the teaching of the OT must be integrated with the NT'. This is more difficult when modular structures with wide student choice are the norm so that students starting a course will have previously studied a variety of modules. This makes it even more crucial that they develop the ability to make links and create structures for themselves. All of these activities enable students to build up their skills.

15. W. Dyrness, *Themes in Old Testament Theology* (Exeter: Paternoster, 1979).
16. E. A. Martens, *Plot and Purpose in the Old Testament* (Leicester: InterVarsity Press, 1981).
17. W. J. Dumbrell, *The Faith of Israel* (Leicester: InterVarsity Press, 1989), p. 40.

Activities

Developing understanding requires more than providing information. Overt activities, provided by seminars, tutorials, laboratory sessions, and other practical sessions and through assignments, are the main means for this. Covert, mental activities occur, or should occur, all the time. Activities need to be focused on the intellectual skills set out in the aims; there needs to be a coherence and consistency which is apparent to students. Developing understanding is illustrated by Wenham's statement that 'ritual needs to be acted out rather than just read' and by his use of student-assessed seminars. Baker stresses the importance of *using* the language being learned. Hess believes that 'the most important application is that of the interpretation of the biblical text'; he emphasizes 'acquisition of methods used in modern interpretation of the text' and uses 'student presentations of their research in small groups'. Barker similarly is seeking to develop students' skills when he gets them to write expository notes.

Assessment

Research has shown that the most significant determinant of students' learning is their perception of the demands of the assessment system.[18] Here again clarity of purpose and consistency with aims and teaching are essential. If students perceive that rote learning is all that is needed, they will not be concerned to develop their deep understanding.

Assignments and examinations need to be of such a kind that they stimulate deep processing leading to learning for understanding. I note with interest that the conference papers give little space to the issue of assessment. Given its crucial importance it might be the focus of a later conference.

18. Becker *et al., Making the Grade*; B. R. Snyder, *The Hidden Curriculum* (New York: Knopf, 1971); C. M. L. Miller and M. Parlett, *Up to the Mark: A Study of the Examination Game* (London: Society for Research into Higher Education, 1974).

Feedback

Commitment to learning requires that students are given feedback on their performance. This occurs both informally and formally. Students receive feedback when their assignments are handed back and I have a feeling that both the nature of the feedback and the use that students make of it are neglected aspects of teaching. Feedback can vary from the instant verbal response to my essays that I received at Oxford nearly forty years ago to a short phrase on an essay handed back a term late. I suggest that feedback on performance needs to be focused on relating student performance to the aims of the course and it should be rapidly available. Students should be encouraged to use feedback as a serious learning experience. What is required is a shared commitment to learning between student and teacher.

It is clear from the conference papers that the teaching of the Old Testament, which they describe, is innovative and imaginative. There is no doubt in my mind that the elements of teaching are taken seriously, providing subject matter knowledge, setting up learning activities, setting assignments, and providing feedback. At the Open University our equivalent actions are focused on the design of our teaching materials. Teaching texts, still the main medium, are carefully put together, integrating different media, introducing new material so that students can relate it to existing knowledge, including exercises or self assessment exercises to stimulate active learning and provide feedback on learning. Materials are developmentally tested to establish quality and teaching effectiveness.

However, I would suggest that this focus, subconsciously perhaps, is still on teaching rather than on learning. Even when teaching exhibits all the positive aspects that I have mentioned it is still possible for students to fail to put it all together and to remain ineffective as learners. It is particularly important for us at the Open University to look at the learning issue as the level of previous education and knowledge of our students falls and we become increasingly aware that many cope only at a superficial level. This problem, though different in degree, is not, I suspect, confined to the Open University. There is a need across levels to concentrate more on developing students' potential for learning. This is necessary firstly so that they can effectively acquire the knowledge and skills of the discipline, in your case of studying the Old Testament, but secondly so that students can become increasingly independent learners able to design their own learning experiences with decreasing assistance from human teachers.

Reflection

There can be a gap in students' learning experience in which they do not bring together the elements of their learning situations in such a way that they become part of a whole in their continuing learning experience. There is a clear view that what learners need is the opportunity to reflect on their learning experience and their approach to learning in order to move to more meaning-oriented ways of learning. To be effective such opportunities for reflection have to be built into mainstream learning. This concern for student reflection has its theoretical grounding in the field of experiential learning.[19] It offers a practical means to alter conceptions of learning, to open up to students the potential of actively seeking for meaning and developing understanding through linking course concepts with actual experience. Opportunities can be provided for students to reflect on their learning, how they tackle texts, what they do in lectures, how they make notes (and for what purpose), how they complete assignments, and what use they make of feedback. Reflecting on their experience enables students to move to 'deep', meaning-oriented approaches to learning, and this, in turn, relates to success even in conventional examinations.[20] Various ways can be used to achieve this. For example, students can be asked to keep a learning diary as part of a learning file in which they record their reflections and which can form the basis of seminars or tutorials.

Assignments could include a requirement to give a commentary on how the question was tackled and what difficulties were experienced. Building in opportunities for reflection is not easy. The importance of this stress on learning has to be accepted by academics and by students, both of whom may feel that the time spent would be better

19. D. Boud, R. Keogh *et al.*, *Reflection: Turning Experience into Learning* (New York: Nicholas, 1985).

20. K. Trigwell and M. Prosser, 'Relating Approaches to Study and Quality of Learning Outcomes at the Course Level', *British Journal of Educational Psychology* 61 3 (1991), pp. 265-75.

allocated to teaching or learning the subject matter. Thorpe records the comments of one student, already a graduate:[21]

> This is the first time I have experienced this sort of integration being required in an OU course (*i.e.,* the integration of student's experience with academic content). I took my degree through the OU and took (the course) as associate last year.

It may well be argued and has been argued that there are a range of excellent books on how to study. Indeed there are, but experience shows that it is those students who need help who find it most difficult to put into practice general advice which does not seem to relate to their real study experience. I would liken it to telling a man with a broken leg that what he really needs is to go for a good run. He knows that; his problem is that he can't do it! Reflection in the context of actual learning enables students to identify the nature of their problems and to select or reject advice on how to study. The Open University's Access Group has produced *The Good Study Guide*[22] and this is widely used by OU students, but it is also built into the reflective approach so that students can relate its advice to their own experience. (Subject customised versions are now being produced for management and mathematics, technology and science students.) Then they can try out advice on particular approaches. Most important of all reflection offers the opportunity for students to recognize that learning is a skill that they can improve and that they have the potential to develop their learning competences. Indeed this step of recognition is the most important one. Once it is taken the battle is won.

The initial use of reflection, using a learning file with a diary and reflective exercises, in an OU course was in courses for adult educators. While evaluation showed that it was successful the question remained whether it would work for students studying courses in other subject areas. Learning skill development activities have been successfully built into the technology foundation course. A new group of first mathemat-

---

21. M. Thorpe, 'Reflective Learning at a Distance', in F. G. Lockwood and M. Valke (eds.), *Research in Relation to New Developments in Distance Education Materials* (Heerlen, The Netherlands: Open universiteit, 1993), p. 48.

22. A. Northedge, *The Good Study Guide* (Milton Keynes: Open University Press, 1990).

ics courses is being designed with learning files as a central part. Initial developmental testing has produced a favourable response, with students feeling less anxious about mathematics and being willing to undertake new approaches. Further courses such as the new science level one course are considering taking up the approach. How reflection on learning is built into teaching will vary with circumstances. What matters is that its importance is recognised.

Conclusion

What is needed is an extra dimension to be added to the concept of teaching, that of enabling students to learn or rather, to develop as learners. Much of what students learn will date, but skills as learners will endure. This means that teachers even in higher education have to take seriously how their students learn. They may even, dare I say, consider making this a subject for their research (though I admit that in saying this I am resembling the legendary shoemaker who said that there was nothing like leather!). Such a concern with learning in all its aspects needs to be seen as part of the professional competence of academics. We must move away from the concept of academics as professional researchers and amateur teachers. Acceptance that learning is important will mean teachers focusing on 'the process of learning running parallel with their teaching process and a person who is learning and managing that process'.[23]

23. M. Thorpe, 'The Challenge Facing Course Design', in F. G. Lockwood (ed.), *Open and Distance Learning Today* (London: Routledge, 1995), p. 179.

Annotated Old Testament Bibliography

M. DANIEL CARROLL R. and RICHARD S. HESS

What follows is a printed edition of the Annotated Old Testament Bibliography that appears in the *Denver Journal,* at the Denver Seminary web site (http://www.gospelcom.net/densem/). It is regularly updated at the web site.

For the most part, this list considers English language studies and exegetical commentaries that have appeared within the last two decades. However, there is much of value that predates this period. For one of the most useful and wide-ranging bibliographies of earlier works, see Brevard S. Childs, *Old Testament Books for Pastors and Teachers* (Westminster, 1977).

A special note of appreciation is due to Robert Hubbard and the late Robert Alden, whose earlier bibliography formed the basis for what follows.

The following categories are found below:

Introductions
Theology
Histories of Israel
Archaeology
Atlases
Translated Collections of Ancient Near Eastern Texts
Ancient Near Eastern Histories
Hebrew Lexicons

Biblical-Theological Dictionaries
Concordances
Hebrew Grammars
Old Testament Canon/Textual Criticism
Sociological and Anthropological Studies
Feminist, Minority, and Third World Studies
Literary Approaches
Israelite Religion
Commentaries by Bible Book (following the order of the Protestant canon)

Abbreviations:

AB	Anchor Bible
BST	The Bible Speaks Today
BETL	Bibliotheca ephemeridum theologicarum lovaniensium
CBC	Cambridge Bible Commentary
CC	Communicator's Commentary
ConC	Continental Commentary
DSB	Daily Study Bible
FOTL	Forms of Old Testament Literature
HCOT	Historical Critical Commentary of the Old Testament
Herm	Hermeneia
ICC	The International Critical Commentary
Int	Interpretation
JPS	Jewish Publications Society Torah Commentary
JSOTSup	*Journal for the Study of the Old Testament* Supplement Series
NAC	New American Commentary
NCBC	New Century Bible Commentary
NICOT	New International Commentary on the Old Testament
OBT	Overtures to Biblical Theology
OTL	The Old Testament Library
TBC	Torch Bible Commentary
TOTC	Tyndale Old Testament Commentaries
WBC	Word Biblical Commentary
WEC	Wycliffe Exegetical Commentary
*	Exemplary in its category

Introductions

Archer, Gleason, Jr. *A Survey of Old Testament Introduction.* Revised ed. Moody, 1994. A conservative, occasionally polemical, always detailed and informative introduction.

Childs, B. S. *Introduction to the Old Testament as Scripture.* Fortress, 1979. A canonical approach to the text and books.

Dillard, Raymond, and Tremper Longman III. *An Introduction to the Old Testament.* Zondervan, 1994. A helpful, up-to-date evangelical contribution. Longman finished the project after the death of Dillard.

Eissfeldt, O. *The Old Testament: An Introduction.* Trans. P. R. Ackroyd. Harper and Row, 1965. The classic liberal Protestant introduction.

Harrison, R. K. *An Old Testament Introduction.* Eerdmans, 1979. A comprehensive evangelical discussion of introductory issues for its time.

*LaSor, W. S., D. A. Hubbard, and F. W. Bush. *Old Testament Survey.* Eerdmans, 1982. 2nd ed., 1996. A reasonably up-to-date introduction from a balanced evangelical perspective.

Soggin, J. Alberto. *Introduction to the Old Testament.* OTL. Westminster, 1989. The current standard in place of Eissfeldt; weak on literary approaches.

Series

Forms of Old Testament Literature. Eerdmans. Analyses of books of the Old Testament in terms of their structure and the forms of literature found in them.

Guides to Biblical Scholarship: Old Testament Series. Fortress. The best set of paperback surveys of methods of biblical interpretation.

Moody Press: Four volumes by H. Wolf (Pentateuch), D. Howard (Historical Books), and C. H. Bullock (Poetic Books and Prophetic Books).

Old Testament Guides. Sheffield Academic Press. These are the most useful for current discussions of the major interpretive issues and approaches on each book of the Old Testament.

The Oxford Bible. Oxford University. These volumes deal with collections of books (e.g., the prophets by J. F. A. Sawyer) and genres (e.g., poetry by S. E. Gillingham).

Sources for Biblical and Theological Study. Eisenbrauns. Collections of the most important articles in the particular field, whether specific biblical texts (e.g., R. Hess and D. Tsumura on Genesis 1-11) or on methods (e.g., C. E. Carter and C. L. Meyers on social sciences approaches).

Theology

Brueggemann, Walter. *Theology of the Old Testament: Testimony, Dispute, Advocacy.* Fortress, 1997. A provocative approach that structures the discussion around the metaphor and imagery of the courtroom.

Childs, Brevard S. *Old Testament Theology in a Canonical Context.* Fortress, 1986. Classic on canon with a sensitivity to the New Testament.

*Eichrodt, W. *Old Testament Theology.* 2 vols. OTL. Philadelphia: Westminster, 1961-67. Emphasis on the covenant.

Hasel, Gerhard. *Old Testament Theology: Basic Issues in the Current Debate.* Eerdmans, 1995. 4th ed. Detailed survey of authors and issues.

*Kaiser, W. C., Jr. *Toward an Old Testament Theology.* Zondervan, 1978. Evangelical. Emphasis on promise themes.

Ollenburger, Ben C., Elmer A. Marten, and Gerhard F. Hasel, eds. *The Flowering of Old Testament Theology.* Sources for Biblical and Theological Study. Eisenbrauns, 1992. A collection of classic articles.

Preuss, H. D. *Old Testament Theology.* 2 vols. OTL. Westminster/John Knox, 1995-96. Focus on Yahweh.

Rad, G. von. *Old Testament Theology.* 2 vols. Harper and Row, 1962-65. Salvation-history approach.

Sailhamer, John H. *Introduction to Old Testament Theology: A Canonical Approach.* Zondervan, 1995. Evangelical. Structured study on how to do Old Testament theology.

Terrien, S. *The Elusive Presence: Toward a New Biblical Theology.* Harper and Row, 1978. Focus on the wisdom literature.

Zuck, Roy B., ed. *A Biblical Theology of the Old Testament.* Moody, 1991. Evangelical. Dallas seminary faculty contribute their perspectives.

Special Studies

*Satterthwaite, Philip E., Richard S. Hess, and Gordon J. Wenham, eds. *The Lord's Anointed: Interpretation of Old Testament Messianic Texts.* Baker and Paternoster, 1995. A current assessment of the exegesis of key Old Testament texts.

Histories of Israel

Ahlström, Gösta W. *The History of Ancient Palestine from the Palaeolithic Period to Alexander's Conquest.* With a contribution by G. O. Rollefson. Edited by D. Edelman. JSOTSup 146. Sheffield Academic Press, 1993. The most up-to-date of the major histories of ancient Israel, though affected by the author's unconventional opinions and perspectives.

Bright, J. *A History of Israel.* 3rd ed. Westminster, 1981. Standard of the last generation, heir of the Albright school.

Hayes, J. H., and J. Maxwell Miller. *A History of Ancient Israel and Judah.* Westminster/John Knox, 1986. The critical alternative to Albright.

Merrill, Eugene. *Kingdom of Priests: A History of Old Testament Israel.* Baker, 1987. Evangelical and conservative.

*Shanks, Hershel, ed. *Ancient Israel: A Short History from Abraham to the Roman Destruction of the Temple.* Prentice-Hall, 1988. Popular writing by leading historians. In need of updating.

Soggin, J. Alberto. *A History of Ancient Israel: From Beginnings to the Bar Kochba Revolt, A.D. 135.* Westminster, 1985. A classic liberal interpretation of Israel's history that, though now out of date, represents an important synthesis of Continental scholarship.

Special Studies in History

*Long, V. Philips. *The Art of Biblical History.* Foundations of Contemporary Interpretation 5. Zondervan, 1994. The balance of historicity, literary art, and theology in the history writing of the Old Testament.

Millard, Alan R., James K. Hoffmeier, and David W. Baker, eds. *Faith, Tradition, and History: Old Testament Historiography in Its Near Eastern Context.* Eisenbrauns, 1994. Important articles on the methods and interpretation of various Old Testament passages in the light of ancient Near Eastern comparisons.

Archaeology

Aharoni, Y. *The Archaeology of the Land of Israel.* Trans. A. F. Rainey. Westminster, 1982. A classic work.

Stern, Ephraim, ed. *The New Encyclopedia of Archaeological Excavations in the Holy Land.* Simon and Schuster, 1995. Essential reference guide for sites.

Ben-Tor, Amnon, ed. *The Archaeology of Ancient Israel.* Trans. R. Greenberg. Yale, 1992.

*Levy, Thomas E., ed. *The Archaeology of Society in the Holy Land.* Facts on File, 1995. Although it covers a larger period than that of the biblical time, it is the first systematic presentation of social archaeology in Israel as written by leading archaeologists.

Mazar, Amihai. *Archaeology of the Land of the Bible: 10,000-586 B.C.E.* Doubleday, 1992. A more recent work by an experienced Israeli archaeologist.

Meyers, Eric M., ed. *The Oxford Encyclopedia of Archaeology in the Near East.* Five vols. Oxford University, 1997.

Special Studies

In a rapidly changing field, the following studies and periodicals can be useful guides:

Brooke, George J., Adrian H. W. Curtis, and John F. Healey, eds. *Ugarit and the Bible. Proceedings of the International Symposium on Ugarit and the Bible. Manchester, September 1992.* Ugaritisch-Biblische Literatur 11. Ugarit-Verlag, 1994. Continues to be the most useful collection of essays on this key subject.

The Ancient Near East (formerly *Biblical Archaeologist*)

Biblical Archaeology Review

Atlases

*Aharoni, Yohanan, Michael Avi-Yonah, Anson F. Rainey, and Zeev Safrai, eds. *The Macmillan Bible Atlas.* 3rd ed. Macmillan, 1993. New edition of a standard atlas that provides individual maps for many significant Bible events.

*Beitzel, B. *The Moody Atlas of Bible Lands.* Moody, 1985. Evangelical with detailed geographical discussion and good integration of maps and commentary.

*Bimson, J., and J. Kane. *New Bible Atlas.* Tyndale, 1985. Excellent combination of price, color maps and illustrations, and archaeological commentary. Evangelical.

Cleave, Richard. *The Holy Land, a Unique Perspective: Photography and Satellite Cartography.* Lion, 1993. Stunning aerial and satellite photography.

Pritchard, J. B., ed. *Harper's Atlas of the Bible.* Harper and Row, 1987. Best on indices and gazetteer in relation to the maps.

Rasmussen, C. G. *Zondervan NIV Atlas of the Bible.* Zondervan, 1989. Stronger on photos and maps of Israel itself than of neighboring lands.

Rogerson, J. *The Atlas of the Bible*. Facts on File, 1985. Visually dazzling color photographs as well as discussion of geography and archaeology.

Special Studies

The following are useful teaching tools:

Abingdon Bible Map Transparencies. Abingdon. This is a wonderful set of full-color maps for both Old and New Testament events and places. One of the best for overhead projection.

Smith, George Adam. *The Historical Geography of the Holy Land*. 25th ed. Hodder & Stoughton, 1936; Harper & Row, 1966. This is an 1894 classic with vivid word pictures of the Holy Land.

Survey of Israel Maps. Survey of Israel, continuously updated. Hebrew and English. This is a set of scale 1:100,000 maps that cover the entire area occupied by modern Israel. Includes all significant political and topographic features with many sites of antiquity noted.

Translated Collections of Ancient Near Eastern Texts

Beyerlin, W., ed. *Near Eastern Religious Texts Relating to the Old Testament*. OTL. Westminster, 1978.

*Hallo, William W., and K. Lawson Younger, Jr., eds. *The Context of Scripture. Volume 1: Canonical Compositions from the Biblical World*. Brill, 1997. The first of a projected three-volume series. This is the new *Ancient Near Eastern Texts*.

Pritchard, J. B., ed. *Ancient Near Eastern Texts Relating to the Old Testament*. 3rd ed. Princeton University Press, 1969. Two volumes of a paperback epitome of this larger volume have also appeared.

Ancient Near Eastern Histories

Gurney, O. R. *The Hittites*. Revised ed. Penguin, 1990. A classic on a culture with important relevance to the Bible.

Hallo, W. W., and W. K. Simpson. *The Ancient Near East: A History*. Harcourt Brace Jovanovich, 1971. One of the most widely used brief histories.

Hoerth, Alfred, Gerald Mattingly, and Edwin Yamauchi, eds. *Peoples of the

Old Testament World. Baker, 1994. Updating of Wiseman's *Peoples of Old Testament Times* by U.S. evangelicals.

*Kemp, Barry J. *Ancient Egypt: Anatomy of a Civilization.* 2nd ed. Routledge, 1991. A social study of Egyptian life and culture.

Oppenheim, A. Leon. *Ancient Mesopotamia.* University of Chicago, 1977.

Von Soden, Wolfram. *The Ancient Orient: An Introduction to the Study of the Ancient Near East.* Trans. D. G. Schley. Eerdmans, 1993. Traditional approach to ancient Near Eastern history.

Wiseman, D. J., ed. *Peoples of Old Testament Times.* Oxford, 1973. Contributions by (mostly British) outstanding scholars in their areas.

Hebrew Lexicons

Brown, F., S. R. Driver, and C. A. Briggs. *Hebrew and English Lexicon of the Old Testament.* Hendrickson, 1979. The best of the older lexicons.

Clines, David J. A., ed. *The Dictionary of Classical Hebrew.* 8 vols. Sheffield Academic Press, 1993-. Three volumes have appeared. Designed for a contextual and usage approach to understanding the meaning of words.

Holladay, W. L. *A Concise Hebrew and Aramaic Lexicon of the Old Testament.* Eerdmans, 1971. Useful, quick reference.

*Koehler, L., and W. Baumgartner et al., eds. *The Hebrew and Aramaic Lexicon of the Old Testament.* 3rd ed. 4 vols. Brill, 1994-. Three volumes have appeared to date. A translation of the most complete Hebrew-German lexicon.

Biblical-Theological Dictionaries

*Botterweck, G. J., H. Ringgren, H.-J. Fabry, eds. *Theological Dictionary of the Old Testament.* Eerdmans, 1977-. 8 volumes have appeared. Translation of a German publication. The standard work.

Harris, R. L., G. L. Archer, Jr., and B. K. Waltke, eds. *Theological Wordbook of the Old Testament.* 2 vols. Moody, 1980. Brief discussions from an evangelical perspective.

Jenni, E., and C. Westermann, eds. *Theological Lexicon of the Old Testament.* 3 vols. Hendrickson, 1997.

VanGemeren, Willem A., ed. *New International Dictionary of Old Testament*

Theology and Exegesis. 5 vols. Zondervan, 1997. The most recent and complete evangelical contribution.

Concordances

*AcCordance 2.1 on CD-ROM. Gramcord, 1996. The most comprehensive computer concordance for Masoretic Text, Septuagint, and English versions. Available for PC and Macintosh computers.

*Even-Shoshan, E. *A New Concordance of the Old Testament Using the Hebrew and Aramaic Text.* 2nd ed. Baker, 1989. The best concordance for the Hebrew text of the Old Testament.

Goodrick, E. W., and J. R. Kohlenberger, III. *The NIV Exhaustive Concordance.* Zondervan, 1990.

Hebrew Grammars

Cowley, A. E., and E. Kautzsch, eds. *Gesenius' Hebrew Grammar.* 2nd English edition. Oxford, 1910. Traditionally the best of the reference grammars.

Kelley, P. *Biblical Hebrew: An Introductory Grammar.* Eerdmans, 1992. Continues and updates the Weingreen approach to learning Hebrew.

Seow, C. L. *A Grammar for Biblical Hebrew.* Revised ed. Abingdon, 1995. Continues and updates the Lambdin approach to learning Hebrew.

*Waltke, B. K., and M. O'Connor. *An Introduction to Biblical Hebrew Syntax.* Eisenbrauns, 1990. An integration of modern linguistic approaches.

Old Testament Canon/Textual Criticism

Beckwith, R. *The Old Testament Canon of the New Testament Church.* Eerdmans, 1985. An affirmation of the Old Testament canon.

Brotzman, E. *Old Testament Textual Criticism: A Practical Introduction.* Baker, 1994. Good evangelical introduction. Special guides for using *Biblia Hebraica Stuttgartensia.*

Tov, Emmanuel. *The Text-Critical Use of the Septuagint in Biblical Research.* Revised ed. Jerusalem Biblical Studies 8. Simor, 1997. The most important introduction to the study of the Septuagint for biblical scholars.

*Tov, Emmanuel. *Textual Criticism of the Hebrew Bible.* Fortress, 1992. The best introduction to the subject.

Würthwein, Ernst. *The Text of the Old Testament.* 2nd ed. Eerdmans, 1995. Classic discussion of the Hebrew texts and the versions.

Sociological and Anthropological Studies

Carter, Charles E., and Carol L. Meyers, eds. *Community, Identity, and Ideology: Social Science Approaches to the Hebrew Bible.* Sources for Biblical and Theological Study 6. Eisenbrauns, 1996. A collection of important essays dealing with method and case studies from ancient Israel's society and history.

*Clements, Ronald E., ed. *The World of Ancient Israel: Sociological, Anthropological and Political Perspectives.* Cambridge, 1989. A key introduction to these categories by a collection of mainly British writers.

Matthews, Victor H., and Don C. Benjamin. *Social World of Ancient Israel 1250-587 BCE.* Hendrickson, 1993. Application of anthropology to social roles and institutions within ancient Israel. Can be a bit fanciful at times.

*Overholt, Thomas W. *Cultural Anthropology and the Old Testament.* Guides to Biblical Scholarship. Fortress, 1996. An excellent introduction to the use of anthropology in the study of the prophets. Good bibliography.

Rogerson, John W. *Anthropology and the Old Testament.* The Biblical Seminar. JSOT Press, 1984. Documents the misapplication of anthropology in Old Testament studies.

Feminist, Minority, and Third World Studies

*Bird, Phyllis A. *Missing Persons and Mistaken Identities: Women and Gender in Ancient Israel.* OBT. Fortress, 1997. A collection of significant essays written over the last twenty years by an important Old Testament feminist scholar.

Boff, Clodovis, and George V. Pixley. *The Bible, the Church, and the Poor.* Orbis, 1989. Presents from a liberationist perspective a biblical basis for a theology of the poor and pastoral work among the disadvantaged.

Croatto, J. Severino. *Exodus: A Hermeneutics of Freedom.* Orbis, 1981. Utilizes modern philosophical hermeneutical theory for contextualizing the Exodus and the prophets to modern Latin America.

Felder, Cain Hope. *Troubling Biblical Waters: Race, Class, and Family*. Orbis, 1989. Designed to surface the existence of blacks in the Bible and to explore how to find the significance of the Bible for contemporary social issues.

————, ed. *Stony the Road We Trod: African American Biblical Interpretation*. Fortress, 1991. Essays that try to bring an African-American perspective to the analysis and application of the Bible.

Newsom, Carol A., and Sharon H. Ringe, eds. *The Women's Bible Commentary*. SPCK, Westminster/John Knox, 1992. A one-volume feminist commentary on the entire Bible. Each entry has a bibliography for further reading.

Pixley, Jorge. *Biblical Israel: A People's History*. Fortress, 1992. The application of a sociological approach in order to present the history of Israel as one of peasants' struggles against oppressors.

*Sugirtharajah, R. S., ed. *Voices from the Margin: Interpreting the Bible in the Third World*. 2nd ed. Orbis/SPCK, 1995. A collection of essays from around the world that interpret particular biblical texts from a liberationist and pluralist perspective.

Trible, Phyllis. *Texts of Terror: Literary-Feminist Readings of Biblical Narratives*. OBT. Fortress, 1984. A classical work that combines literary and feminist criticism to highlight the tragedy and violence in the stories of four women in the Old Testament.

Literary Approaches

*Alter, Robert. *The Art of Biblical Narrative*. Basic Books, 1981. Still one of the best introductory guides for the beginner in interpreting narrative.

————. *The Art of Biblical Poetry*. Basic Books, 1985. An excellent introduction to biblical poetry, especially the dynamics of parallelism.

————. *The World of Biblical Literature*. Basic Books, 1992. A useful supplement to Alter's earlier work.

————, and Frank Kermode, eds. *The Literary Guide to the Bible*. Harvard University Press, 1987. An application of the literary method to each book of the Bible.

Bar-Efrat, Shimon. *Narrative Art in the Bible*. Bible and Literature Series 17. Sheffield Academic Press, 1989. An important contribution to techniques of literary interpretation.

Berlin, Adele. *Poetics and Interpretation of Biblical Narrative.* Almond, 1983. A very helpful introduction to the various elements of a literary approach.

Gunn, David M., and Danna Nolan Fewell. *Narrative in the Hebrew Bible.* The Oxford Bible Series. Oxford University Press, 1993. A counterpoint to Sternberg.

Polzin, Robert. *Moses and the Deuteronomist: A Literary Study of the Deuteronomic History.* Seabury, 1980. One of the earliest and best discussions of narrative analysis in the historical books.

Ryken, Leland, and Tremper Longman III, eds. *A Complete Literary Guide to the Bible.* Zondervan, 1993. An evangelical counterpart to Alter and Kermode.

*Sternberg, Moshe. *The Poetics of Biblical Narrative: Ideological Literature and the Drama of Reading.* Indiana University Press, 1985. Probably the most important and thorough guide to philosophy and technique of narrative writing in the Old Testament.

Israelite Religion

Albertz, Rainer. *A History of Israelite Religion in the Old Testament Period.* 2 vols. Old Testament Library. Westminster/John Knox, 1994. This detailed study uses a classic liberal reconstruction of the history of Old Testament literature and interacts with recent discussions and discoveries.

De Moor, Johannes C. *The Rise of Yahwism: The Roots of Israelite Monotheism.* BETL 91. Peeters, 1990. Important evidence and arguments for Israel's worship of one God in Mosaic and later times.

Grabbe, Lester L. *Priests, Prophets, Diviners, Sages: A Socio-Historical Study of Religious Specialists in Ancient Israel.* Trinity Press International, 1995. Sometimes assumes too much, but overall a useful study of these professional groups and their activities in Israel and surrounding cultures.

*Keel, Othmar, and Christoph Uelinger. *Gods, Goddesses, and Images of God in Ancient Israel.* Trans. Allan W. Mahnke. Fortress, 1997. The most important survey of the archaeological data, and especially the iconography, related to Israelite religion.

Mettinger, Tryggve N. D. *No Graven Image? Israelite Aniconism in Its Ancient Near Eastern Context.* Coniectanea Biblica Old Testament Series 42. Almqvist & Wiksell, 1995. Explores a combination of archaeological, textual, and biblical evidence to consider the practice of Israel's worship of God without images.

Smith, Mark S. *The Early History of God: Yahweh and the Other Deities in Ancient Israel.* Harper & Row, 1990. A detailed synthesis of archaeological, textual, and biblical evidence for the worship of Yahweh and other deities in Old Testament times. This approach argues for a convergence of various deities to "create" Israel's God as he is known in the Bible.

*Tigay, Jeffrey H. *You Shall Have No Other Gods: Israelite Religion in the Light of Hebrew Inscriptions.* Harvard Semitic Studies 31. Scholars Press, 1987. A brief but thorough survey of written evidence, especially personal names, this study argues that monotheism was present during the Israelite monarchy as the official religion of the southern and perhaps northern kingdoms.

van der Toorn, Karel. *Family Religion in Babylonia, Syria and Israel: Continuity and Change in the Forms of Religious Life.* Studies in the History and Culture of the Ancient Near East 7. Brill, 1996. Studies ancestor worship and Israelite monotheism from the beginnings and through the Monarchy.

*————, Bob Becking, and Pieter W. van der Horst, eds. *Dictionary of Deities and Demons in the Bible.* Brill, 1995. An essential reference work on the subject.

Commentaries by Bible Book

Blenkinsopp, Joseph. *The Pentateuch: An Introduction to the First Five Books of the Bible.* AB. Doubleday, 1992.

Genesis

Atkinson, D. *The Message of Genesis 1–11.* BST. InterVarsity, 1990. Helpful exposition for laypeople and pastors. Evangelical.

Brueggemann, W. *Genesis.* Int. Westminster/John Knox, 1982. Theological reading with application.

Cassuto, U. *Commentary on Genesis.* Trans. I. Abrahams. 2 vols. Magnes, 1964. A Jewish scholar situates Genesis in Rabbinic and Hebrew interpretative traditions. A classic alternative to the documentary approach. Includes only chapters 1-11.

Hamilton, Victor. *The Book of Genesis: Chapters 1–17* and *The Book of Genesis:*

Chapters 18–50. NICOT. Eerdmans, 1990, 1995. Emphasis on comparative Semitics. Evangelical.

Kidner, D. *Genesis: An Introduction and Commentary.* TOTC. InterVarsity, 1967. An elegant interpretation of the book. Evangelical.

Mathews, Kenneth A. *Genesis 1–11:26.* NAC. Broadman, 1996. Most up to date.

Rad, G. von. *Genesis.* OTL. Westminster, 1972. A classic theological interpretation from a higher critical perspective.

Ross, Allen P. *Creation and Blessing: A Guide to the Study and Exposition of Genesis.* Baker, 1988. An evangelical theological exposition with emphasis on preaching the text.

Sarna, N. M. *Genesis.* The Jewish Publication Society Torah Commentary. Jewish Publication Society, 1989. A recent Jewish exegesis of the Hebrew text with appreciation for traditional Rabbinic exegesis.

*Wenham, G. J. *Genesis 1–15* and *Genesis 16–50.* WBC. Word, 1987, 1994. The best all-around evangelical commentary; introduces the reader to the major interpretative issues and provides clear writing on the exegesis and theological significance.

Westermann, C. *Genesis.* 3 vols. Augsburg, 1984-86. The largest of the resources; with an emphasis on collecting exegetical data.

Exodus

Cassuto, U. *Commentary on Exodus.* Trans. I. Abrahams. Magnes, 1967. Important for study of the Hebrew text.

*Childs, B. S. *The Book of Exodus.* OTL. Westminster, 1974. The application of the canonical approach to a higher critical commentary. Includes a history of interpretation for each passage.

Durham, J. I. *Exodus.* WBC. Word, 1987. Follows the method of Childs.

Houtman, Cornelis. *Exodus: Volume 1 (1:1–7:13)* and *Exodus: Volume 2 (7:14–19:25).* HCOT. Kok Pharos, 1993 and 1996. Updating of classic historical critical approach to the book.

Sarna, Nahum. *Exodus.* JPS. Jewish Publication Society, 1991. See above for Genesis.

Leviticus

Harrison, R. K. *Leviticus: An Introduction and Commentary.* TOTC. InterVarsity, 1980. Evangelical.

Hartley, J. *Leviticus.* WBC. Word, 1992.

Levine, B. A. *Leviticus*. JPS. Jewish Publication Society, 1989. A specialist in Ugaritic studies looks at Leviticus.

Milgrom, J. *Leviticus 1–16*. AB. Doubleday, 1992. Major Jewish scholarly commentary on the book.

*Wenham, G. J. *The Book of Leviticus*. NICOT. Eerdmans, 1979. Evangelical application of anthropology to categories of holiness. Oriented toward New Testament applications.

Numbers

Ashley, T. R. *The Book of Numbers*. NICOT. Eerdmans, 1993. Evangelical focus on the text's final form with attention to translational issues.

Davies, Eryl W. *Numbers*. NCB. Eerdmans, 1995. Focus on sources and their development to form the book.

Levine, Baruch A. *Numbers 1–20*. AB. Doubleday, 1993. Large commentary with ancient Near Eastern detail and philological discussion.

Milgrom, J. *Numbers*. JPS. Jewish Publication Society, 1990. Commentary on the Hebrew text that accepts a substantial historicity of the accounts.

*Wenham, G. *Numbers: An Introduction and Commentary*. TOTC. InterVarsity, 1981. Evangelical perspectives on the literary structure of the book.

Deuteronomy

Christensen, Duane L. *Deuteronomy 1–11*. WBC. Word, 1991. Evangelical study of the structure of the book as a poem with five concentric units.

*Craigie, P. C. *The Book of Deuteronomy*. NICOT. Eerdmans, 1976. Evangelical, clearly written study using Ugaritic and other ancient Near Eastern evidence.

Miller, P. D., Jr. *Deuteronomy*. Int. John Knox, 1990. Important theological application of the book.

Rad, G. von. *Deuteronomy*. OTL. Westminster, 1966. Theological.

Thompson, J. A. *Deuteronomy: An Introduction and Commentary*. TOTC. InterVarsity, 1974. Helpful on Ancient Near Eastern backgrounds. Evangelical.

Tigay, J. H. *Deuteronomy*. JPS. Jewish Publication Society, 1996. A committed source critic studies the book within a Jewish context.

Weinfeld, M. *Deuteronomy 1–11*. Doubleday, 1991. Comments on the text by an authority on Deuteronomic studies.

*Wright, Christopher J. H. *Deuteronomy*. New International Biblical Commentary. Hendrickson, 1996. A leading Old Testament ethicist presents an evangelical interpretation of the text.

Joshua

Boling, R., and G. E. Wright. *Joshua: A New Translation with Introduction and Commentary*. AB. Doubleday, 1982. Aware of the archaeology, although dated.

Butler, T. *Joshua*. WBC. Word, 1983. Emphasis on literary critical aspects of the text as a Deuteronomistic work.

*Hess, R. S. *Joshua: An Introduction and Commentary*. TOTC. InterVarsity, 1996. Integrates recent archaeological discoveries and literary analysis. Evangelical.

Nelson, Richard D. *Joshua*. OTL. Westminster/John Knox, 1997. Joshua as the product of Deuteronomistic redaction.

Woudstra, M. *The Book of Joshua*. NICOT. Eerdmans, 1981. Evangelical; regards the narrative as historical.

Judges

Auld, A. G. *Joshua, Judges, and Ruth*. DSB. Westminster, 1984. A useful, brief commentary.

Boling, R. *Judges*. AB. Doubleday, 1975. Emphasizes the traditions behind the text and places many of them in the pre-Monarchy period.

*Lindars, Barnabas. *Judges 1–5*. T & T Clark, 1995. The beginning of a new ICC stopped by the author's untimely death, this work surveys a breadth of modern scholarship and closely studies the text criticism of the book.

Soggin, J. A. *Judges*. OTL. Westminster, 1981. A classic liberal exegesis by someone who controls much of European scholarship.

Ruth

Bush, Frederic. *Ruth, Esther*. WBC. Word, 1996. An evangelical scholar of the Bible and the ancient Near East brings his knowledge to these two books.

Campbell, E. F., Jr. *Ruth*. AB. Doubleday, 1985. An important theological and archaeological discussion of the book.

Gow, Murray D. *The Book of Ruth: Its Structure, Theme, and Purpose*. Apollos,

1992. Evangelical application of rhetorical and literary techniques to argue for a coherent structure to Ruth.

*Hubbard, Robert L., Jr. *The Book of Ruth.* NICOT. Eerdmans, 1988. A balanced and thorough study with an appreciation of literary criticism from an evangelical perspective.

Nielsen, Kirsten. *Ruth.* OTL. Westminster/John Knox, 1997. The only major English language commentary on Ruth written by a woman with a special interest in intertextuality.

Sasson, Jack M. *Ruth: A New Translation with a Philological Commentary and a Formalist-Folklorist Interpretation.* 2nd ed. Sheffield, 1989. An ancient Near Eastern specialist examines this book.

1 & 2 Samuel

Anderson, A. A. *2 Samuel.* WBC. Word, 1989. Considers the historical context as one in which David and Solomon are presented as rightful occupants of the throne in Jerusalem.

*Bergen, R. D. *1 and 2 Samuel.* NAC. Broadman, 1996. Evangelical, reflecting a knowledge of the Hebrew and modern linguistics.

Fokkelman, J. P. *Narrative Art and Poetry in the Books of Samuel: A Full Interpretation Based on Stylistic and Structural Analyses.* 4 vols. Van Gorcum, 1981-93. More than two thousand pages of careful literary analysis of the books of Samuel.

Gordon, R. P. *1 and 2 Samuel.* Zondervan, 1986. Evangelical historical and grammatical study of the books.

Klein, R. W. *1 Samuel.* WBC. Word, 1983. A commentary concerned with the final form of the text.

*McCarter, P. Kyle, Jr. *I Samuel* and *II Samuel.* AB. Doubleday, 1980, 1984. The most important study of the Hebrew text in relation to Greek and Dead Sea Scroll witnesses.

1 & 2 Kings

*Cogan, M., and H. Tadmor. *II Kings.* AB. Doubleday, 1988. Essential discussion of the Assyrian context of Judah during the latter period of the Monarchy and especially the time of Hezekiah.

DeVries, Simon J. *1 Kings.* WBC. Word, 1985. Useful evangelical commentary written without apology for the difficulties in the book.

Hobbs, T. R. *2 Kings.* WBC. Word, 1985. Evangelical literary and theological interpretation of 2 Kings.

*House, P. R. *1 and 2 Kings*. NAC. Broadman, 1995. Evangelical theological and literary synthesis of recent approaches.

Jones, G. H. *1 and 2 Kings. Volumes I and II*. NCBC. Eerdmans, 1984. Historical and textual criticism dominate the concerns of these volumes.

Knoppers, Gary N. *Two Nations under God: The Deuteronomistic History of Solomon and the Dual Monarchies*. 2 vols. Scholars, 1993, 1994. A doctoral dissertation that provides a historical and critical commentary on Kings.

Long, Burke O. *1 Kings and 2 Kings*. FOTL. Eerdmans, 1984, 1991. A study of the genres and literary forms used in the books.

Nelson, R. *First and Second Kings*. Int. John Knox, 1987.

*Provan, Iain W. *1 and 2 Kings*. New International Biblical Commentary. Hendrickson, 1995. Evangelical literary reading of the text.

Walsh, Jerome T. *1 Kings*. Berit Olam. Liturgical, 1996. Commentary in the context of a study of literary and narrative forms of 1 Kings.

Wiseman, Donald J. *1 and 2 Kings*. InterVarsity, 1993. Evangelical application of archaeological and historical studies to the interpretation and application of the message of Kings.

1 & 2 Chronicles

Braun, R. *I Chronicles*. WBC. Word, 1986. An evangelical contribution with appreciation of the historical worth of the text.

Dillard, R. B. *II Chronicles*. WBC. Word, 1987. Similar to Braun for 1 Chronicles, with appreciation of Williamson's work in several cases.

*Japhet, Sara. *I & II Chronicles*. OTL. Westminster/John Knox, 1993. A detailed theological commentary that is sensitive to Chronicles as history.

Selman, Martin J. *1 Chronicles, 2 Chronicles*. 2 vols. TOTC. InterVarsity, 1994. Evangelical study with special emphasis upon theological significance and application.

Thompson, John A. *1 and 2 Chronicles*. NAC. Broadman, 1995. Evangelical appreciation of the books as historically reliable.

Williamson, H. G. M. *1 and 2 Chronicles*. NCBC. Eerdmans, 1982. Presents the books as basically historical with creative development for theological purposes.

Ezra & Nehemiah

Blenkinsopp, J. *Ezra-Nehemiah*. OTL. Westminster, 1988. An important discussion reflecting opinions held by many scholars and stressing the importance of the period for Judaism.

Breneman, Mervin. *Ezra, Nehemiah, Esther.* NAC. Broadman, 1993. An evangelical, conservative review of the recent discussions and applications regarding these books.

Clines, D. J. A. *Ezra, Nehemiah, Esther.* NCBC. Eerdmans, 1984. Strong bibliographies and introductions. In Esther God's existence is a premise not requiring mention.

Fensham, F. C. *The Books of Ezra and Nehemiah.* NICOT. Eerdmans, 1982. Evangelical focus on the historical and archaeological background.

Kidner, D. *Ezra and Nehemiah.* TOTC. InterVarsity, 1979. Evangelical discussion of the theological message of the book.

Throntveit, Mark A. *Ezra-Nehemiah.* Int. John Knox, 1992. A more up-to-date discussion of theological and interpretative issues.

*Williamson, H. G. M. *Ezra-Nehemiah.* WBC. Word, 1985. A judicious survey of the historical and major exegetical issues with an awareness of the archaeological component.

Esther

(See also commentaries listed above for Ruth and for Ezra & Nehemiah.)

Baldwin, J. G. *Esther.* TOTC. InterVarsity, 1984. Evangelical, with a strong introduction and discussion of the book's contemporary theological relevance.

Fox, Michael V. *Character and Ideology in the Book of Esther.* University of South Carolina Press, 1991. A text-critical and literary study that stresses how open-ended the book is, with uncertainty about many aspects, including the role of God.

Levenson, Jon D. *Esther.* OTL. Westminster/John Knox, 1997. A master of biblical theology from a Jewish perspective examines the book of Esther.

Job

*Alden, Robert A. *Job.* NAC. Broadman, 1994. A balanced and evangelical discussion of the biblical text.

Anderson, F. I. *Job.* TOTC. InterVarsity, 1976. Evangelical and linguistic study of the text.

Clines, D. J. A. *Job 1–20.* WBC. Word, 1989. Important literary study with a vast bibliography.

Gordis, R. *The Book of Job: Commentary, New Translation and Special Studies.* Ktav, 1978. A Jewish perspective with attention to the interpretation of difficult words and phrases.

Hartley, J. *Job.* NICOT. Eerdmans, 1988. Good evangelical survey and interaction with relevant secondary literature.

Janzen, J. G. *Job.* Int. John Knox, 1985. Existentialist approach stressing the element of free will in creation; at times more technical in its discussion.

Psalms

Allen, L. C. *Psalms 101–150.* WBC. Word, 1983. A balanced and comprehensive evangelical survey of exegesis in these psalms.

Cohen, A. *Psalms: Hebrew Text, English Translation and Commentary.* Revised by E. Oratz. Soncino, 1992. A Jewish perspective on the interpretation of the Psalms.

*Craigie, P. *Psalms 1–50.* WBC. Word, 1983. A clearly written evangelical combination of comparative Ugaritic studies and theological insights with practical application.

Kidner, D. *Psalms 1–72* and *Psalms 73–150.* TOTC. InterVarsity, 1973, 1975. An evangelical musical artist and theological exegete brings the psalms to life.

Kraus, H.-J. *Psalms 1–59* and *Psalms 60–150.* Trans. H. C. Oswald. ConC. Fortress, 1988, 1989. A comprehensive review of scholarship and detailed commentary on the Psalms.

*Mays, J. L. *Psalms.* Int. Westminster/John Knox, 1994. This is a theological and practical commentary set within the contexts of the canon of Scripture and the history of interpretation.

Tate, M. E. *Psalms 51–100.* WBC. Word, 1990. An evangelical focus on review of scholarship, exegesis, and word studies, and the relation of psalms to one another.

Weiser, A. *Psalms.* OTL. Westminster, 1962. Focus on annual festivals and the psalms' role in these festivals.

Williams, D. M. *Psalms.* CC. 2 vols. Word, 1986. Evangelical.

Proverbs

Alden, Robert L. *Proverbs: A Commentary on an Ancient Book of Timeless Advice.* Baker, 1983. Evangelical exegesis.

*Garrett, Duane A. *Proverbs, Ecclesiastes, Song of Songs.* NAC. Broadman,

1993. Evangelical discussion of these three Solomonic books with useful exegesis and theological application.

Hubbard, D. A. *Proverbs: Mastering the Old Testament.* CC. Word, 1989. Evangelical exposition and application.

*Kidner, D. *Proverbs.* TOTC. InterVarsity, 1964. Evangelical, balanced reflections on the meaning of each of the proverbs.

McKane, W. *Proverbs: A New Approach.* OTL. Westminster, 1970. Learned discussion based on original secular wisdom that evolved into theologically oriented wisdom literature.

Ecclesiastes

Crenshaw, J. L. *Ecclesiastes.* OTL. Westminster, 1987. A master of biblical wisdom literature considers this book.

Eaton, Michael A. *Ecclesiastes: An Introduction and Commentary.* TOTC. InterVarsity, 1983. Evangelical appreciation of a positive interpretation to the book as an apologetic in a world of faithlessness.

Gordis, R. *Koholeth: The Man and His World.* Schocken, 1951. A philological commentary on the Hebrew text that remains useful.

*Longman, Tremper, III. *Ecclesiastes.* NICOT. Eerdmans, 1998. An important evangelical contribution with good balance in linguistic study and theological application.

Murphy, Roland E. *Ecclesiastes.* WBC. Word, 1992. Lengthy introduction with standard exegesis; the author adds a monologue on the traditional wisdom that the book challenged.

*Seow, C.-L. *Ecclesiastes.* AB. Doubleday, 1997. Important summary of recent research with a careful exegesis of what is regarded as a Persian period book.

Whybray, R. N. *Ecclesiastes.* NCBC. Eerdmans, 1989. Good survey of secondary literature with exegesis that argues a middle-of-the-road position for the Hellenistic author.

Song of Songs

Carr, G. Lloyd. *The Song of Solomon. An Introduction and Commentary.* TOTC. InterVarsity, 1984. Evangelical discussion of this book as love poetry.

Keel, Othmar. *Song of Songs.* Trans. F. J. Geiser. ConC. Fortress, 1994. An authority on Israelite iconography interprets the images of the book.

*Murphy, R. E. *The Song of Songs.* Herm. Fortress, 1990. A thorough commentary with theological as well as exegetical insight.

Pope, M. H. *Song of Songs.* AB. Doubleday, 1977. A large commentary with frequent digressions into comparative customs.

Isaiah

Kaiser, Otto. *Isaiah 1–12* and *Isaiah 13–39.* OTL. Westminster, 1983 (2nd ed.), 1974. Emphasis of discussion is often on authenticity and historical reconstruction instead of theology from a critical perspective.

*Oswalt, John. *Isaiah 1–39* and *Isaiah 40–66.* NICOT. Eerdmans, 1986, 1998. Solid exposition of biblical text. Introduction could be stronger. Evangelical.

Watts, John D. W. *Isaiah.* 2 vols. WBC. Word Books, 1985, 1987. His unique approach to Isaiah as drama has not won much support. Evangelical.

*Westermann, Claus. *Isaiah 40–66.* OTL. Westminster, 1969. A standard critical commentary.

Wildberger, Hans. *Isaiah 1–12.* ConC. Fortress, 1991. Part of the same German series as some of the Hermeneia volumes. Very detailed form-critical approach.

Young, Edward J. *The Book of Isaiah.* 3 vols. (reprint of 1965-72 editions). Eerdmans, 1993. A standard of an earlier generation. Amillennial. Evangelical.

Jeremiah

Carroll, Robert P. *Jeremiah.* OTL. Westminster, 1986. Argues that the text is an ideological creation.

Clements, Ronald E. *Jeremiah.* Int. John Knox, 1988. An effort by a critical scholar to deal with the final form of the text.

Craigie, Peter C., Page H. Kelley, and Joel F. Drinkard, Jr. *Jeremiah 1–25.* WBC. Word, 1991. Completed by the other authors after the death of Craigie. Accordingly, it is uneven in amount and quality of detail. Evangelical.

*Holladay, William L. *Jeremiah 1–25* and *Jeremiah 26–52.* Herm. Fortress, 1986, 1989. A massive technical commentary with a wealth of textual and exegetical notes.

Keown, Gerald L., Pamela J. Scalise, and Thomas G. Smothers. *Jeremiah 26–52.* WBC. Word, 1995. Evangelical.

McKane, William. *A Critical and Exegetical Commentary on Jeremiah 1–25; Jeremiah 26–52.* ICC. Edinburgh: T. & T. Clark, 1986, 1989. Focus on textual and philology issues.

Thompson, John A. *The Book of Jeremiah*. NICOT. Eerdmans, 1980. The standard evangelical commentary for the last two decades.

Lamentations

*Hillers, Delbert R. *Lamentations: A New Translation with Introduction and Commentary*. 2nd ed. Doubleday, 1992. Update of 1972 commentary. Attentive to poetry and structure.

Provan, Iain. *Lamentations*. NCBC. Eerdmans, 1991. A timely commentary by an author known for literary sensitivity. Evangelical.

Ezekiel

Allen, Leslie C. *Ezekiel 1–19* and *Ezekiel 20–48*. WBC. Word, 1990. The first volume replaces the earlier initial volume by Brownlee. Helpful commentary with concern for ancient Near Eastern background. Evangelical.

Blenkinsopp, J. *Ezekiel*. Int. John Knox, 1990. An effort by a critical scholar to judiciously utilize scholarship for preaching concerns.

Block, Daniel I. *Ezekiel 1–24* and *Ezekiel 25–48*. NICOT. Eerdmans, 1997, 1998. The standard evangelical commentary on this prophetic book.

Craigie, P. C. *Ezekiel*. DSB. Westminster, 1983. Good example of a devotional commentary that incorporates serious exegesis. Evangelical.

Eichrodt, Walter. *Ezekiel*. OTL. Westminster, 1970. The classical critical commentary of a generation ago.

Greenberg, M. *Ezekiel 1–20* and *Ezekiel 21–37*. AB. Doubleday, 1983, 1997. Sees work as substantially from the hand of the prophet and focuses on final form of the prophetic text. Jewish.

*Zimmerli, Walther. *Ezekiel 1–24* and *Ezekiel 25–48*. 2 vols. Herm. Fortress, 1979, 1983. Massive commentary within the form-critical and tradition-history traditions.

Daniel

Baldwin, Joyce G. *Daniel*. TOTC. InterVarsity, 1978. Helpful with attention to background, textual, and theological issues. Evangelical.

*Goldingay, John. *Daniel*. WBC. Word, 1989. Detailed comments with comparisons with biblical and nonbiblical parallels. Defends a late date. Evangelical.

Hartman, Louis F., and Alexander A. DiLella. AB. Doubleday, 1978. Places comments against a late reconstruction of background. Roman Catholic.

Montgomery, J. A. *Daniel.* ICC. T. & T. Clark, 1927. Though now dated in many ways, this critical commentary is still a benchmark in terms of textual data and philology.

Porteous, N. *Daniel.* OTL. 2nd ed. Westminster Press, 1979. An important critical commentary of a generation ago. The second edition has a supplement to update the original 1962 commentary.

Young, Edward J. *The Prophecy of Daniel.* Eerdmans, 1949. A classical commentary of earlier decades. Much attention given to millennial debates. Evangelical.

Hosea

Andersen, Francis I., and David N. Freedman. *Hosea.* AB. Doubleday, 1980. Detailed commentary with attention to literary unity and style.

Davies, G. I. *Hosea.* NCBC. Eerdmans, 1992. Brief comments coupled with a unique understanding of the relationship between the prophet and Gomer.

Harper, William Rainey. *Hosea and Amos.* ICC. T & T Clark, 1905. The classic commentary of early critical scholarship. Much attention to textual and philological matters.

Hubbard, David A. *Hosea.* TOTC. InterVarsity, 1989. Helpful commentary with some concern for literary features. Evangelical.

Mays, James L. *Hosea.* OTL. Westminster, 1969. A concise and well-written commentary from the form-critical perspective.

McComiskey, Thomas Edward, ed. *The Minor Prophets: An Exegetical & Expository Commentary,* vol. 1: Hosea-Amos. Baker, 1992. Separate, but parallel, textual and expositional comments. Quality of commentary on each book varies according to the contributor. Evangelical.

*Stuart, Douglas. *Hosea — Jonah.* WBC. Word, 1987. Solid textual and expositional commentary. Stresses covenantal background. Evangelical.

Wolff, Hans W. *Hosea.* Herm. Fortress, 1974. A detailed form-critical commentary.

Joel

*Allen, Leslie C. *The Books of Joel, Obadiah, Jonah and Micah.* NICOT. Eerdmans, 1976. Careful and informed exegesis with an attempt to locate texts against possible historical background. Evangelical.

Crenshaw, James L. *Joel*. AB. Doubleday, 1995. Interest in literary structure and features.

Finley, T. J. *Joel, Amos, Obadiah*. WEC. Moody, 1990. Exegesis from a conservative evangelical point of view.

Hubbard, David A. *Joel and Amos*. TOTC. InterVarsity, 1989. Helpful commentary with concern for literary features. Evangelical.

McComiskey, Thomas Edward, ed. *The Minor Prophets: An Exegetical & Expository Commentary*, vol. 1: Hosea-Amos. See above under *Hosea*.

Stuart, Douglas. *Hosea — Jonah*. See above under *Hosea*.

*Wolff, Hans W. *Joel and Amos*. Herm. Fortress, 1977. The classic form-critical study of these two prophetic books.

Amos

Andersen, Francis I., and David N. Freedman. *Amos*. AB. Doubleday, 1989. A massive commentary that takes the book as substantially from the hand of the prophet.

Finley, T. J. *Joel, Amos, Obadiah*. See above under *Joel*.

Hubbard, David A. *Joel and Amos*. See above under *Joel*.

Mays, James L. *Amos*. OTL. Westminster, 1969. A concise, well-written commentary from the form-critical perspective.

McComiskey, Thomas Edward, ed. *The Minor Prophets: An Exegetical & Expository Commentary*, vol. 1: Hosea-Amos. See above under *Hosea*.

*Paul, Shalom. *Amos*. Herm. Fortress, 1991. Excellent analysis of text with an emphasis on ancient Near Eastern parallels and backgrounds.

*Smith, G. V. *Amos*. Zondervan, 1988. Solid exegesis with attention to theological concerns. Evangelical.

Stuart, Douglas. *Hosea — Jonah*. See above under *Hosea*.

Wolff, Hans W. *Joel and Amos*. See above under *Joel*.

Obadiah

*Allen, Leslie C. *The Books of Joel, Obadiah, Jonah and Micah*. See above under *Joel*.

Baker, D. W., T. D. Alexander, and B. K. Waltke. *Obadiah, Jonah, Micah*. TOTC. InterVarsity, 1988. Helpful, but sometimes brief. Evangelical.

Finley, T. J. *Joel, Amos, Obadiah*. See above under *Joel*.

McComiskey, Thomas Edward, ed. *The Minor Prophets: An Exegetical & Expository Commentary*, vol. 2: Obadiah-Habakkuk. Baker, 1993. Separate, but parallel, textual and expositional comments. Quality of commentary on each book varies according to the contributor. Evangelical.

Stuart, Douglas. *Hosea — Jonah.* See above under *Hosea.*

Wolff, H. W. *Obadiah and Jonah.* Augsburg, 1985. Form-critical perspective. Not as detailed as some of Wolff's other commentaries.

Jonah

Allen, Leslie C. *The Books of Joel, Obadiah, Jonah and Micah.* See above under *Joel.*

Alexander, T. D., D. W. Baker, and B. K. Waltke. *Obadiah, Jonah, Micah.* See above under *Obadiah.*

McComiskey, Thomas Edward, ed. *The Minor Prophets: An Exegetical & Expository Commentary,* vol. 2: Obadiah-Habakkuk. See above under *Obadiah.*

*Sasson, Jack M. *Jonah.* AB. Doubleday, 1990. Detailed commentary with attention to literary nuances.

Stuart, Douglas. *Hosea — Jonah.* See above under *Hosea.*

Wolff, H. W. *Obadiah and Jonah.* See above under *Obadiah.*

Micah

*Allen, Leslie C. *The Books of Joel, Obadiah, Jonah and Micah.* See above under *Joel.*

Hillers, Delbert R. *Micah.* Herm. Fortress, 1984. A bit brief, with emphasis on textual issues.

Mays, James L. *Micah.* OTL. Westminster, 1976. A well-written commentary from the form-critical perspective, although it has not been as well received as his works on Amos and Hosea.

McComiskey, Thomas Edward, ed. *The Minor Prophets: An Exegetical & Expository Commentary,* vol. 2: Obadiah-Habakkuk. See above under *Obadiah.*

Waltke, B. K., D. W. Baker, and T. D. Alexander. *Obadiah, Jonah, Micah.* See above under *Obadiah.*

Smith, Ralph L. *Micah-Malachi.* WBC. Word, 1984. Not as detailed as Stuart's commentary on Hosea-Jonah in the same series.

Wolff, Hans Walter. *Micah: A Commentary.* Augsburg, 1990. A detailed form-critical approach.

Nahum

Baker, David W. *Nahum, Habakkuk, Zephaniah.* TOTC. InterVarsity, 1988. Helpful but sometimes overly concise. Evangelical.

McComiskey, Thomas Edward, ed. *The Minor Prophets: An Exegetical & Expository Commentary,* vol. 2: Obadiah-Habakkuk. See above under *Obadiah.*

*Roberts, J. J. *Nahum, Habakkuk, and Zephaniah.* OTL. Westminster/John Knox, 1991. Focuses on textual and grammatical issues.

*Robertson, O. Palmer. *The Books of Nahum, Habakkuk, and Zephaniah.* NICOT. Eerdmans, 1990. Clear exposition with theological concerns. Evangelical.

Smith, Ralph L. *Micah-Malachi.* See above under *Micah.*

Habakkuk

Baker, David W. *Nahum, Habakkuk, Zephaniah.* See above under *Nahum.*

McComiskey, Thomas Edward, ed. *The Minor Prophets: An Exegetical & Expository Commentary,* vol. 2: Obadiah-Habakkuk. See above under *Obadiah.*

*Roberts, J. J. *Nahum, Habakkuk, and Zephaniah.* See above under *Nahum.*

*Robertson, O. Palmer. *The Books of Nahum, Habakkuk, and Zephaniah.* See above under *Nahum.*

Smith, Ralph L. *Micah-Malachi.* See above under *Micah.*

Zephaniah

Baker, David W. *Nahum, Habakkuk, Zephaniah.* See above under *Nahum.*

Berlin, Adele. *Zephaniah.* AB. Doubleday, 1994. A literary approach to the book.

*Roberts, J. J. *Nahum, Habakkuk, and Zephaniah.* See above under *Nahum.*

*Robertson, O. Palmer. *The Books of Nahum, Habakkuk, and Zephaniah.* See above under *Nahum.*

Smith, Ralph L. *Micah-Malachi.* See above under *Micah.*

Haggai

Baldwin, Joyce G. *Haggai, Zechariah, Malachi.* TOTC. InterVarsity, 1972. Clear exposition with theological sensitivity; defends integrity of text. Evangelical.

*Meyers, Carol L., and Eric M. Meyers. *Haggai, Zechariah 1–8.* AB. Doubleday, 1987. Very detailed commentary with attention to possible historical backgrounds and parallels.

Petersen, David L. *Haggai, Zechariah 1–8.* OTL. Westminster, 1984. Well-written and balanced critical approach, with an attempt to link with historical background.

Smith, Ralph L. *Micah-Malachi.* See above under *Micah.*

*Verhoef, Pieter A. *The Books of Haggai and Malachi.* NICOT. Eerdmans, 1987. Exposition with an eye to theological implications. Evangelical.

Wolff, H. W. *Haggai.* Augsburg, 1988. Form-critical perspective. Not as detailed as some of Wolff's other commentaries.

Zechariah

Baldwin, Joyce G. *Haggai, Zechariah, Malachi.* See above under *Haggai.*

*Meyers, Carol L., and Eric M. Meyers. *Haggai, Zechariah 1–8* and *Zechariah 9–14.* Doubleday, 1987, 1993. See the first title under *Haggai.*

Petersen, David L. *Haggai, Zechariah 1–8.* See above under *Haggai.*

———. *Zechariah 9–14 and Malachi.* OTL. Westminster, 1995. Well-written and balanced critical approach, with an attempt to link with historical background.

Smith, Ralph L. *Micah-Malachi.* See above under *Micah.*

Malachi

Baldwin, Joyce G. *Haggai, Zechariah, Malachi.* See above under *Haggai.*

*Hill, Andrew E. *Malachi: A New Translation with Introduction and Commentary.* AB. Doubleday, 1998. Written by an evangelical, this is the most detailed and up-to-date exegetical commentary on the book available in the English language.

*Petersen, David L. *Zechariah 9–14 and Malachi.* See above under *Zechariah.*

Smith, Ralph L. *Micah-Malachi.* See above under *Micah.*

Verhoef, Pieter A. *The Books of Haggai and Malachi.* See above under *Haggai.*